Women in Media

Recent Titles in the

CONTEMPORARY WORLD ISSUES

Series

World Oceans: A Reference Handbook
David E. Newton

First Amendment Freedoms: A Reference Handbook
Michael C. LeMay

Medicare and Medicaid: A Reference Handbook
Greg M. Shaw

Organic Food and Farming: A Reference Handbook
Shauna M. McIntyre

Civil Rights and Civil Liberties in America: A Reference Handbook
Michael C. LeMay

GMO Food: A Reference Handbook, Second Edition
David E. Newton

Pregnancy and Birth: A Reference Handbook
Keisha L. Goode and Barbara Katz Rothman

Hate Groups: A Reference Handbook
David E. Newton

Plastics and Microplastics: A Reference Handbook
David E. Newton

Prescription Drugs: A Reference Handbook
David E. Newton

The U.S.-Mexico Border: A Reference Handbook
Michael C. LeMay

Homelessness in America: A Reference Handbook
Michele Wakin

The Judicial System: A Reference Handbook
Michael C. LeMay

Foster Care in America: A Reference Handbook
Christina G. Villegas

Books in the **Contemporary World Issues** series address vital issues in today's society such as genetic engineering, pollution, and biodiversity. Written by professional writers, scholars, and nonacademic experts, these books are authoritative, clearly written, up-to-date, and objective. They provide a good starting point for research by high school and college students, scholars, and general readers as well as by legislators, business-people, activists, and others.

Each book, carefully organized and easy to use, contains an overview of the subject, a detailed chronology, biographical sketches, facts and data and/or documents and other primary source material, a forum of authoritative perspective essays, annotated lists of print and nonprint resources, and an index.

Readers of books in the Contemporary World Issues series will find the information they need in order to have a better understanding of the social, political, environmental, and economic issues facing the world today.

CONTEMPORARY WORLD ISSUES

Women in Media

A REFERENCE HANDBOOK

Amy M. Damico

An Imprint of ABC-CLIO, LLC
Santa Barbara, California • Denver, Colorado

Library of Congress Cataloging-in-Publication Data

Names: Damico, Amy M., author.
Title: Women in media : a reference handbook / Amy M. Damico.
Description: Santa Barbara, California : ABC-CLIO, [2022] | Series: Contemporary world issues | Includes bibliographical references and index.
Identifiers: LCCN 2022012543 | ISBN 9781440876059 (hardcover) | ISBN 9781440876066 (ebook)
Subjects: LCSH: Women in mass media.
Classification: LCC P94.5.W65 D36 2022 | DDC 302.23/082—dc23/eng/20220503
LC record available at https://lccn.loc.gov/2022012543

ISBN: 978-1-4408-7605-9 (print)
978-1-4408-7606-6 (ebook)

26 25 24 23 22 1 2 3 4 5

This book is also available as an eBook.

ABC-CLIO
An Imprint of ABC-CLIO, LLC

ABC-CLIO, LLC
147 Castilian Drive
Santa Barbara, California 93117
www.abc-clio.com

This book is printed on acid-free paper ∞

Manufactured in the United States of America

As this book goes to press, the United States is emerging from the COVID-19 pandemic, a historic and tragic global event that has resulted in millions of deaths worldwide and over a half a million deaths in the United States alone, with some reports indicating that fatalities in the United States could ultimately top 900,000 (Sullivan 2021). During much of 2020, numerous businesses shut down or altered their operations, and many Americans were forced to change their work, school, and recreational routines, staying home much more than they typically would. For most Americans, pandemic life increased reliance on home screens—televisions, computers, and portable devices—for work, school, information, and entertainment. According to MarketWatch, for example, streaming service subscriptions increased by 32 percent in 2020 (Watson 2021).

The pandemic highlighted what we already know: in the United States, media plays a significant role in many of our lives. Given this, it is important to critically consider the representations of people, groups, and ideas in the films, television programs, advertisements, and news reports that entertain, engage, and inform us. This book looks at the participation and representation of women in American entertainment and news media, especially in the areas of movies, scripted television, advertising, news, and sports. It provides an overview of ways in which women have been historically present and absent in these media forms. Engaging with this history and reading about current issues related to this topic will help readers better understand why women's engagement in media—in such roles as performers, journalists, producers, and writers—is important. It also provides a framework for understanding the positive and problematic media representations of women that influence the daily lives of girls and women across the United States.

Few readers who pick up this book will be surprised to find that women are still fighting for equitable representation in American media industries. Harmful stereotypical images of women and girls persist in the news, on television programs, in advertising, in movies, and in other sectors of the entertainment industry. At the same time, however, remarkable changes and reforms have unfolded across these same media industries. Women are anchoring newscasts, portraying complex women characters in movies and television, and defying the traditional gender status quo in advertising and other promotional messaging.

This book summarizes and synthesizes information that addresses these topic areas and offers readers a one-stop resource for gaining a better understanding of the broad and complex topic of women in media. The content found in the following chapters is informed by published research, critical perspectives, and scholarly essays—research initiatives that are ongoing as scholars continue to document women's participation and portrayal in media content.

- Chapter 1, "Background and History," offers a broad overview of the evolution of how women have been portrayed and how they have helped shape media industries in the United States. This chapter examines how evolving and sometimes contradictory representations of women in magazines, films, news, television programs, and advertising aligned shifting cultural ideas about women in the United States. The chapter also defines relevant concepts and terms and reviews how representations of women in media are studied. It additionally summarizes the ideas of some often referenced gender and media scholars.

- Chapter 2, "Problems, Controversies, and Solutions," presents some of the contemporary challenges and problems confronting girls and women in their relationships to media in the United States, both as subjects and as members. Focus areas in this chapter address current research about women in narrative film and scripted television; the presence and portrayal of women in news, politics, and sports; and representation trends in contemporary advertising and on social media. This chapter also summarizes some of the solutions and reforms proposed by experts to address gender inequality in these industries and sectors of American life.
- Chapter 3, "Perspectives," is composed of nine essays written by professionals and scholars who offer their viewpoints on specific aspects of women in media. The essays address such topics as the emergence of women superheroes; representations of various female demographic groups in television, film, and social media; sports coverage of women athletes; and constructions of women and teenage characters on television.
- Chapter 4, "Profiles," highlights some of the many women who have impacted the film, television, news, sports, or advertising industries by way of contributing to the field's advancement or working in ways that resulted in more equitable and positive representations of women. A few notable media texts are profiled in this chapter as well.
- Chapter 5, "Data and Documents," provides additional insights into the relationship between gender and American media and how that relationship is changing. The data section of the chapter compiles summaries of relevant research findings, while the documents section presents excerpts of relevant primary texts that offer further illumination on the topic.
- Chapter 6, "Resources," offers an annotated list of sources for readers interested in learning more about aspects of this topic. This chapter highlights useful books, research

organizations, digital resources, audio/visual content, and relevant scholarly journals.

- Chapter 7, "Chronology," presents a timeline of important events and milestones to help readers better understand the history of women and media in the United States.

The book concludes with a succinct glossary of relevant terms for reader reference and a comprehensive subject index.

Bibliography

Johnson, Catherine, and Lauren Dempsey. 2020. "How Corona Virus May Have Changed TV Viewing Habits for Good—New Research." The Conversation, November 11, 2020. https://theconversation.com/how-coronavirus-might-have-changed-tv-viewing-habits-for-good-new-research-146040

Mitchell, Amy, Mark Jurkowitz, J. Baxter Oliphant, and Elisa Shearer. 2020. "Americans' Attention to News about the Coronavirus Pandemic Remains Steady in November as Cases Surge." Pew Research Center, December 5, 2020. https://www.journalism.org/2020/12/15/americans-attention-to-news-about-the-coronavirus-pandemic-remains-steady-in-november-as-cases-surge/

Sullivan, Becky. 2021. "New Study Estimates More Than 900,000 People Have Died of COVID-19 in US." National Public Radio, May 6, 2021. https://www.npr.org/sections/coronavirus-live-updates/2021/05/06/994287048/new-study-estimates-more-than-900-000-people-have-died-of-covid-19-in-u-s

Watson, R. T. 2021. "Global Streaming Subscriptions Top 1B during COVID." MarketWatch, March 18, 2021. https://www.marketwatch.com/story/global-streaming-subscriptions-top-1b-during-covid-2021-03-18

Women in Media

Introduction

If prompted to conjure historical images of women in American media, some may point to glamorous "flappers" from the 1920s, a woman character from a 1950s television show, or the iconic image of Rosie the Riveter. Others may think of film stars during the Golden Age of Hollywood, models featured in advertisements for beauty products, or one of the many problematic stereotypes of nonwhite women in twentieth-century popular culture. The presence and portrayal of women in U.S. media is a broad and widely studied topic. Many scholars today focus on the ways portrayals of women in media have changed over the decades. They examine specific types of representations, including portrayals of women in print, film, and television; their roles as journalists; and their participation as writers, producers, and editors in both news and entertainment. As mediated images of women can be tremendously influential, scholars continually examine the potential impact and effects of these images on the culture and its audience. Finally, acknowledging that individuals process messages differently, scholars investigate how audiences engage with, and respond to, mediated images of women.

This image from *Godey's Lady's Book* (1862), a popular magazine with women in the 18th century, shows women in fashionable clothing. Before the middle of the century, magazines were primarily text oriented; the inclusion of drawings and engravings eventually became part of the magazines form. (Library of Congress)

The purpose of this chapter is to provide a broad overview of some of this work, synthesizing some of the research and identifying some of the shifting historical trends in portrayals of women in popular magazines, film, scripted television, news, and advertising. A review of this history provides the necessary context one needs to make sense of the current media landscape, where representations of women in American media are an ongoing topic of discussion and area of tension. Critical and cultural studies scholars argue the social, economic, gendered, and other structures that inform social reality both influence members of the culture and are influenced by members of the culture themselves (Guba and Lincoln 1994). Therefore, a discussion of images of women in media—and how those images are received in the United States—should take into account the historical moment when they were produced.

Representations of women in popular media have clearly contributed to the culture's shifting perspectives on women. As mass media industries developed and expanded through the nineteenth, twentieth, and twenty-first centuries, mainstream representations of women in the United States changed and expanded. Portrayals of women in magazines, film, and some news sources challenged the status quo, encouraged political engagement, and mirrored progressive changes in the culture.

At the same time, though, problematic stereotypes of women often dominated mainstream media and offered limited definitions of what a *woman* is. In many cases, magazine imagery and content, news stories, advertisements, and portrayals in film, television, and online contributed to constructions of unachievable beauty standards, racial and ethnic stereotypes, and trivialization of women's contributions and narratives.

Representations of women in media can also be considered in light of the sources responsible for crafting and disseminating those images and messages. The history of the development of mass media demonstrates how many news reports, film narratives, television story lines, and advertisements were created by men who did not represent ideas and perspectives offered by women. This has changed. However, as we venture more deeply into the second decade of the twenty-first century, problems around media representations of women and women's equitable engagement in media industries persist, some of which echo trends present in early media texts.

The New Woman in Early Media

During the end of the 1800s through the early 1900s, as newspapers and magazines were increasing in circulation and film was emerging as a mass medium, cultural ideas about what it meant to be a woman were changing. The media at the time reflected, advanced, and challenged these ideas, resulting in a proliferation of images of women and the emergence of particular characterizations and stereotypes. Scholars refer to women who came of age between 1890 and 1920 as "the New Woman," one who "challenged gender norms and structures by asserting a new public presence through work, education, entertainment and politics, while also denoting a distinctly modern appearance that contrasted with Victorian ideals" (Rabinovitch-Fox 2017).

The emerging popularity and increased circulation of magazines during this time paralleled a time period of progressive reform for women; women advocated for the right to vote, became active in politics, advocated for social causes, and pursued college and careers to an extent never before seen (Kitch 2001). Lived experiences of the New Woman varied across race, economic class, and geographic lines. Media depictions of women during this time contribute to an understanding of the different ways shifting ideas about women were produced, distributed, and received, despite their largely limited focus on the white middle- to upper-middle-class demographic.

Scholars identify the nineteenth-century magazine as the first form of mass media because it was the first media successfully developed for a national audience (Kitch 2001). Though magazines had been in existence in colonial America, advances in technology and mail delivery contributed to the form's development, increased circulation, and eventual success. Before the mid-1800s, newspapers and magazines were primarily text oriented. By the middle of the century, however, the inclusion of drawings and engravings became central to the magazine's form. For example, such magazines as *Godey's Lady's Book* and *Peterson's Magazine* included hand-colored fashion plates that supplemented the magazines' stories, essays, and poetry (Endres 2012b). By the end of the nineteenth century, the magazine industry was thriving. In 1890, 4,500 magazines were being published across the United States; by 1905, 6,000 were in circulation (Campbell, Martin, and Fabos 2016; Kitch 2001). Several popular magazines, including *Godey's Lady's Book*, the *Saturday Evening Post*, and *Ladies' Home Journal*, were produced with women readers specifically in mind. By the early 1900s, magazines such as the *Saturday Evening Post* and *Ladies' Home Journal* boasted more than a million subscribers (Kitch 2001).

In the mid-1800s, such magazines constructed what scholars refer to as the "cult of domesticity," emphasizing "the characteristics commonly associated with the 19th century 'lady': piety, purity, domesticity and submissiveness" (Endres 2012b, 435). However, these magazines underwent incremental but steady change as ideas about the New Woman permeated the culture. Magazine images of women, content for women, and articles about women contributed to and reflected cultural ideas about women at the turn of the century. For example, columns and fiction by female writers appealed to women in the *Saturday Evening Post*, and the magazines *Vogue* and *Harper's Bazaar* developed into early versions of modern fashion magazines for women (Kitch 2001; Endres 2012b). Additionally, *Ladies' Home Journal*'s editorial content evolved with the changing times, reflecting new and progressive ideas about women's roles in homes, communities, and the wider culture (Kitch 2001).

These mainstream magazines primarily focused on the mainstream white female culture. Numerous African American publications represented aspects of the African American woman's experience in different ways. For example, the fashion magazine

Ringwood's Afro-American Journal of Fashion addressed fashion "as a means of uplifting the African American race as a whole and distancing African American women from outmoded associations with slavery, violence, and sexual vulnerability" (Rooks 2004, 65). These periodicals discussed the history and experiences of enslaved women, the migration of African American populations, and various quests for social justice, equality, and access to professional work. Popular African American magazines offered constructions of women that presumably influenced their Black readers. Additionally, popular magazines such as *Crisis*, produced by the National Association for the Advancement of Colored People (NAACP), challenged racist, stereotypical images of the time by distributing positive portrayals of African American women and men (Kitch 2001). Images of Black women in these magazines were complicated, however. They consciously included Black women in their coverage, but in so doing, they adhered to dominant white middle-class notions of the ideal woman (Patterson 1995; Kitch 2001).

In her historical analysis of the portrayal of women in magazines, scholar Carolyn Kitch argues that magazine imagery provided limited, rather than diverse, images of women. "As the American Women's sphere widened and her opportunities grew in real life, she was increasingly portrayed in popular culture as a girl. In the new century, a group of male illustrators would rise to fame and fortune by showing the public what that new American Girl looked like" (Kitch 2001, 36). The various ways women were depicted on magazine covers by men became the first mass media stereotypes of women—recognizable representations that evoked some sort of shared cultural understanding (Kitch 2001, 5).

Male Depictions of the Ideal "Girl"

The first of these stereotypes emerged in the late 1800s. The Gibson Girl was a white woman depicted in a series of pen-and-ink drawings by Charles Dana Gibson. The so-called Gibson

Girl became a fixture in many popular magazines, including *Life*, *Good Housekeeping*, *McCall's*, and *Ladies' Home Journal.* The Gibson Girl was slim, beautiful, tall, well dressed, confident, and white, and "her rapid rise to fame created a blueprint for the commercial uses of such a stereotype" (Kitch 2001, 37). While Gibson's definition of the ideal American woman persisted for about two decades, other male artists emerged during the first two decades of the twentieth century to present other idealized images of "girls." For example, Harrison Fisher's "Fisher Girls" and Howard Chandler Christy's "Christy Girls" depicted women as active, fit, and college educated.

While these evolving images of "girls" were conceived by male artists, their drawings represented changing ideas concerning women and their place in American society. Harrison Fisher, for example, depicted seventeen women graduating from college on a magazine cover in 1913. As the scholar Carolyn Kitch points out, "Whether or not she was portrayed as educated or athletic, the magazine cover girl of this era was almost always shown outside the home, a rhetorical shift that acknowledged real change in women's societal roles" (Kitch 2001, 54). The magazines, however, presented mixed messages to their readers. Editorial content often warned women about the dangers of being independent and pursuing careers (Kitch 2001).

The dominant image of the New Woman shifted during the 1920s. Dubbed "the flapper," this slim, youthful, somewhat androgynous image was a departure from the curvy representations of women preceding it. Einav Rabinovitch-Fox (2017) explains, "As depicted in advertisements and popular media, [the flapper] was associated with a range of consumer products that denoted modern living: cars, cosmetics, clothing and electrical appliances." Scholars suggest the flapper marked a shift in presentations and cultural understandings of sexuality; it emphasized sexual agency and enjoyment for women and gave them an identity divorced from procreating and mothering (Fields 2007; Benshoff and Griffin 2009). While dominant images of flappers were white, women across many ethnic and racial groups adopted the look, and the Black press created their own interpretation of the style (Rabinovitch-Fox 2017).

The pervasiveness of the changing images of the New Woman were influential. In her book *The Body Project: An Intimate History of American Girls* (1997), social historian Joan Jacobs Brumberg documents how aspects of culture, including media, contributed to women's, teens' and girls' emphasis and focus on their bodies, often defining themselves in terms of what their bodies look like. Brumberg asserts that "before the twentieth century, girls simply did not organize their thinking about themselves around their bodies" (Brumberg 1997, 97). The beauty standards that nineteenth-century girls aspired to were defined by fashionable clothing, jewelry, and hairstyles. However, as cultural expectations changed—partially powered by advertising messages—a new focus on the female body emerged. Early twentieth-century advertising emphasized pretty faces and white teeth, and images of women began to feature exposed legs and ankles. Fashion and film in the 1920s promoted freedom from binding clothing and, as Brumberg writes, "encouraged a massive 'unveiling' of the female body which meant that certain body parts—such as arms and legs—were bared and displayed in ways they never had been before" and thus needed to be maintained with "beauty regimens" and dieting (Brumberg 1997, 98).

Indeed, while the image of the flapper may have challenged previous conceptions of women, its popularity also brought its own set of limitations and problems. As film scholars note, "A flapper's independence was chiefly defined by her freedom to buy things in order to reconcile her personal style, and not by any kind of radical political critique: in most novels and films in which she appeared, the flapper was still out to find a husband" (Benshoff and Griffin 2009, 222). Historian Einav Rabinovitch-Fox also points out that "for women who could not conform to the flapper ideal, particularly non-white, older, and more stout women, adopting 'flapperism' also required adopting a strict regimen of dieting, grooming, chest-binding, and makeup wearing" (Rabinovitch-Fox 2017).

Stereotypes of Women in Early Movies

Portrayals of women in early film can also be considered in light of changes in the culture and the emergence of the New Woman. Early American films generally presented "good" women as those who adhered to gender roles of the Victorian era, innocent, virtuous women who existed to marry and have children (Benshoff and Griffin 2009). Eager to reinforce traditional ideas about women's sexuality, early films presented women in a binary called the *virgin-whore complex*, whereby women were judged based on their sexual choices (Benshoff and Griffin 2009). In this restrictive dynamic, "good" women are virgins until marriage, and sexually active women are described as unworthy of marriage. Although film representations of female sexuality have diversified and improved since then, aspects of this construct can still be seen in contemporary films.

Another female stereotype in early American films was what is now referred to as the *vamp*. Initially present in silent films, the stereotypical vamp character is an immoral woman, often played by a "foreign" (nonwhite) actress, who leads to the male protagonist's downfall. The central characterization of the vamp as an evil temptress informed pervasive stereotypes in later films. One notable example is the "femme fatale" of film noir, a character whose seductive and selfish ways threaten the happiness or life of the male hero (Creed 1994). Interest in cinematic stereotypes of women like the vamp is driven by the idea that stereotypes "tell us very little about [the] woman herself, but a great deal about male fears and desires about women" (Creed 1994, 409). Film portrayals of independent women also spoke to a certain reluctance to accept changing gender norms. Even as women's involvement in increasing feminist activism and participation in work outside of the home became evident in the early decades of the twentieth century, popular films of that era often painted independent women as harmful forces (Benshoff and Griffin 2009).

Portrayals of Women during Hollywood's Golden Age

As the 1920s moved into the 1930s and the country dealt with the Great Depression, the film industry evolved into what is variously known as Classical Hollywood cinema or Hollywood's Golden Age. During this period, glamorous female movie stars such as Mae West, Greta Garbo, Joan Crawford, and Katharine Hepburn became powerful players in the industry. These women—and other actresses as well—played strong, confident female characters who were comfortable with their sexuality and, at times, even challenged traditional conceptions of gender roles (Benshoff and Griffin 2009).

Classical Hollywood did not, however, feature women of color in prominent roles. When they were cast in films, nonwhite women often played roles that fueled stereotypes, such as domestic servants or characters who were clearly subservient. The situation only marginally improved for women in front of and behind the camera over the subsequent decades. *Variety* writers Steven Gaydos and Tim Gray contend that

> the history of show business is a history of bias, which can be broken down into three general eras: Humiliation (1905–42), when grossly demeaning terms like "coon" and vile treatment were "normal"; protest (1942–49), when voices were raised in simple requests that demeaning stereotypes and racist images be removed from entertainment; and the struggle for equality (1949–2016), when groups began confronting the absence of people of color in key above- and below-the-line fields. For those who still do not quite understand the fury behind the current demands for change, it should be noted that this third phase is now approaching its 70th year. (Gaydos and Gray 2016)

A cultural reaction to the film flapper, the permissive Hollywood culture of which she was a part, and the unsavory actions (drug use, murder allegations) of some in Hollywood eventually provoked protests, particularly among conservative and religious groups. This backlash prompted the emergence of a period of Hollywood film censorship at the end of the 1920s (Modello 2008). The Motion Picture Production Code adopted by the Motion Pictures Producers and Distributors of America (MPPDA; now known as the Motion Picture Association, or MPA) informed filmmakers about what presentations of content on-screen were acceptable. Screenwriters were not permitted to advance progressive images of women and had to adhere to conservative presentations of gender roles and female sexuality (Wilson 2018). The Motion Picture Production Code prohibited such content as nudity, passionate scenes, suggestive dances, ridicule of religion, and anything that "lowered the moral standards of those who see it" (Modello 2008). Eventually, with the advent of more permissive television content and evolving cultural standards, the Motion Picture Production Code became obsolete and was ultimately replaced with the film rating system in 1968.

Women in Developing Media Industries

The media industry includes, but is not limited to, film, print media, radio, and television. When considering women's historical roles in these developing media industries, one might consider how the gender composition of the entertainment world's most powerful executives and creative talents impacted the types of news being reported, the nature of the stories created on large and small screens, and the various ways women—in fact and in fiction—were constructed, represented, and presented. Without gender equality and ample diversity throughout all levels of media industries, news stories, film narratives, television programs, and popular songs and literature often produced limited and problematic representations and perspectives on women, women's issues, and women's stories. While much of the history of the developing media industries is dominated by men, numerous women did contribute to the development and maturation of various news and entertainment media. Many women worked hard to challenge the status quo, tell their own stories, and influence industry change.

News

In the eighteenth and nineteenth centuries, the majority of newspapers and magazines were controlled by men. Some women worked as reporters, photographers, publishers, and writers, but they were in the minority. For example, Elizabeth Timothy became publisher of the *South Carolina Gazette* after her husband died in 1739, writer Anne Newport Royall began publishing the newspaper *Paul Pry* in 1831, Sarah Joseph Hale began editing the women's magazine *Godey's Lady's Book* in 1837, and Margaret Fuller worked as a literacy critic and foreign war correspondent in the mid-1800s (Earman 2000; Huhulea 2016; Lucey 2005). For the most part, however, mainstream news organizations attempted to engage women as readers of fashion and society stories; women were perceived to be consumers, rather than producers, of news and were not considered suitable to pursue jobs in the field (Chambers, Steiner, and Fleming 2004).

After the Civil War ended in 1865, women activists and suffragists became frustrated with the reluctance of most newspapers to report fairly on their ideas and goals; instead, they were written about in ways that suggested their views and advocacy did not have merit (Byerly 2012). During this time, when women were fighting for equal rights (an era often referred to as *first-wave feminism*), women who did not defer to men or who resisted being pigeonholed as wives and mothers "risked being characterized as inappropriate, insane or misfits" by news reporters (Byerly 2012). Similarly, "if they demanded equality with men, the media depicted them as either curiosities or as loud, militant and aggressive" (Byerly 2012). In response to this unfair and sexist reporting, some women established their own publications. For example, Elizabeth Cady Stanton and Susan B. Anthony founded *Revolution* in 1868, a newspaper that advocated for a number of progressive reforms, including voting rights for women (Landers 2016).

Other changes also prompted more involvement by women in the news industry. As advertising became central to the economic survival of news publications in the late 1800s, women were hired to write stories that appealed to female readers. These stories often appeared alongside advertisements specifically targeted toward women (Chambers, Steiner, and Fleming 2004). Women who wrote for newspapers and magazines were mainly tasked with writing stories focused on the arts, domesticity, fashion, gossip, and human-interest stories—stories their male supervisors believed would appeal to other women (Chambers, Steiner, and Fleming 2004). However, as journalism as a profession continued to develop in the late 1800s and early 1900s, women such as Ida Tarbell, Rheta Childe Dorr, and Nellie Bly achieved success with powerful and highly publicized investigative reports. As the United States entered World War I, journalistic opportunities for women increased. Notable contributors to the news sphere in the first half of the twentieth century included popular journalist, broadcaster, and columnist Dorothy Thompson; photojournalist Margaret Bourke-White; and journalist and war correspondent Martha Gellhorn.

During the middle of the twentieth century, the way women were reported on in news stories mirrored some of the trends seen in the late 1800s and early 1900s, when traditional ideas about women were dominant and coverage of women's issues, workplace challenges, access to education, and quests for independence was slim (Tuchman, Daniels, and Benét 1978). In 1978, sociologist Gaye Tuchman argued, based on her analyses of representations of women in news and other media texts, that women were often symbolically annihilated in media content; they were often excluded, stereotyped, and trivialized.

Tuchman's assertions echoed the voices of many activists and academics during the period of what is sometimes referred to as *second-wave feminism*, a cultural women's movement advocating for women's equality (the term *first-wave feminism* is associated with the time period leading up to the establishment of women's legal right to vote). While the press covered the women's movement and its outcome, the reporting was often narrow in scope or constructed along stereotypical gender lines (Sanmiguel 2000). Additionally, "women of color, including Latina American, Asian-Pacific American, and Native American women, have historically received scant attention in the news media. The presence of lesbian and bisexual women in the news has been confined largely to stock butch/femme images pulled from 'gay pride' marches and other public events" (Sanmiguel 2000, 1121).

By the mid-twentieth century, more women were working as newsroom professionals, even though the news business generally remained male dominated. Women reporters and editors continued to primarily work in areas deemed of interest to women consumers. Eventually, however, a series of "first woman" achievements by smart, talented women began to break down myths that women could not, or should not, participate in hard news reporting. The successful careers of such journalists as Helen Thomas, Carole Simpson, and Barbara Walters led the way for other women to succeed in the news industry.

In the 1980s and 1990s, when the number of women pursuing professional careers and working outside the home increased, news coverage of these trends was largely negative. In her 1991 book *Backlash*, journalist Susan Faludi argued that criticisms and condemnations of the feminist movement in news reporting, entertainment, and advertising actually hurt both women and wider American society. In Faludi's view, the media helped perpetuate a "powerful counterassault on women's rights, a backlash, an attempt to retract the handful of small and hard-won victories that the feminist movement did manage to win for women" (Faludi 1991, 9). Faludi argued that the conservative media like to frame the contemporary challenges women face as attributable to the gains achieved by the women's movement: "It stands the truth boldly on its head and proclaims that the very steps that have elevated women's position have actually led to their downfall" (Faludi 1991, 9–10).

The Global Media Monitoring Project (GMMP) has been studying the representation and portrayal of women in worldwide news since 1995. According to the organization, their research "demonstrates that women are dramatically underrepresented in news, even as representations of women has marginally increased from 1995–2015." According to their findings, only 24 percent of "news subjects—the people who are interviewed or whom the news is about—are female." GMMP also finds that when women are present in news coverage, they are seen as ordinary people in contrast to their male counterparts, who are seen more often as authority figures and professionals. Additionally, the Women's Media Center (WMC) regularly highlights problematic news coverage of women leaders and authority figures, particularly in political campaigns, calling attention to the ways female candidates are framed in sexist ways as opposed to their male opponents.

Observers, including the WMC, have blamed this state of affairs, at least in part, on the continued dominance of men—especially white men—in the news and journalism industry. "We live in a racially and ethnically diverse nation that is 51 percent female, but the news media itself remains staggeringly limited to a single demographic [of white straight males]," charged the WMC in 2017. "The media is the single most powerful tool at our disposal. It has the power to educate, effect social change, and determine the political policies and elections that shape our lives. . . . Diversifying the media landscape is critical to the health of our culture and democracy" (Women's Media Center 2017).

However, despite some gains, female equity, particularly among nonwhite women, in news and journalism fields across the nation has yet to be achieved. According to a 2018 WMC report examining data from the almost 40 percent of newsrooms that responded to an annual survey, about 52 percent of all newsroom staff are white men, and about 31 percent are white women. Additionally, among newsroom leaders—people in positions to make choices about news coverage and the use of newsroom resources—about 54 percent are white men, and 33 percent are white women.

WMC's research also highlights that according to Radio Television Digital News Association (RTDNA) data, the local television news industry is composed of about 44 percent white men, 31 percent white women, 12 percent nonwhite men, and 13 percent nonwhite women. The WMC points out that news media professionals make decisions every day about what news events to prioritize, and they identify what is important to report. It is thus crucial to have a diverse slate of people writing and reporting on what is happening in the country that is reflective of the experiences of those living here. However, male journalists continue to report most news; a 2019 WMC study found that 69 percent of newswire bylines are men, 63 percent of television prime-time news broadcasts feature male anchors and correspondents, 60 percent of online news is written by men, and 59 percent of print news is written by men.

Film

In the early twentieth century, Hollywood established itself as the center of the American movie industry, and women were active participants in its development. Women worked both in front of and behind the camera as producers, writers, directors, editors, and actors prior to 1925, and such notable stars as Mary Pickford and Gloria Swanson formed their own production companies (Mahar 2001).

Over time, however, Hollywood became increasingly masculinized due to several factors, including the framing of the use of developing film technology as masculine, the establishment of film organizations and clubs that were primarily for men, and the persistence of traditional ideas of what women can and should do in American society (Mahar 2001). As historian Karen Ward Mahar notes, the film industry eventually became seen as a "big business" that women were not qualified to participate in, even though women had previously demonstrated their successful filmmaking capabilities. According to Mahar, "The efficient, masculinized business-man filmmaker—the type most admired by the investment community and the emerging studio system—became the Hollywood ideal in the years following World War I" (Mahar 2001, 102).

During the period from 1930 to around 1960, the only women with meaningful stature and influence in the film industry were actors; female writers, editors, and costume designers had low status in the industry (Giannetti 2008). Despite their presence on-screen, female stars were discriminated against: they did not earn as much money as men, they rarely garnered top billing as stars, and their careers often ended prematurely because although men played leading roles into their sixties, women were perceived as being too old for romantic roles past the age of forty (Giannetti 2008). If women managed longer careers in acting, they were often forced to accept roles as "grotesque caricatures" (Giannetti 2008, 476).

This environment partly stemmed from a business model known as the *Hollywood studio system*, which dominated American moviemaking from the late 1920s through the late 1940s. Under this studio system, five major film production companies controlled all aspects of the U.S. film industry. A comprehensive analysis of over 26,000 American movies produced between 1911 and 2010 demonstrates that the establishment of the Hollywood studio system was "strongly associated with lower levels of female representation among directors, screenwriters and actors" and informed the resulting gender disparity in filmmaking even after the studio system broke up and the industry became more diversified (Amaral et al. 2020).

While the narrative of absent and disempowered women in the film industry through the end of the studio system is a common one, film historian J. E. Smyth (2018) argues that male film historians largely omitted women's contributions to the industry in their historical scholarship, highlighting popular actresses but disregarding women's roles as producers, creatives, and writers. Smyth asserts that during the years of the studio system, women worked in all aspects of the film industry, had considerable power, held numerous leadership positions, and were recognized for their contributions. Crediting film directors as the sole creators, Smyth points out, ultimately erases the complex process of filmmaking, a process of which women were a part.

After the studio system crumbled, however, women were no longer prominent leaders in labor unions such as the Screen Writers Guild and the Screen Actors Guild. They were no longer department heads at major studios either, and their employment opportunities decreased as production companies downsized, dealt with the fallout of the communist scare blacklist (a 1950s list of film industry workers who allegedly had communist ties), and attempted to compete with television. "The studio era—long dismissed as corporate patriarchy by historians and critics—remains the most important and empowering chapter in women's employment in the film industry" (Smyth 2018, 23–24).

Television

As the medium of television developed and became a central part of American culture in the 1950s and 1960s, a host of patriarchal practices informed television's development. Developing television technology was adopted and supported by male executives of radio networks, and much of radio programming eventually migrated and adapted to television. Overall, women were not routinely included as valuable contributors to the business side of television. In their book *Women Television Producers: Transformation of the Male Medium* (2001), Robert Alley and Irby Brown point out that the first decades of television are "almost exclusively the story of men shaping programming without evident regard for equality" (9). They explain that although many women starred in television comedies and dramas in the late 1940s, only a few appeared in show production credits. During the 1950s and 1960s, though, television studios increasingly sought to attract viewing audiences by employing former Hollywood actresses such as Jane Wyman, Donna Reed, Barbara Stanwyck, and Loretta Young after they had "aged out" of starring roles in the movies. Additionally, Lucille Ball became a popular top-paid television star after early career success in film and radio. Eventually, female involvement in all components of the television industry began to increase, particularly after the women's movement. However, despite these advances, inequality still exists today; just 31 percent of key behind-the-scenes jobs are held by women in the television industry (Lauzen 2019).

World War II Propaganda

The now iconic image of Rosie the Riveter is often used to evoke ideals of female empowerment. The story of this image, and others encouraging similar ideas about women and their capacity to competently tackle challenging and important work, can be traced to government propaganda from World War II that encouraged women to work in jobs traditionally reserved for men serving in the military. However, it is perhaps important to note that dominant mainstream media images of women during the pre–World War II years were of white middle-class women. Given this reality, the range of diversity of women's working experiences was rarely represented. For example, many women from poor or working-class households were employed outside the home even before women began entering the workforce in greater numbers in the late nineteenth and early twentieth centuries (Enstad 1999). Other women, some married, had been working prior to World War I, while others entered after the war began (Greenwald 1990).

The Great Depression, World War II, and the post–World War II years advanced "dramatically different cultural messages about proper female behavior" (Douglas 1994, 45). During the 1930s, women were warned about taking jobs from men, and women who worked outside the home were limited to what American culture deemed to be traditionally feminine jobs (e.g., secretaries, maids, saleswomen, teachers). Once World War II began, however, factories and other businesses found themselves desperate to fill positions that had been left vacant by the men who had gone off to war. Women were encouraged to reconceptualize what kinds of jobs they could and should do, as were male supervisors, managers, and business owners. A widespread government propaganda campaign asked women to work in fields that ranged from manufacturing to the air force (Douglas 1994). The media was central to distributing this message, and while Rosie the Riveter is perhaps the most recognized icon used to encourage women to work, the Office of War Information (OWI) recruited magazine publishers, advertisers, and film and radio producers to include similar messages in their products (Honey 1985).

During World War II, images of women engaged in what was then considered to be masculine work permeated film newsreels, radio programs, advertisements, and fictional stories in popular magazines (Douglas 1994; Honey 1985). The U.S. National Archives and Records Administration (n.d.) describes the influential images of women in the following way: "Poster and film images glorified and glamorized the roles of working women and suggested that a woman's femininity need not be sacrificed. Whether fulfilling their duty in the home, factory, office, or military, women were portrayed as attractive, confident, and resolved to do their part to win the war." Messaging about women's participation in the workforce focused on what the country needed in wartime rather than challenging conceptions of gender roles and femininity. As scholar Maureen Honey writes, "War work became a vehicle for women to shoulder their civic and moral responsibilities as good citizens rather than a way to become more independent and powerful" (Honey 1985, 6).

After the war, the campaign to encourage women to work morphed into a campaign to encourage women to go back to their traditional prewar roles as homemakers and mothers (Douglas 1994). Mediated images after the war prioritized the place of women—white middle-class women—in the home. Many media messages from this period insisted that the patriotic women who had worked in factories during World War II were relieved to resume their former roles as homemakers. The reality was quite different, however. Middle-class housewives were not the only women who had participated in the war effort; women from other socioeconomic groups, single women, and students, many of whom had worked before, had also participated (Honey 1985).

Portrayals of Women in Postwar Entertainment Media

As World War II ended and the United States' Cold War conflict with the Soviet Union began, tensions and hostility between the two nations and fear of nuclear war dominated national concerns. The United States implemented a policy of "containment" toward the Soviets in which national security would be ensured by stopping, or containing, the spread of communism. Meanwhile, during the 1950s, television became deeply integrated into American culture and an increasingly prominent leisure-time activity. Depictions of stable families on popular television programs, particularly situation comedies (or *sitcoms*, as they later came to be known), promoted an ideology of "domestic containment," a belief that "stable family life [was] necessary for personal and national security as well as supremacy over the Soviet Union" (De Hart 2001, 125).

On many popular sitcoms, as well as in popular books, cookbooks, advertisements, and films, white women were dominantly portrayed as homemakers whose job it was to care for the house and children while their "breadwinner" husbands went off to the office or factory (Douglas 1994; Allan and Coltrane 1996). Such portrayals defined women as nurturing mothers and housewives and confined them to private domestic spaces. Nonwhite women, many of whom worked outside the home and often dealt with issues of social and economic inequality, were not usually present in television narratives.

Instead, the dominant portrayal of family and domestic contentment consisted of white suburban nuclear families who modeled happiness and stability in environments where women and men adhered to traditional gender roles (Damico and Quay 2017). Single women portrayed on television during the 1950s and 1960s were often concerned with securing romantic relationships even as they worked in gendered jobs as teachers, secretaries, or nurses (Douglas 1994). Some portrayals, however, complicated these ideas. *I Love Lucy*, an enormously popular show that starred actress, comedian, and producer Lucille Ball, consistently featured story lines in which her character sought work outside of her homemaker role. While these initiatives were played for laughs, they also implied a dissatisfaction with traditional gender roles even as her character returned "to domesticity" at the end of many episodes (Egge 2015). Ball continues to be remembered today not only for her long and successful career but also for her enduring influence in several sectors of the entertainment industry.

Films produced by Hollywood studios during this time often reinforced traditional gender roles. Women in many films were portrayed as sex objects, and sympathetic female characters were supportive of their men or devoted to pursuing a traditional life path with marriage and children; powerful, independent, and career-oriented women were largely absent or portrayed negatively in film narratives (Holtzman and Sharpe 2014). Women were most often seen in such particular genres as domestic family dramas, romantic comedies, musicals, and dramas focused on "'typical' female concerns such as getting (or holding onto) a man, raising children, or balancing a career with marriage" (Giannetti 2008, 477). Examples of films that illustrate these ideas include *Father of the Bride* (1950), *How to Marry a Millionaire* (1953), *Seven Brides for Seven Brothers* (1954), and *High Society* (1956) (Holtzman and Sharpe 2014).

American Entertainment Media and Feminism

While traditional definitions of gender roles were dominant in the 1950s through the early 1960s, an activist movement known today as "the women's movement" or the "feminist movement" eventually challenged this status quo. Americans began to question the norms established by the era of domestic containment, ushering in a new period of women's liberation and civil rights. In *The Feminine Mystique* (1963), a book now credited with being a key text of the movement, Betty Friedan challenged the widespread cultural belief that women were always happy in their traditional roles as wives and mothers and did not want to pursue careers or dreams outside the home.

During the era of women's liberation, women advocated for equal opportunity and pay in the workplace, quality childcare, civil rights, and equality in relationships (Holtzman and Sharpe 2014; Faludi 1991). Even though the metaphor of the "waves" of feminism is critiqued because it implies activism and attention to women's social issues and inequality were not taking place during particular times in history, labeling periods of activism as "waves" is often used as an organizational tactic, and the term *second-wave feminism* refers to this particular time period.

As the women's movement gained momentum and the United States experienced other turbulent events of the 1960s, ranging from Vietnam War protests to increased experimentation with sex and drugs, images of women in the visual media began to reflect the changing culture. Representations of women in the media slowly began to expand. In 1965, Helen Gurley Brown (author of the 1962 self-help book *Sex and the Single Girl*) became the first female editor of *Cosmopolitan* magazine.

She transformed the publication, a former traditional women's magazine, into one that prioritized content of interest to a young and liberated female audience. Gurley Brown began to craft what is referred to as the "Cosmo girl" lifestyle by publishing articles on career options, premarital sex, birth control, and fashion. At a time when many women's magazines remained more domestic and conservative in their focus, *Cosmopolitan* advocated for sexual liberation for women, encouraged readers to be comfortable with their own bodies, and suggested women should look for satisfying work (Zimmerman 2012).

While *Cosmopolitan* aimed to liberate female readers in one way, the launch of the news magazine *Ms.* perhaps liberated female readers in another. In 1972, Gloria Steinem, one of the leaders in the feminist movement, cofounded *Ms.* magazine as a periodical focused on women's issues. The magazine's leadership committed itself to reporting on stories focused on areas that impacted the lives of women, diverging from content seen in typical women's magazines at the time. Steinem and her team also challenged the status quo of how advertising functioned in magazines and advocated for a more progressive advertising model more in line with the messages *Ms.* was promoting (Steinem 1990). According to the *Ms.* website, in just over a week after the publication of its first regular issue, 26,000 subscription orders were submitted, demonstrating a significant interest in the subject matter the publication focused on. Later, other feminist magazines such as the teen publication *Sassy* (1988–1996), *Bust* (1993–present), and *Bitch: Feminist Response to Pop Culture* (1996–present) offered alternative content to the messages present in more mainstream women's magazines.

Television programming also changed in response to the feminist movement. Long-standing mainstream representations of the nuclear family, with the contented homemaker mother, were still plentiful. But other constructions of family life also emerged. As television scholar Lynn Spigel (1991) points out, two new types of family situation comedies emerged in the

1960s: the "broken family sitcom" (where the nuclear family structure is not dominant) and the "fantastic family sitcom" (where elements of magic or science fiction are part of the story). Spigel argues that the family compositions on these shows "corresponded to the rising divorce rates of the 1960s," while the fantastic-oriented sitcoms modeled demographic changes and "provided narrative situations and themes that suggested a clear departure from the conventions of the suburban family sitcoms that preceded them" (Spigel 1991, 215–216).

Beginning in the late 1960s, television programming increasingly featured working women who were successful at their careers. Programs such as *That Girl* (1966–1971), *Julia* (1968–1971), *The Mary Tyler Moore Show* (1970–1977), *Laverne & Shirley* (1976–1983), *Police Woman* (1974–1978), and *Charlie's Angels* (1976–1981) presented independent and ambitious young women in a sympathetic and appealing light. Other popular programs, such as *One Day at a Time* (1975–1984), presented single mothers raising teenagers. In the 1980s and 1990s, television shows featured women—some with children, some childless—who were successful in their professional lives. Portrayals of working mothers during this period helped inform the cultural concept of the "supermom" or "superwoman," monikers suggesting women could easily manage both home and career; they could "have it all." During the last decades of the twentieth century, television programs and films such as *Maude* (1972–1978), *Kramer vs. Kramer* (1979), *Roseanne* (1988–1997), and *Murphy Brown* (1988–1998) provided alternative perspectives on working families, single motherhood, and divorce. Network television dramas featured women in a variety of roles, and the establishment of basic and premium cable programming expanded television's offerings of comedies, dramas, and reality-based programming that provided more diverse representations of women.

However, even as representations of women in some media broadened, female characters still largely adhered to traditional ideas of gender. As scholar Susan Douglas writes, women in the early 1970s were underrepresented and often "typecast as homemakers, secretaries, nurses, and, with increasing frequency, victims" in television programming. Douglas describes how female representation changed in the popular culture landscape, with women's progress toward gender equality celebrated in some cases, although girls and women were still ultimately encouraged to conform to stereotypical ideals of gender identity (Douglas 1994, 200).

Bonnie Dow's 1996 analysis of women on prime-time television is founded on similar principles. She points out that while women were seen outside of the home on television, their roles did not necessarily change. For example, although *The Mary Tyler Moore Show* presents independent women and feminist plotlines, Dow argues that "within her family of co-workers, Mary functions in the recognizable roles of idealized mother, wife and daughter—roles familiar from decades of reinforcement in popular culture generally and sitcoms specifically" (Dow 1996, 40).

Toward the end of the twentieth century, the diversity of portrayals of women in media had increased, but men still dominated the media landscape. For example, on prime-time television, the majority of major characters continued to be men, and programs were largely written, produced, and directed by men as well (Vande Berg and Streckfuss 1991; Glascock 2001). An extensive analysis of television programs, commercials, movies, music videos, and teen magazine content by scholar Nancy Signorelli (1997) revealed a number of mixed messages present during this time. First, while women were often depicted as independent, honest, and intelligent in American entertainment in the 1990s, they were underrepresented in comparison to men. She also found that while men in the media were depicted via their occupation, women were more likely to be seen via a relationship context. Finally, Signorelli documented that while women were often portrayed as strong role models, they also prioritized their appearance and had thin physiques.

Criticism was also levied toward filmic representations of women, despite some increases in women's participation. In 1985, as a part of her comic strip *Dykes to Watch Out For*, Allison Bechdel created a character who will only see a movie if it has three elements: (1) the film has to have at least two women in it, (2) the women have to talk to one another, and (3) the women's conversations have to be about something other than a man (Bechdel 2005). Now widely known as the "Bechdel test," this rubric of representation resonated with those frustrated with the quality of representation of women in film. While the test itself is limiting—it does not address issues of diversity or quality of female representations and interactions—research on women in film has demonstrated the central point of Bechdel's critique: films often to do not feature many women, and when they do, women's story lines center around relationships with men. Despite some gains in more equitable representation that materialized toward the end of the twentieth century and into the twenty-first century, women are not equally represented in movies, and the trend of featuring younger female film stars over older women persists (Neville and Anastasio 2019).

The presence of lesbian characters in media began to increase after the women's movement emerged and as American culture moved toward being more accepting of nonheterosexual sexual orientations. While films in the 1960s and 1970s featured stereotypical or trivialized lesbian characters, this began to change toward the end of the century. Independent films such as *Go Fish* (1994), *The Incredibly True Adventures of Two Girls in Love* (1995), and *Chasing Amy* (1998) presented complex representations of gay women (Holtzman and Sharpe 2014). Additionally, such television programs as *Roseanne* (1988–1997), *Law and Order* (1990–2010), *Northern Exposure* (1990–1995), and *Buffy the Vampire Slayer* (1997–2003) featured prominent lesbian characters. In 1997, comedian Ellen DeGeneres's character Ellen Morgan came out as gay on her sitcom *Ellen* (1994–1998), and DeGeneres herself indicated that she was a lesbian on the *The Oprah Winfrey Show*.

While conservative organizations protested the growing representation of sympathetic gays and lesbians on television, wider audiences, particularly gay teens, supported the inclusion. At the end of the twentieth century, the overall representation of lesbians on prime-time television was quite low (Epstein 1999), but representation of LGBTQ+ characters increased in television and film in the early twenty-first century. For example, in 2004 Showtime's groundbreaking *The L Word* debuted, presenting complicated portrayals of lesbian, gay, and transgender characters. *Transamerica*, a film that centers on a character transitioning from man to woman, was released in 2005. While these and other shows and movies featuring LGBTQ+ characters were sometimes criticized about the nature of their LGBTQ+ portrayals in one respect or another, they collectively represented a shift toward inclusion.

Approaches to Analysis: How Representations of Women in Media Are Studied

A new focus on media's representations of women emerged during the era of women's liberation in the 1960s and 1970s. Media studies and the study of mass communication emerged as disciplines in American colleges and universities around this time, as did women's studies programs. Scholars, activists, and audiences began discussing, protesting, and documenting the ways women were portrayed—or not portrayed—in news reports, television shows, films, and advertisements. Additionally, activists and organizations collected data on the number of women working behind the scenes in media industries and how many of these women were in positions of power. In the decades that followed, an ever-expanding focus on women in media has provided various tools, perspectives, and theories used to document and critique mediated representations of women. Many of these formative approaches and theories are referenced today.

Scholars often discuss and analyze media representations of women through the lens of gender ideology, pointing out certain traditional ideas about women and men that are often advanced in media texts. As scholar Carolyn Kitch points out, "Mass media exist not only to make money but also to make meaning. For a century, they have disseminated a particular group of visual stereotypes of womanhood and manhood (though mainly womanhood) that stand for not just gender ideas but also issues of what it means to be 'typically' American and what it takes to have status in American culture" (Kitch 2001, 191).

Scholarship in this area tends to focus on the dominant ways women are portrayed in media and how often they are present, usually as compared to their male counterparts. Additional analysis, often informed by aspects of feminist theory, may examine the various ways women are present in specific films, television programs, news reports, and the like. Media studies scholars often emphasize the role individual audience members may play when looking at media, acknowledging one's active, rather than passive, engagement in interpreting media texts. Research shows not everyone interprets a television show, advertisement, or film in the same way, and the audience's "reading" of texts may be impacted by their social circumstances, demographics, and station in life (Brooker and Jermyn 2003).

However, media texts are also viewed as socializing agents, meaning such products as television shows, magazine covers, and movies advance ideas about, in this case, gender and help shape popular public perceptions of what constitutes "normal" or "typical" gender presentation and behavior. As such, scholars of social cognitive theory argue audiences learn from media representations of gender; portrayals contribute to how people make sense of the social roles of men and women, and they perhaps use this information to inform their own thoughts and behaviors (Bandura 2001; Nabi and Oliver 2009). Additionally, researchers have documented how repeated exposure to particular representations over time can influence audiences' ideas about the world. This phenomenon is called the *cultivation effect* or *cultivation theory*. Scholars demonstrate that audiences adopt, or cultivate, thoughts, attitudes, and behaviors that are similar to ones seen on television and other types of media (Gerbner et al. 1994).

Researchers employ a variety of methods to study and document the representation of women in media. Content analysis is a method used to describe and quantify the presence of women in films, television programs, video games, advertising, and other media. This type of research can systematically document how women (and men) are presented. Other scholarship investigates the potential effect of particular representations—in this case gender—on an audience's thoughts, attitudes, and behaviors. For example, scholars have examined how media portrayals potentially impact audiences' perspectives on gender roles and demographic groups. A large body of research examines relationships between images of female beauty and women's and girls' self-esteem and body confidence. Research has consistently shown that pervasive media images that define *attractive* women as tall and thin contribute to the adoption of unrealistic beauty standards, a focus on achieving an "ideal" body type, and the development of bulimia, anorexia, and similar eating disorders (Groesz, Levine, and Murnen 2002).

Scholars usually define *gender* as a social construct—an understanding of what it means to be a particular gender and what characteristics inform masculinity and femininity during a particular historic moment. Whereas sex is biological, gender scholars Patricia Leavy and Adrienne Trier-Bienick write that socially constructed gender "consists of the ideas we have about masculinity and femininity and how we apply these notions to people based on their sex assignment" (Leavy and Trier-Bienick 2014, 2). Another way to think about this distinction is to associate "sex" with the "categories of male and female" and their associated biological and physiological differences and "gender" with the "categories of masculine and feminine," which refer to culturally constructed differences (Ott and Mack 2014, 218). Gender theorist Judith Butler argues that one's biological sex does not inform one's gender but rather that gender is a performance; her ideas have informed many approaches to analyses of mediated images of women in the field of gender studies (Butler 1990).

The framework of "the binary where masculinity and femininity are seen as polar opposites" is often used by scholars as a way of explaining how media presentations of gender are often oversimplified or stereotyped (Leavy and Trier-Bienick 2014). One approach to this work is to look at how characteristics of traditional ideas or beliefs, or gender ideologies, are present in media texts. Holtzman and Sharpe's list of "Traditional Gender Ideology" traits offers a summary of characteristics historically associated with men and women. They list the following as "male traits of the traditional ideology": "rough and tumble, athletic, tough, high-status job, supports the family financially, in charge at work, active, adventurous, powerful, strong, unemotional, confident, rational, and competent." Their list of "female traits of the traditional ideology" includes the following: "sweet, pretty, tender, low-status job, supports the family emotionally, in charge at home, sensitive, supportive, nurturing, patient, emotional, dependent, irrational, and helpless" (Holtzman and Sharpe 2014, 112). As Levy and Trier-Bienick point out, "Our socially constructed ideas about gender often originate in, and are reinforced by, dominant narratives in the popular culture" (13). Consistent and repetitive presentations of traditional gender ideologies may thus impact how audiences perceive and define gender roles and characteristics.

Approaches to examining women in media texts have also included examinations of images of women from various racial and ethnic groups. However, the examination of media representations of race and ethnicity is complex. While the "historical experiences of various immigrant and racial groups in the United States are profoundly different from one another," mediated representations of these groups, and subsequently, academic research on such representations, may not acknowledge or address the complexities of each race (Holtzman and Sharpe

2014, 309). Discussions of representations are often positioned as studies of homogenized groups (e.g., Asians, Native Americans). This can be problematic because the approach may result in a lack of acknowledgment of individual cultures, but studying such representations also provides important information about portrayals of various groups that reinforce or challenge previously established stereotypes. The *absence* of portrayals of different racial and ethnic groups can be just as "powerfully negative and potentially damaging as the *presence* of stereotypes" (Holtzman and Sharpe 2014, 316; italics in original).

Theoretical Approaches

Additionally, theoretical work informs the ways women in media are studied. For example, theorists Laura Mulvey and John Berger theorize how constructed visuals communicate ideas about gender and power. In her often-cited essay "Visual Pleasure and Narrative Cinema" (1975), Mulvey argues that the ways films are edited situate all viewers of film to adopt a "male gaze," whereby they experience the film from the male perspective, embracing the man as the hero and the woman in a supporting "love interest" role. This positioning, Mulvey argues, helps to maintain ideas of traditional gender power relations in the culture. In *Ways of Seeing* (1977), Berger et al. collectively argue in a series of essays that there is a long history of image creation in Western art that sets up a dynamic where women are passive subjects to be looked at by men. The authors point out a similar dynamic is present in visual media, particularly advertising, where women are objectified for presumed male pleasure (Berger et al. 1977).

The "beauty myth" is a term theorized by feminist writer Naomi Wolf in her 1990 book *The Beauty Myth*. Wolf uses the term to describe or refer to the idea that a pervasive and ongoing slew of media messages routinely pressure women and girls to look beautiful, thin, and (for some) young (Wolf 1990). She argues that despite societal gains made by women during the feminist movement, women still find themselves trying to achieve physical perfection and flawless beauty as seen in media—despite the fact that such "perfection" is often achieved by digitally altering images to eliminate "flaws" and trim body physique using computer editing techniques. In further discussions of unrealistic idealized images of beauty, many explain that historically mainstream media texts define *beauty* in rather limited ways, privileging young white women with figures largely unrepresentative of the population at large. These unrealistic ideal images of beauty are referenced by researchers who study their potential influences on women struggling with eating disorders, self-esteem, and body dissatisfaction (Groesz, Levine and Murnen 2002).

There are many branches of feminist thought and many ways to use aspects of feminist theory to examine representations of women in such media texts as news reports, advertising, films, and television shows. As Cirksena and Cuklanz (1992) point out, liberal feminist approaches operate under the assumption that women and men are equal in most ways and that women should not be prevented from securing voting rights, education, equal pay, or domestic equality, among other issues, just because past generations subscribed to the myth that women were too emotional and fragile to fully participate in American society. An analysis of media via a liberal feminist lens may examine how women's participation is presented in various media forms. Those using the frame of socialist feminism, which, in part, examines the cultural divide that supports the presence of men in the public sphere and confines women to the private sphere, might investigate how women are portrayed in the home and workplace. Scholars also look at whether media portrayals of women are more concerned with romance and relationships than with work or current events.

Other research examines how active women are in media narratives and whether their individual successes, goals, and choices are a priority (Ott and Mack 2014). A large body of scholarship focuses on the sexual objectification of women and how mainstream images of women promote particular beauty standards (Groesz, Levine, and Murnen 2002). Scholars who focus on representations of women of color consider whether women are exploited in media texts or defined and presented from a Western perspective, one that is often oppressive and limiting (Kamran 2017).

Other research focusing on women of color documents and discusses representations of demographic groups that have been historically marginalized and stereotyped in mainstream media. For example, the feminist scholar bell hooks (the lack of capitalization is intentional) advocates for diversifying approaches to feminism. She argues that the feminist movement has not always acknowledged the diversity of the female experience, particularly along race and socioeconomic class lines. She also contends that the country's mainstream white culture dominates, marginalizes, and stereotypes Black women and men in its media representations (hooks 1992). Finally, she warns that the pervasiveness of problematic images of "Blackness" may prompt women, communities of color, and other marginalized audiences to internalize these negative ideas about themselves—thus perpetuating those same negative ideas and bolstering the existing white- and male-dominated power structure.

Black feminist scholars also call attention to mainstream media's attempts to define who they are. They urge Black women to create their *own* understanding of who they are in defiance of media constructions (Collins 1991). Other scholars have examined representations of such groups as Latina women, Native American women, and Asian women, among others, while considering other aspects of the representation at the same time, such as their economic status or profession. Scholar Kimberlé Crenshaw uses the historical term "intersectionality" to suggest women's gender, race, and socioeconomic class are interconnected and inform women's individually unique lives. Her work is often referenced when considering experiences of diverse women and, by extension, their media representations (Crenshaw 1989). Additionally, strands of scholarship in audience studies focus on women as active audience members, highlighting how and why women engage with and enjoy media that represent and portray women in problematic ways.

Common Stereotypes and Evolving Images of Women in Media

As the diversity of portrayals of women in visual media has increased over time, cultural and empirical research has revealed particular trends. As previously discussed, portrayals of women in media texts are often complex and offer mixed messages to audiences. However, it is perhaps useful to identify some common stereotypical portrayals of women in mainstream media. Versions of these characterizations are often referred to in media, gender, and feminist scholarship as well as in educational materials designed to increase critical awareness of media depictions of women.

When scholars discuss stereotypical portrayals of women in media, they are usually referring to presentations conforming to traditional ideas about gender characteristics and gender roles. A *stereotype*, by definition, is an oversimplified idea or conception of a particular person, group, or thing. Gender stereotypes, then, are ones that assign oversimplified traditional ideas about what it means to be a man to all men and what it means to be a woman to all women. In comparison, complex representations of men and women may include so-called stereotypical characteristics, but only as part of more fully developed and nuanced portrayals.

Indeed, research has demonstrated that traditional presentations of gender continue to be present in mainstream twentieth- and twenty-first-century media. Media stereotypes of women are ones that "portray women as submissive, less intelligent than men, sexual objects, and preoccupied with their roles as 'sexy' wives and mothers" (Roessner 2012, 329). In general, women are presented as more passive, more emotional, and more likely to be seen in private spaces like the home than their male counterparts; they are also more likely to be portrayed as sex objects (Ott and Mack 2014). SAS Scholar Rachel Silverman writes that stereotypes about gender and sexuality "perpetuate the idea that only male and female genders exist," while framing men as promiscuous, aggressive, brutish and detached and women as sexually repressed, demure, passive, and nurturing (Silverman 2012, 373).

Researchers have documented a history of multiple stereotypical representations of diverse women in media that build upon long-standing cultural ideas about gender, race, and ethnicity. For example, female Asian stereotypes include the sexual "Dragon Lady," the submissive and subservient "China Doll," and the "Madame Butterfly"—Asian women who suffer heartbreak after becoming involved with white men over Asian men (Keith 2016).

Native American women are often portrayed in American cinema, television, literature, and other media as underdeveloped older women or maidens or as victims of violence, or they are represented in stereotypically Native roles that emphasize tribal tropes. They also function in many media narratives as figures whose main purpose in the story is to support, culturally instruct, and fall in love with the usually white male lead (Nagle 2018).

Popular media images of African American women often took the form of domestic figures like the mammy, a matronly woman who often cared for white children and completed other domestic tasks, and the Aunt Jemimah, a stereotype of a cook who was appropriated to sell pancake mix (Jewel 1993). These glaringly racist representations have faded away in recent decades, but other problematic stereotypes of Black women have been more persistent, including the bossy, argumentative "Sapphire" and the sexual "Jezebel" (Jewel 1993). Remnants of these more historical representations still inform depictions of Black women in media today; contemporary stereotypes include the sassy or "angry Black woman" and the lazy "welfare mother" (Ward 2015).

Simplistic stereotypes of Latina girls and women also abound. Examples that include the "fat mamacita," the "Mexican spitfire," and the "sexy senorita" have long dominated American entertainment (Gutiérrez n.d.). Another Latina character stereotype is that of the subservient and passive woman, which as one scholar notes, "corresponds to the complementary and active role of Latino men. The logic seems to be that since Latino men are macho, Latinas must be passive. This has resulted in a stereotype that portrays Latinas as inarticulate, subservient, passive and gullible. This negative stereotype tends to limit mass media portrayals of Latinas to roles as either maids or sex objects" (Cortese 2008, 106).

However, while stereotypical images persist, decades of scholarship from the latter part of the twentieth century and early twenty-first century demonstrate a complex evolution of portrayals of women in American popular culture. For example, late twentieth-century research on popular nighttime television soap operas finds women are portrayed as independent, career oriented, and powerful (Geraghty 1991). Additionally, while crime-oriented films may not feature many women in significant roles, strong female characters emerged in this genre of television programming at the beginning of the twenty-first century (Byerly and Ross 2006). In the introduction to her edited book *Action Chicks: New Images of Tough Women in Popular Culture*, Sherrie Inness summarizes how scholars who examine media's "tough women" of the late twentieth and early twenty-first century often highlight the complexities and contradictions present in their portrayals that seem, in many ways, to challenge the gender status quo. However, Inness writes, while characters such as Xena, of *Xena: Warrior Princess*; Buffy Summers, of *Buffy the Vampire Slayer*, Sarah Pezzini, of *Witchblade*; and Sarah Connor, of the *Terminator* films, are tough, heroic, and powerful, they are often "still expected to be feminine, attractive and heterosexually appealing" (Inness 2004, 14).

Similarly, in late twentieth-century and early twenty-first-century fantasy and science fiction texts, women are more likely to be positioned as equal to men, even as characterizations of their traditional femininity often undermine their power (Byerly and Ross 2006). These genres also present more complex representations of women. While they sometimes affirm gender stereotypes, female characters in many of the popular *Star Wars* films, *Star Trek* television shows, *Lord of the Rings* films and *Harry Potter* narratives play important roles even though the male narrative is often the priority. However, film scholars point out that many mainstream Hollywood films continue to convey traditional ideas about gender. "Many dramas emphasize women's struggles with expectations for their gender; most other well-known dramatic films starring women center on romance, doomed love, or love gone wrong. On the other hand, male dominated dramas emphasize stories about corruption, loyalty and war" (Adney 2014, 110).

In the last twenty years, numerous high-quality programs featuring women protagonists became central to the television and streaming landscape. Additionally, choices by some to employ diverse producers, directors, and writers resulted in a range of portrayals of women on big and small screens that better reflected the shifting cultural norms and expectations around the capabilities and full humanity of women. For example, shows such as *The Closer* (2005–2012), *Fringe* (2008–2013), *Scandal* (2012–2018), and *Grey's Anatomy* (2005–present) present educated, experienced professional women who are central to the program's narrative. And characters on programs such as *Damages* (2007–2012), *House of Cards* (2013–2018), and *Homeland* (2011–2020) feature developed, nuanced women protagonists—who are excellent at their job but who also possess poor parenting skills. *The Hunger Games* series of films feature a strong female lead, and such blockbuster films as *Wonder Woman* (2017) and *Black Panther* (2018) are positively recognized for their strong portrayals of female characters. Additionally, versions of *Ghostbusters* (2016) and *Oceans 8* (2018) with all-female casts were moderately successful. While issues still remain around aspects of representations of women on and behind the screens, the landscape has changed.

Finally, unscripted "reality" television shows generally feature a diverse slate of women. The emergence and popularity of the reality-based television genre featuring "average" people on programs with various foci—from talent competitions (e.g., *American Idol* (2002–present)) to makeover shows (e.g., *What Not to Wear* (2003–2013)) to dating shows (e.g., *The Bachelor* (2002–present)). Some reality-based programs are praised for addressing social issues relevant to women through their programming, but these same shows are sometimes criticized for reinforcing other messages seen as damaging to women and girls. For example, the popular *America's Next Top Model* (2003–2018) addressed issues related to body image, eating disorders, sexuality, and gender and featured LGBTQ+ participants. At the same time, however, the show was challenged for the ways it critiqued and focused on physical beauty (Friedman 2015). Even though reality-based television shows present women from a range of racial, socioeconomic, and other demographic groups, the ways these women are framed can be problematic. For example, Jervette Ward's (2015) edited book of essays explores the representation of Black women on reality-based television. It highlights problematic stereotypes and racist practices on the shows in addition to other, more positive, portrayals.

Women in Advertising

Advertising messages aim to reach target audiences who will consider purchasing the advertiser's product or service. In so doing, ads may target men and women differently, advancing ideas about gender and the cultural roles of men and women through their messaging. In 1976, sociologist Erving Goffman offered an analysis of how advertising images communicate and construct cultural expectations of gender in his often referenced book *Gender Advertisements.* Using more than 500 advertisements as evidence, Goffman documented how women in many ads during the twentieth century are presented as passive, submissive, childlike, or vulnerable, thus defining femininity along these lines. They are positioned as subordinate to men, who are typically presented in advertising of the period as confident, active, and/or intimidating. Much of Goffman's analysis is derived from his attention to the ways women and men are posed in advertising photographs. As he noted, advertisements often show women lying down, standing with one knee bent, or touching a part of their body or tilting their head in ways that present femininity as soft, passive, and submissive.

For decades following the publication of *Gender Advertisements,* scholars applied Goffman's ideas to more contemporary promotional materials, demonstrating there is not much change in the representations of women and the respective construction of gender roles—women were portrayed as passive, sexualized, and feminine (Belknap and Leonard 1991). In *Provocateur: Images of Women and Minorities in Advertising,* an analysis of late twentieth- and early twenty-first-century advertising, scholar Anthony Cortese points out several trends reminiscent of Goffman's initial findings. He writes that women's body parts are focused on without showing their faces and that women's bodies are often infused with inanimate objects, such as an image of a handbag on a table where the table's legs are women's legs in high heels (Cortese 2016).

Cortese also documents that when men and women are seen in advertisements together, it is common for men to have the more prominent and active role, with women serving a decorative background part. Further, when women are actively portrayed in advertising, men are more likely to be absent altogether rather than placed in a secondary role, something that contributes to the power imbalance between men and women in advertising representations (Cortese 2016). While Cortese acknowledges some positive shifts in recent advertising that elevates new ideas about beauty and self-worth, he points to the many ways contemporary advertising continues to objectify and sexualize women. In discussions of racial-ethnic representations in advertising, he points out that nonwhite women are often presented in contexts that white women in advertising are seen in; there is little acknowledgment of the cultural, socioeconomic, or physical characteristics that might define these groups and their identities.

Other advertising analysis utilizes the lens of the binary from feminist theory to demonstrate that women in ads are often passive, rather than active, participants; are often associated with the private space of the home rather than the workplace; and are often defined by their sexually objectified bodies rather than their intellect (Ott and Mack 2014). In her books, lectures, and documentaries, Jean Kilbourne points out that advertisements featuring women are often problematic because they contribute to a "toxic cultural environment" where pressure is put on girls and women to look, act, and be a particular way—feminine and sexy but also virginal and successful but not aggressive—adopting a "false self" (Kilbourne 1999, 130). She additionally argues, using multiple examples of advertisements as her evidence, that images of women in advertising prompt women to develop and define their identities as connected to products and the use of them, encourage dangerous messages about alcohol and tobacco use, and pressure women to strive to achieve an unattainable body size and beauty standard.

In their 2011 review of advertising research during what they categorize as the prefeminist period (pre-1950s–early 1960s), the feminist period (1960s–1970s), and the postfeminist period (post-1985), John Mager and James Helgeson identify trends from multiple studies on presentations of gender in advertising during those time frames. During the prefeminist period, they write, advertising research documents that women were primarily seen in the home, had little power to make important decisions, were often seen as sexual objects, and were reliant on men. In the feminist period, images of women in advertising changed a bit; they were depicted as sex objects and dependent on men less frequently, although female body parts were often spotlighted. In the postfeminist period, less stereotypical presentations of women increased in advertising, but women continued to be situated in the home, as housewives, as fixated on their attractiveness, and as sex objects (Mager and Helgeson 2011).

Mager and Helgeson point out that the complicated response to the feminist sexual revolution may help explain why women seen as sex objects in advertising persisted during the postfeminist period studied: "Conflict in feminist thought regarding sexual freedom made it easy for advertising to incorporate female sexuality in ads and may have promoted its use" (Mager and Helgeson 2011, 240). Advertisers appropriated other aspects of feminist ideas in advertising as well—perhaps to appear supportive of the ideas of the feminist movement while ultimately using these ideas in ways to promote their products. One particularly notable example of this is the Virginia Slims cigarette advertising campaign and its slogan, "You've come a long way, baby." In the late 1960s, when the women's movement was underway, this slogan was crafted to target women seeking to be independent and liberated. The tobacco company essentially used the ideals of the feminist movement to sell cigarettes. The words of the slogan evoke the idea of progress toward achieving the equality women were fighting for.

While issues around the portrayal of women in advertising persist, in more recent years, companies have increasingly directed their marketing communication teams to create messaging that deliberately challenges stereotypical and limiting ideas about women. For example, the Dove Campaign for Real Beauty, a marketing communication campaign that began in 2004, aimed to broaden the definition of beauty after internal research indicated just 2 percent of 3,000 surveyed women considered themselves beautiful (Bahadur 2014). The campaign prominently features a diverse group of beautiful "real women" in its imagery, and while the campaign has been critiqued for capitalizing on women's insecurities to sell Dove products by focusing on appearance and beauty, it has also been complimented for challenging stereotypical ideas. Other companies have followed suit. In 2014, American Eagle's Aerie lingerie store launched its Aerie Real campaign, where the company vowed not to use any airbrushing or other digital alteration of their models. The body positive message, which was celebrated by many of the company's shoppers, aimed to challenge "supermodel standards" and to acknowledge research that shows the impact mediated images can have on one's body confidence (Krupnick 2014).

Other campaigns focus on female empowerment. For example, the feminine product company Always launched a Like a Girl campaign in 2014 that encouraged confidence among girls by reappropriating the insult "like a girl" in its display of images and accompanying narratives. In 2017, the company followed up with a new campaign called Keep Going to encourage girls to overcome their fear of failure by using setbacks as a way of building confidence. In 2016, the fashion company H&M launched the She's a Lady campaign that challenged the idea women needed to be "ladylike" with their fashion choices. A 2017 General Electric commercial promoted interest in science and technology by asking what would happen if the culture treated female scientists like celebrities. These types of campaigns have come to be known as *feminist advertising*, an approach critically discussed by those who study women in advertising. On the one hand, scholars acknowledge that the advertisements offer positive messages and perspectives; on the other hand, they critique the alignment of such positive messages with consumerism, challenge the continued focus on women's bodies, and are critical of putting the onus on women to "be confident" in a societal structure that in many ways still favors men (Jennings 2018).

The Digital Age and Feminist Practices

The early years of computer programming were actually pioneered by women, but as with many histories, women's contributions to the formative development of the technology industries have often been erased or unacknowledged (Royal 2014). Over time, technology fields became male dominated, perhaps due in part to gender stereotypes present in the culture that suggested women were not suited for the field and that those who did engage in this type of work were "nerds" (Royal 2014). The culture-changing sites MySpace, Facebook, YouTube, and Wikipedia were designed by men, perhaps due to deep and persistent gender disparities in computer fields that penalized women (Endres 2012a). However, since the beginning of the twenty-first century, women have been prominent participants in new digital media as creators, citizen journalists, producers, blog writers, and engineers. In addition, more high-profile women represented aspects of large technology companies. In addition to information seeking and entertainment, social media is often used by women to communicate with others and engage in online communities (Royal 2014). Unfortunately, some men have used social media to stalk and bully women or to disseminate violent and misogynistic content against women.

The emergence of new technologies and the ability for average citizens to produce and easily distribute content across digital platforms allowed for the creation of media by women that, at times, challenged mainstream views. Expanding digital technologies allowed for anyone to create a website, write a blog, produce and post videos, and engage in social media. This has resulted in new spaces for women to discuss issues, challenge mainstream media representations, and become authors of widely shared work. It also provided new formats of female representations and became a central tool in the next iterations of feminist activism.

Third-Wave Feminism

Beginning in the 1990s, so-called *third-wave feminism* continued to promote the ideals of the second wave while also challenging its underlying assumptions. In rejecting the idea of a unified, collective movement, third-wave feminism aims to consider more completely the diverse experiences of women by more fully reflecting on one's race, ethnicity, socioeconomic status, and identity. Scholar Martha Rampton (2015) points out characteristics of this movement are challenges to universal ideas about what it means to be a woman and previously held constructs of gender and sexuality. Rampton explains the "third wave" breaks boundaries because it "tends to be global, multi-cultural, and it shuns simple answers or artificial categories of identity, gender, and sexuality. Its transversal politics means differences such as those of ethnicity, class, sexual orientation, etc. are celebrated and recognized as dynamic, situational, and provisional. Reality is conceived not so much in terms of fixed structures and power relations, but in terms of performance within contingencies" (Rampton 2015). Third-wave feminists may reject the term *feminist* and challenge previously held ideas about sexualized images of women in popular culture. For example, "third wave feminists tend to highlight women's agency and choice in intimate relationships," focusing on how previously criticized sexual practices and portrayals can be "sites of women's empowerment and pleasure" (Griebling 2012, 107). While so-called *fourth-wave feminism* builds upon some of the third-wave principles, feminist writers suggest this chapter of activism is digitally situated. As *Bustle*'s Kristen Sollee (2015) explains, the internet "drives discourse, from hashtag activism to the digital forums that create community, foster debate and encourage IRL (in real life) action."

One outcome of third-wave feminism was the riot grrrl movement—a challenge to sexism that emerged from the punk music scene in the 1990s—and the subsequent creation and publication of *zines*, or handmade newsletters or magazines. Riot grrrls, appropriating a new spelling of the word *girl* to reclaim the term they viewed being used in a patronizing way, aimed to aggressively challenge discriminatory practices affecting all marginalized groups (Marcus 2010). Their photocopied zines, and subsequent inspired e-zines (or electronic zines, shared via digital methods) created by other women, provided a "woman e-zines -only space" where diverse voices were heard and traditional gender boundaries were crossed (Rampton 2015).

Today, mainstream social media platforms such as Facebook, Twitter, Tumblr, TikTok, and Instagram are fixtures in the culture. Mobile phone use is pervasive, and consumers engage in using social media platforms for sharing photos and messaging; the popularity of visual platforms like Instagram and Pinterest created new opportunities for women to participate in media creation, activism, and community building—essentially representing aspects of themselves. Through the use of hashtags (#, the number sign character) on Twitter, women engage in hashtag activism, where ideas, protests, and calls to action are organized by the use of a hashtag. Activism campaigns include #WomenShould, where sexism toward women was identified in Google searches; #EverydaySexism, where women are encouraged to note their problematic experiences, no matter how small; #TimesUp, whose goal is to draw attention to, and end, sexual misconduct in the workplace; and #MeToo, which was initially created as a safe space for girls to connect but later popularized and used as a mechanism for women to identify times they had experienced sexual assault (UN Women 2019).

The ubiquitous integration of Web 2.0 technology and social media—platforms that allow for social interaction—resulted in the production of volumes of content by users that is easily shared. In her discussion of what this means from a gender perspective, scholar Cory Armstrong explains, "The significance of gender representations can now be felt across three dimensions: Traditional mainstream content, which generally comes from informational, entertainment or persuasive content developed by professionals in the field of media production; media (primarily online) in which women control and share their own images, such as websites, social media or blogs; and media content (primarily online) shared about women but without their consent or (potentially) knowledge" (Armstrong 2013, 222).

An area of scholarly focus is an examination of how gender is constructed and performed in online spaces. Initially, as blogs, video sharing, and social media platforms became popular, it was anticipated women could use these vehicles to create their own content and perhaps provide alternatives to mainstream media stereotypes and traditional conceptions of gender (Webb and Temple 2016). However, scholars Lynne Webb and Nicholas Temple point out that because social media sites, in particular, are corporate owned, they tend to feature advertising that reiterates traditional constructions of what it means to be a woman (or man). Webb and Temple note research that suggests users internalize messages encouraging women to adhere to traditional definitions of femininity, including an emphasis on an attractive, and often sexy, appearance. At the same time, however, online platforms can give women greater opportunities to challenge traditional ideas about gender and sexuality, engage in gender-based activism, and communicate their own interests. Blogging in particular is identified as a site of female empowerment for many women, and blogging platforms foster connections, community, and activism among diverse women who write about parenting, politics, and social issues.

Conclusion

The ways women are represented in media texts have certainly expanded from the traditional "homemaker" depictions of women in nineteenth-century magazines. In the ever-expanding media landscape, audiences have an extensive menu of content to choose from. Items on this menu offer a range of entertainment and information options that advance diverse representations of women, challenge traditional conceptions of gender, and offer viewers the opportunity to engage with complex and interesting characters. At the same time, many portrayals of women—in film, on television, in advertising, and on the news—still adhere to traditional ideas about gender roles and reinforce long-running gender stereotypes. Additionally, while women are employed in greater numbers today as directors, writers, producers, and editors in the television and film arenas, the news industry, and in promotional fields, these industries remain male dominated. The lack of the equitable inclusion of women and underrepresented groups in all areas of the mainstream media industry presents a range of problems and controversies, although many are currently working hard to advocate for solutions that will result in meaningful change.

Bibliography

Adney, Karley. 2014. "Film: Hollywood." In *Encyclopedia of Gender in Media*, edited by Mary Kosut, 110–113. Thousand Oaks, CA: Sage.

Allan, Kenneth, and Scott Coltrane. 1996. "Gender Displaying Television Commercials: A Comparative Study of Television Commercials in the 1950s and 1980s." *Sex Roles* 35 (3/4): 185–203.

Alley, Robert, and Irby Brown. 2001. *Women Television Producers: Transformation of the Male Medium*. Rochester, NY: University of Rochester Press.

Amaral, Luis Nunes, Joao Moreira, Murielle Dunand, Heliodoro Tejedor Navarro, and Ada Lee Hyojun. 2020. "Long-Term Patterns of Gender Imbalance in an Industry without Ability or Level of Interest Differences." *PLoS ONE* 15 (4). https://doi.org/10.1371/journal.pone.0229662

Armstrong, Cory. 2013. "The Next Frontier in Gender Representation." In *Media Disparity*, edited by Cory Armstrong, 217–226. Lanham, MD: Rowman & Littlefield.

Bahadur, Nina. 2014. "Dove 'Real Beauty' Campaign Turns 10: How a Brand Tried to Change the Conversation about Female Beauty." *HuffPost*, January 1, 2014. https://www.huffpost.com/entry/dove-real-beauty-campaign-turns-10_n_4575940

Bandura, Albert. 2001. "Social Cognitive Theory: An Agentic Perspective." *Annual Review of Psychology* 52: 1–26.

Bechdel, Alison. 2005. "The Rule." *Dykes to Watch Out For*, August 16, 2005. https://dykestowatchoutfor.com/the-rule/

Belknap, Penny, and Wilbert M. Leonard. 1991. "A Conceptual Replication and Extension of Goffman's Study of Gender Advertisements." *Sex Roles* 25: 103–118.

Benshoff, Harry, and Sean Griffin. 2009. *America on Film: Representing Race, Class, Gender and Sexuality at the Movies*. 2nd ed. Malden, MA: Wiley-Blackwell.

Berger, John, Sven Blomberg, Chris Fox, Michael Dibb, and Richard Hollis. 1977. *Ways of Seeing*. London: Penguin Books.

Bosker, Bianca. 2013. "New Selfie-Help Apps Are Airbrushing Us All into Fake Instagram Perfection." *HuffPost*, December 5, 2013. https://www.huffpost.com/entry/selfie-instagram_n_4391220

Brooker, Will, and Deborah Jermyn, eds. 2003. *The Audience Studies Reader*. New York: Routledge.

Brumberg, Joan Jacobs. 1997. *The Body Project: An Intimate History of American Girls*. New York, Random House.

Butler, Judith. 1990. *Gender Trouble*. London: Routledge.

Byerly, Carolyn M. 2012. "Women and the Media." In *Global Women's Issues: Women in the World Today, Extended Version*, [Open Source e-book]. Bureau of International Information Programs, United States Department of State. https://opentextbc.ca/womenintheworld/

Byerly, Carolyn M., and Karen Ross. 2002. *Women & Media: A Critical Introduction*. Malden, MA: Blackwell Publishing.

Campbell, Richard, Christopher Martin, and Bettina Fabos. 2016. *Media and Culture*. 10th ed. Boston: Bedford/St. Martins.

Cantor, Muriel G. 1991. "The American Family on Television: From Molly Goldberg to Bill Cosby." *Journal of Comparative Family Studies* 22 (2): 205–216.

Chambers, Deborah, Linda Steiner, and Carole Fleming. 2004. *Women and Journalism*. London: Routledge.

Cirksena, Kathryn, and Lisa Cuklanz. 1992. "Male Is to Female as __ Is to __: A Guided Tour of Five Feminist Frameworks for Communication Studies." In *Women Making Meaning: New Feminist Directions in Communications*, edited by Lana Rakow, 18–43. London: Routledge.

Collins, Patricia Hill. 1991. *Black Feminist Thought: Knowledge, Consciousness, and the Politics of Empowerment*. New York: Routledge.

Cortese, Anthony. 2008. *Provocateur: Images of Women and Minorities in Advertising*. 3rd ed. Lanham, MD: Rowman & Littlefield.

Cortese, Anthony. 2016. *Provocateur: Images of Women and Minorities in Advertising*. 4th ed. Lanham, MD: Rowman & Littlefield.

Creed, Barbara. 1994. "Vamp." In *The Woman's Companion to International Film*, edited by Annette Kuhn and Susannah Radstone, 408–410. Berkeley: University of California Press.

Crenshaw, Kimberlé. 1989. "Demarginalizing the Intersection of Race and Sex: A Black Feminist Critique of Antidiscrimination Doctrine, Feminist Theory and Antiracist Politics." *University of Chicago Legal Forum* 1 (8): 139–167. https://chicagounbound.uchicago.edu/cgi/viewcontent.cgi?article=1052&context=uclf

Damico, A., and S. Quay. 2017. "Domestic Containment in Early Cold War Popular Culture." In *Pop Culture Universe: Icons, Idols, Ideas*, edited by Richard Hall, Edward Lordan, Tiffini Travis, and Nita Lang. [ABC-CLIO Solutions: Academic editions database.] Santa Barbara, CA: ABC-CLIO.

De Hart, Jennifer. 2001. "Containment at Home: Gender, Sexuality, and National Identity in Cold War America." In *Rethinking Cold War Culture*, edited by Peter Kuznick and James Gilbert, 124–155. Washington, DC: Smithsonian Books.

Douglas, Susan. 1995. *Where the Girls Are: Growing Up Female with the Mass Media*. New York: Times Books.

Dow, Bonnie. 1996. *Prime-Time Feminism: Television, Media Culture and the Women's Movement since 1970*. Philadelphia: University of Pennsylvania Press.

Earman, Cynthia. 2000. "An Uncommon Scold." *Library of Congress Information Bulletin* 59 (1). https://www.loc.gov/loc/lcib/0001/royall.html

Egge, Sara. 2015. "'I Love Lucy' Confronts the American Housewife Ideal." Norton Center for the Arts, February 2, 2015. http://nortoncenter.com/2015/02/02/i-love-lucy-confronts-the-1950s-american-housewife-ideal/

Endres, Kathleen. 2012a. "New Media." In *Encyclopedia of Gender in Media*, edited by Mary Kosut, 253–256. Thousand Oaks, CA: Sage.

Endres, Kathleen. 2012b. "Women's Magazines: Fashion." In *Encyclopedia of Gender in Media*, edited by Mary Kosut, 434–439. Thousand Oaks, CA: Sage.

Enstad, Nan. 1999. *Ladies of Labor, Girls of Adventure: Working Women, Popular Culture, and Labor Politics at the Turn of the Twentieth Century*. New York: Columbia University Press.

Epstein, Jeffrey. 1999. "Prime Time for Gay Youth (Gay Characters on Television)." *The Advocate*, April 27, 1999: 4–6.

Faludi, Susan. 1991. *Backlash: The Undeclared War against American Women*. New York: Crown Publishing Group.

Fields, Jill. 2007. *An Intimate Affair: Women, Lingerie, Sexuality*. Berkeley: University of California Press.

Friedan, Betty. 1963. *The Feminine Mystique*. New York: W. W. Norton & Company.

Friedman, Vanessa. 2015. "America's Next Top Model, Deconstructed." *New York Times*, December 4, 2016.

https://www.nytimes.com/2015/12/06/fashion/americas-next-top-model-deconstructed.html

Gaydos, Steven, and Tim Gray. 2016. "A Telling Look Back at the Century-Old Quest for Diversity in Entertainment." *Variety*, February 23, 2016. https://variety.com/2016/film/news/diversity-history-movies-tv-1201712294/

Geraghty, Christine. 1991. *Women and Soap Opera: A Study of Prime Time Soaps*. Cambridge, UK: Polity Press.

Gerbner, George, Larry Gross, Michael Morgan, and Nancy Signorelli. 1994. "Growing Up with Television: The Cultivation Perspective." In *Media Effects: Advances in Theory and Research*, edited by Jennings Bryant and Dolf Zillmann, 17–41. Hillside, NJ: Lawrence Erlbaum Associates, Inc.

Giannetti, Louis 2008. *Understanding Movies*. 11th ed. Upper Saddle River, NJ: Prentice Hall.

Glascock, Jack. 2001. "Gender Roles on Prime-Time Network Television: Demographics and Behaviors." *Journal of Broadcasting & Electronic Media* 45 (4): 656–669. https://doi.org/10.1207/s15506878jobem4504_7

Global Media Monitoring Project. n.d. "Background." Who Makes the News. Accessed May 1, 2020. http://whomakesthenews.org/about-us

Goffman, Erving. 1976. *Gender Advertisements*. New York: Harper & Row.

Greenwald, Maurine Weiner. 1990. *Women, War, and Work. The Impact of World War I on Women Workers in the United States*. Ithaca, NY: Cornell University Press.

Griebling, Brittany. 2012. "Feminist Theory: Third Wave." In *Encyclopedia of Gender in Media*, edited by Mary Kosut, 106–108. Thousand Oaks, CA: Sage.

Groesz, Lisa, Michael Levine, and Sara Murnen. 2002. "The Effect of Experimental Presentation of Thin Media

Images on Body Satisfaction: A Meta-Analytic Review." *International Journal of Eating Disorders* 31 (1): 1–16. https://doi.org/10.1002/eat.10005

Guba, Evon, and Yvonnna Lincoln. 1994. "Competing Paradigms in Qualitative Research." In *Handbook of Qualitative Research*, edited by Norman K. Denzin and Yvonna S. Lincoln, 105–117. Thousand Oaks, CA: SAGE Publications.

Gutiérrez, Felix. n.d. "More Than 200 Years of Latino Media in the United States." *American Latinos and the Making of the United States: A Theme Study.* National Park System Advisory Board (NPSAB) for the National Park Service (NPS). Accessed May 1, 2020. https://www.nps.gov/articles/latinothemestudymedia.htm

Holtzman, Linda, and Leon Sharpe. 2014. *Media Messages: What Film, Television, and Popular Music Teach Us about Race, Class, Gender, and Sexual Orientation*. Armonk, NY: M.E. Sharpe.

Honey, Maureen. 1985. *Creating Rosie the Riveter: Class, Gender and Propaganda during World War II*. Amherst: University of Massachusetts Press.

hooks, bell. 1992. *Black Looks: Race and Representation*. Boston: South End Press.

Huhulea, Irene. 2016. "Infographic: The History of Women's Media." A Woman's Thing, August 11, 2016. https://awomensthing.org/blog/history-womens-media/

Inness, Sherrie. 2004. *Action Chicks: New Images of Tough Women in Popular Culture*. New York: Palgrave MacMillan.

Jennings, Rebecca. 2018. "Why Feminist Advertising Doesn't Make Us Better Feminists." Vox, November 5, 2018. https://www.vox.com/the-goods/2018/11/5/18056004/feminist-advertising-empowered-sarah-banet-weiser

Jewel, K. Sue. 1993. *From Mammy to Miss America and Beyond: Cultural Images and the Shaping of U.S. Policy*. London: Routledge.

Kamran, Gabriella. 2017. "Feminism 101: What Is Postcolonial Feminism?" *FEM*, April 18, 2017. https://femmagazine.com/feminism-101-what-is-postcolonial-feminism/

Keith, Zak. 2016. "Hollywood Asian Stereotypes." Keith Productions. http://www.zakkeith.com/articles,blogs,forums/hollywood-asian-stereotypes.htm

Kilbourne, Jean. 1995. *Slim Hopes: Advertising and the Obsession with Thinness* [documentary]. Directed by Sut Jhally. Northampton, MA: Media Education Foundation.

Kilbourne, Jean. 1999. *Deadly Persuasion: Why Women and Girls Must Fight the Addictive Power of Advertising*. New York: Free Press.

Kitch, Carolyn. 2001. *The Girl on the Magazine Cover: The Origins of Visual Stereotypes in American Mass Media*. Chapel Hill: University of North Carolina Press.

Krupnick, Ellie. 2014. "Aerie's Unretouched Ads 'Challenge Supermodel Standards' for Young Women." *HuffPost*, January 17, 2014. https://www.huffpost.com/entry/aerie-unretouched-ads-photos_n_4618139

Landers, Jackson. 2016. "For Susan B. Anthony, Getting Support for Her 'Revolution' Meant Taking On an Unusual Ally." *Smithsonian Magazine*, March 24, 2016. https://www.smithsonianmag.com/smithsonian-institution/susan-anthony-getting-support-revolution-taking-on-an-unusual-ally-180958480/

Lauzen, Martha. 2019. *Boxed In 2018–19: Women on Screen and behind the Scenes in Television*. Center for the Study of Women in Television & Film, San Diego State University, September 2019. https://womenintvfilm.sdsu.edu/wp-content/uploads/2019/09/2018-19_Boxed_In_Report.pdf

Leavy, Patricia, and Adrienne Trier-Bienick. 2014. "Introduction to Gender & Pop Culture." In *Gender & Pop Culture: A Text Reader*, edited by Adrienne Trier-Bienick and Patricia Leavy, 1–26. Rotterdam, Netherlands: Sense Publishers.

Lucey, Bill. 2005. "Women in Journalism: Newspaper Milestones." New York State Library, March 14, 2005. https://www.nysl.nysed.gov/nysnp/refsources.htm

Mager, John, and James Helgeson. 2011. "Fifty Years of Advertising Images: Some Changing Perspectives on Role Portrayals along with Enduring Consistencies." *Sex Roles* 64 (3–4): 238–252. https://doi.org/10.1007/s11199-010-9782-6

Mahar, Karen Ward. 2001. "True Womanhood in Hollywood: Gendered Business Strategies and the Rise and Fall of the Woman Filmmaker, 1896–1928." *Enterprise & Society* 2 (1): 72. https://doi.org/10.1093/es/2.1.72

Marcus, Sara. 2010. *Girls to the Front: The True Story of the Riot Grrrl Revolution*. New York: Harper Perennial.

May, Elaine Tyler. 1988. *Homeward Bound: American Families in the Cold War Era*. New York: Basic Books.

Modello, Bob. 2008. "Remembering Hollywood's Hays Code 40 Years On." National Public Radio, August 8, 2008. https://www.npr.org/templates/story/story.php?storyId=93301189

Mulvey, Laura. 1975. "Visual Pleasure and Narrative Cinema." *Screen* 16 (3): 6–18.

Nabi, Robin, and Mary Beth Oliver. 2009. *The SAGE Handbook of Media Processes and Effects*. Thousand Oaks, CA: SAGE Publications.

Nagle, Rebecca. 2018. "Media Representation of Native Women: Invisibility, Stereotypes, Whitewashing." Women's Media Center, June 12, 2018. https://womensmediacenter.com/news-features/media-representation-of-native-women-invisibility-stereotypes-whitewashing

Neville, Conor, and Phyllis Anastasio. 2019. "Fewer, Younger, but Increasingly Powerful: How Portrayals of Women, Age, and Power Have Changed from 2002 to 2016 in the 50

Top-Grossing U.S. Films." *Sex Roles* 80 (7/8): 503–514. https://doi.org/10.1007/s11199-018-0945-1

Ott, Brian, and Robert Mack. 2014. *Critical Media Studies: An Introduction, Second Edition*. Malden, MA: Wiley-Blackwell.

Patterson, Martha. 1995. "'Survival of the Best Fitted': Selling the American New Woman as Gibson Girl, 1895–1910." *ATQ* 9 (1): 73–87.

Rabinovitch-Fox, Einav. 2017. "New Women in Early 20th-Century America." *Oxford Research Encyclopedia of American History*. Retrieved March 16, 2020. https://doi.org/10.1093/acrefore/9780199329175.013.427

Rampton, Martha. 2015. "Four Waves of Feminism." *Pacific Magazine* (Fall 2008). Updated October 25, 2015. https://www.pacificu.edu/magazine/four-waves-feminism

Roessner, Lori. 2012. "Sexism." In *Encyclopedia of Gender in Media*, edited by Mary Kosut, 327–333. Thousand Oaks, CA: SAGE Publications.

Rooks, Noliwe M. 2004. *Ladies' Pages: African American Women's Magazines and the Culture That Made Them*. New Brunswick, NJ: Rutgers University Press.

Royal, Cindy. 2014. "Gender and Technology: Women's Usage, Creation and Perspectives." In *Gender & Pop Culture: A Text Reader*, edited by Adrienne Trier-Bienick and Patricia Leavy, 174–189. Rotterdam, Netherlands: Sense Publishers.

Sanmiguel, Lisa. 2000. "Images of Women: North America." In *Routledge International Encyclopedia of Women: Global Women's Issues and Knowledge*, edited by Dale Spencer and Cheris Kramarae, 1120–1123. New York: Routledge.

Signorelli, Nancy. 1997. "Reflections on Girls in the Media: A Content Analysis: A Study of Television Shows and Commercials, Movies, Music Videos, and Teen Magazine Articles and Ads." Children Now and the Kaiser Family Foundation. https://eric.ed.gov/?id=ED444213

Silverman, Rachel. 2012. "Stereotypes." In *Encyclopedia of Gender in Media*, edited by Mary Kosut, 372–375. Thousand Oaks, CA: SAGE Publications.

Smyth, J. E. 2018. *Nobody's Girl Friday: The Women Who Ran Hollywood*. New York: Oxford University Press.

Sollee, Kristen. 2015. "6 Things to Know about 4th Wave Feminism." *Bustle*, October 30, 2015. https://www.bustle.com/articles/119524-6-things-to-know-about-4th-wave-feminism

Spigel, Lynn. 1991. "From Domestic Space to Outer Space: The 1960s Fantastic Family Sit-Com." In *Close Encounters: Film, Feminism and Science Fiction*, edited by Constance Penley, 205–235. Minneapolis: University of Minnesota Press.

Steinem, Gloria. 1990. "Sex, Lies & Advertising." *Ms.* (July/August 1990): 18–28. https://www.academia.edu/31540089/STEINEM._Sex_lies_e_advertising.pdf

Tuchman, Gaye, Arlene Kaplan Daniels, and James Benét, eds. 1978. *Hearth and Home: Images of Women in the Mass Media*. New York: Oxford University Press.

UN Women. 2019. "Hashtag Women's Rights: 12 Social Media Movements You Should Follow." Medium, June 28, 2019. https://medium.com/@UN_Women/hashtag-womens-rights-12-social-media-movements-you-should-follow-6e31127a673b

U.S. National Archives and Records Administration. n.d. "Powers of Persuasion." Accessed January 6, 2020. https://www.archives.gov/exhibits/powers-of-persuasion

Vande Berg, Leah, and Diane Streckfuss. 1991. "Profile: Prime-Time Television's Portrayal of Women and the World of Work: A Demographic Profile." *Journal of Broadcasting & Electronic Media* 36 (2): 195–208. https://doi.org/10.1080/08838159209364167

Ward, Jervette. 2015. *Real Sister: Stereotypes, Respectability, and Black Women in Reality TV*. New Brunswick, NJ: Rutgers University Press.

Webb, Lynne, and Nicholas Temple. 2016. "Social Media and Gender Issues." In *Handbook of Research on the Societal Impact of Digital Media*, edited by Barbara Guzzetti and Mellinee Lesley, 638–669. Hershey, PA: Advances in Media, Entertainment, and the Arts (AMEA) Books Series, Information Science Reference.

Wilson, Leslie Kreiner. 2018. "Frances Marion, *The Secret Six*, and the Evolving Heroine in 1930s Hollywood." *Historical Journal of Film, Radio & Television* 38 (2): 246–262. https://doi.org/10.1080/01439685.2017.1300003

Wolf, Naomi. 1990. *The Beauty Myth: How Images of Beauty Are Used against Women*. New York: Harper Collins.

Women's Media Center. 2017. *The Status of Women in the U.S. Media 2017*. http://wmc.3cdn.net/10c550d19ef9f3688f_mlbres2jd.pdf

Women's Media Center. 2018. *The Status of Women of Color in the U.S. Media 2018*. http://www.womensmediacenter.com/assets/site/reports/the-status-of-women-of-color-in-the-u-s-media-2018-full-report/Women-of-Color-Report-FINAL-WEB.pdf

Women's Media Center. 2019. *The Status of Women in the U.S. Media 2019*. https://womensmediacenter.com/assets/site/from-bsd/WMCStatusofWomeninUSMedia2019.pdf

Zimmerman, Edith. 2012. "99 Ways to Be Naughty in Kazakhstan." *New York Times*, August 3, 2012. https://www.nytimes.com/2012/08/05/magazine/how-cosmo-conquered-the-world.html

FOX

2 Problems, Controversies, and Solutions

Introduction

This chapter identifies and discusses some of the many contemporary problems and controversies surrounding representations of women in American films, television, news, advertising, and aspects of social media. The chapter is organized into four main sections. The first section, "Women in Film and Television," explores the representation of women in movies and scripted television programs. The second section, "News Coverage and Women," describes how women are presented and portrayed in the categories of news, national political candidate coverage, and sports. The third section, "Women in Advertising and on Social Media," highlights some current trends in how these visual forms are advancing ideas about women through industry- and consumer-driven content. The last section, "Solutions," summarizes reforms designed to address some of the problems and challenges outlined in the preceding chapter sections.

Women in Film and Television

In the last several years, systemic problems in the film and television industries' approaches to representing, including,

---

Award winning writer, creator, television showrunner, and producer Shonda Rhimes is credited with changing the landscape of television with her popular, culturally relevant programs that include *Grey's Anatomy, Private Practice,* and *Scandal.* Her company Shondaland is behind additional programs such as *How to Get Away with Murder, The Catch, Station 19,* and *Bridgerton.* (Carrienelson1/Dreamstime.com)

and interacting with women have been widely documented. In 2014, a pervasive hack of Sony Pictures resulted in a public release of private company documents and communications. Among the proprietary information made public was evidence of significant compensation disparities between male and female employees with the same jobs (Copeland 2014). Subsequent reporting has continued to document what many already know: overall, women get paid less than their male counterparts in the film and television industries. While there are always many reasons for potential differences in pay, the disparity is significant enough to suggest gender discrimination is at play. One study noted, for example, that top female actors earn only 38 percent of top male actors' salaries (Pedace 2019). Other reporting suggests there are double-digit pay disparities and differences in bonus amounts between men and women across multiple sectors of the entertainment industry, although the situation may be improving (Singers 2018).

In 2015, April Reign, a lawyer, popular culture fan, and active Twitter user, tweeted "#OscarsSoWhite they asked to touch my hair" after hearing about the Academy Award nominations announced for twenty white actors. Reign's tweet prompted the adoption of the phrase "Oscars So White" to protest the lack of recognition for actors of color in Hollywood. One year later, in 2016, all of the Academy Award nominees for acting were again white performers. Though some people of color have been recognized by the Academy since then, "Oscars So White" is still a relevant critique (Sperling 2020). As Reign shared with a *New York Times* reporter in 2020, "It could have been a bunch of different things—there were no women in the directors category, there were no visibly disabled people nominated—so #OscarsSoWhite has never just been about race. It's about the underrepresentation of all marginalized groups" (Ugwu 2020).

In response to criticism about its lack of diversity, in 2016, the Academy of Motion Picture Arts and Sciences, the group that bestows the Academy Awards, promised to try to double the number of women and people of color in its membership by 2020. Though the Academy does not release specific demographic data of its membership, reports suggest the membership in 2020 was 32 percent female (up from 25% in 2015) and included 16 percent people of color (up from 8% in 2015; Whitten 2020).

In 2017, activist Tarana Burke founded the nonprofit organization Just Be Inc. to support survivors of sexual assault and harassment, using the phrase "me too" on social media as a way to let such victims know that they were not alone and to underscore how prevalent the problem of sexual abuse and assault is in American culture. The "me too" phrase became popularized by actress Alyssa Milano in October of that year when accusations of sexual assault and harassment by powerful Hollywood producer Harvey Weinstein became a major news story (Langone 2018). The accusations against Weinstein in October 2017 prompted many women to come forward with similar stories of predatory bosses and colleagues. They exposed "powerful men in media, politics, and other high-profile walks of life" who had allegedly engaged in sexual misconduct, a development dubbed the "Weinstein effect" (Maddaus 2018).

Although Milano did not realize that Burke had previously coined the "me too" phrase when she tweeted, "If you've been sexually assaulted write 'me too' as a reply to this tweet," Milano's tweet struck a nerve that resulted in an initial response of over 60,000 replies. The emerging Me Too movement was further boosted by the investigative reporting of journalists such as Ronan Farrow and Jodi Kantor. They revealed patterns of widespread sexual misconduct in media industries and helped provide a space in American society for survivors of sexual assault, harassment, and demeaning sexism to speak up (Langone 2018).

In January 2018, the organization Time's Up was founded by 300 women in the entertainment industry to combat sexism and harassment. It has since been joined by other industries and individuals around the world. Focusing on workplace issues, the organization (which uses the hashtag #timesup on

Twitter to promote its cause) argued that power imbalances in industries set the stage for sexual harassment and other problematic behaviors (Langone 2018). Part of the group's goal was to advocate for policy changes and legislation that promote a more equitable inclusion of women and other underrepresented groups. It also supports a legal defense fund for those who need assistance navigating the justice system around sexual misconduct issues (Langone 2018). In recent years, however, the organization has been criticized for its connections with those in power, including former New York governor Andrew Cuomo, who resigned from office in August 2021 after allegations of sexual harassment, and its involvement in disputes between producers and directors (Kantor et al. 2021).

At the 2018 Golden Globes Awards ceremony, actress Natalie Portman introduced the nominees for best director by saying, "And here are the all-male nominees." At the 2018 Academy Awards, best actress–winner Frances McDormand encouraged other female nominees to stand up, noted that such women (and others) had ideas for projects, and called for the use of an "inclusion rider." In the movie industry, inclusion riders, according to Stacey Smith of the Annenberg Inclusion Initiative, is "the idea that A-list actors have the ability to stipulate in their contracts that diversity be reflected both onscreen and in 'below the line' positions, where women, people of color, and members of LGBT communities are traditionally underrepresented" (Buckley and Victor 2018). A little over a year after McDormand's acceptance speech, however, few film production companies were identified as using the rider. Those who did not do so defended their decision, claiming that diversity hiring policies were already in place or expressing concerns that such riders would place burdensome restrictions on their hiring practices (Buckley 2019). Absence of the rider does not necessarily mean there are not efforts in place to diversify Hollywood hiring practices, although some claim the progress is slow (Sperling 2020).

On January 13, 2020, after reading the Academy Award nominees for best director, the writer and actress Issa Rae pointedly said, "Congratulations to those men." Her remarks highlighted the fact that despite Hollywood's vows to pursue greater gender equity in the industry, only a handful of women have ever been nominated for best director, and at the time only one woman had ever won—Kathryn Bigelow for *The Hurt Locker* (2008). Although gender disparities in Hollywood are well documented, 2019 featured several highly regarded films directed by women, including *Little Women* (directed by Greta Gerwig), *A Beautiful Day in the Neighborhood* (directed by Marielle Heller), and *The Long Farewell* (directed by Lulu Wang), adding to many people's frustrations with the Academy's pattern of "snubbing women" (Gajanan 2020). Rae's line reverberated on Twitter among industry insiders, critics, and fans frustrated by the lack of recognition of female talent in the motion picture industry.

These high-profile comments, hashtag campaigns, and the ideas and work behind them brought increased scrutiny of the prohibitive structures that operate to keep a white male-dominated industry in place. They also further spurred renewed activism that engaged others in calling for increased diversity in the entertainment industry. While some progress has been made, the issue of equitable representation remains a relevant one. Pressure on the entertainment industry to change is inherently and explicitly present in entertainment reporting, investigative pieces, and social media commentary, and the work on these issues is advanced by scholars, organizations, activists, and industry professionals.

Women in Film

A number of organizations and academic institutions have published research documenting the presence of women in front of and behind the camera that consistently shows gender and other demographic inequities. For example, the University of California's Annenberg Inclusion Initiative focuses on studying diversity in the entertainment industry. In 2019, it published "Inequality in 1,200 Popular Films: Examining Portrayals of

Gender, Race/Ethnicity, LGBTQ & Disability from 2017 to 2018," a research study that offers a comprehensive snapshot of how inclusive popular Hollywood films are of diverse characters and creators.

From 2007 through 2018, the Annenberg research team examined the top 100 films for each year, resulting in an examination of 1,200 films (Smith, Choueiti, Pieper et al. 2019). The team found there was little progress in the number of women characters in films over the time period studied. In 2018, only 33.1 percent of that year's films featured female speaking characters, compared to 31.8 percent in 2017, 31.5 percent in 2016, and similar percentages for the years 2007–2015. Similarly, when examining the participation of women behind the camera, the study found that 58 (4.3%) of the 1,335 film directors across the 1,200 films were women (some films had more than one director). In addition, "given that some female directors work more than once, the total number of individual women hired across the 1200 movies is 47. The total number of unique men is 657" (Smith, Choueiti, Pieper et al. 2019).

The Annenberg study also identified areas of progress toward more equitable representation. For example, female character leads are featured in 34, 33, and 39 of each batch of the 100 films studied in 2016, 2017 and 2018, respectively, an increase from the 20 women lead or colead characters identified in the top 100 films of 2007. In 2018, 11 of these female leads were also from underrepresented demographic groups. However, the research also documented continued poor representation of women with disabilities and poor inclusion of LGBT characters.[1] Despite such shortcomings, the Annenberg report also found an increase in the portrayal of underrepresented racial and ethnic characters overall.

Also spotlighting gender, race, and overall diversity trends in the film industry, the UCLA *Hollywood Diversity Report 2020*

[1] Reports and organizations use different monikers to describe the LGBTQ+ community. The descriptors used in this book align with the ones used in the respective report or organization being summarized.

examined representation, profits, award recognitions, and market distribution of 140 films released in 2018 and 146 films released in 2019. Darnell Hunt and Ana-Christina Ramon, the report's lead authors, explained that since the 2008 recession, major Hollywood studios and their subsidiaries have released fewer films. Meanwhile, the ones that were released in 2018 and 2019 featured a rising percentage of films in the action, comedy, and adventure genres and a decrease in the drama category. Pointing out that film executives determine what films to make, the authors documented that in early 2020, at the eleven "major and mid-major" studios, these executives were primarily men and overwhelmingly white, even though some progress in gender equity was evident since the previous analysis completed in 2015 (Hunt and Ramon 2020).

A key feature of the *Hollywood Diversity Report* is an examination of proportionate representation—how the demographics of lead characters in film compare to population demographics. Noting "minorities" make up just over 40 percent of the U.S. population and women make up just over 50 percent of the population, the study found that among the 2018 films it reviewed, only 26.6 percent of leads were people of color, and in the group of 2019 films, 27.6 percent of leads were people of color. Women played 41 percent and 44.1 percent of lead characters in 2018 and 2019, respectively, a jump from 25.6 percent in 2011 and 31.2 percent in 2016 (Hunt and Ramon 2020).

The *Hollywood Diversity Report* also examined overall cast diversity. Again, the research showed film casts have diversified in the past few years. However, the research also revealed that "when individual racial and ethnic groups are considered in isolation, it is clear that women remain underrepresented among cast members for nearly all groups." This white male dominance also extended to writers' rooms. In 2019, for example, 105 out of 144 writers were white men. The authors of the report concluded there are "two Hollywoods," arguing that while women and people of color are increasingly visible in both lead and supporting roles, "white men remain firmly in charge" behind the camera (Hunt and Ramon 2020, 42).

Other recent research documents similar trends. The Center for the Study of Women in Television and Film at San Diego State University has long examined women's participation in film and television both in front of and behind the camera. Martha Lauzen's research on 2019's top-grossing films found that 40 percent of protagonists are women, an increase from 31 percent in 2018 (Lauzen 2020b). The study also found that 37 percent of major characters in those 2019 films are women. When considering the 2,300 characters who appear in the top 100 top-grossing films of 2019, Lauzen reports that only about one out of three (34%) of all speaking characters are women, while 66 percent are men. This research, which also offers a historical comparison of the gender of the main characters and speaking characters since 2002, highlights the ongoing fact that men continue to outnumber women in both categories. Lauzen also notes the lack of diversity in women characters. In the sample of films from 2019, 68 percent of female characters were white, 20 percent were Black, 7 percent were Asian, and only 5 percent were Latina. Lauzen's research also demonstrates that more gender diversity behind the scenes leads to better inclusion on-screen: "Films with at least one woman director and/or writer were more likely than films with no women in these roles to feature higher percentages of females as protagonists, in major roles, and as speaking characters" (Lauzen 2020b, 6).

Gender and other diversity behind the scenes, however, remain an issue. Another study by Lauzen examines the numbers of women employed behind the scenes in the film industry. It found that in 2019, just 20 percent of all directors, writers, producers, editors, and cinematographers working on top-grossing films were women, compared to 16 percent in 2018. Twelve percent of the directors of the 100 top-grossing films in 2019 were women. Inequity among male and female employees persisted when Lauzen expanded the number of top-grossing films in the sample. In the 250 top-grossing films of 2019, "85% had no women directors, 73% had no women writers, 44% had no women exec[utive] producers, 31% had no women producers, 72% had no women editors and 95% had no women cinematographers" (Lauzen 2020a, 4).

Lauzen's recent research documents the participation by women in the film industry during the pandemic years, when film production and moviegoing patterns were disrupted. In 2020, 38 percent of major characters in the hundred top-grossing films were women, and in 2021, 35 percent of major characters were women, decreasing since 2019 (Lauzen 2022). This study also documents that 85 percent of 2021 top-grossing films featured more male characters than female characters and that female protagonists (characters from whose point of view the story is told) were featured in 29 percent of 2020's top-grossing films and 31 percent of 2021's top-grossing films. However, Lauzen stipulates this data needs to be looked at in the current historical context: "Due to the closure of many theaters in 2021 and 2020 and the resulting drop in box office grosses, comparisons between the last two years and previous years should be made with caution" (2).

Focusing on the top-grossing family films from 2007 to 2017, the Geena Davis Institute on Gender in Media has also investigated the representations of women, people of color, LGBTQ+ characters, and characters with disabilities. One 2017 analysis demonstrates upward movement in creating and casting women in lead character roles but found that, overall, male lead characters "vastly outnumber female leads 71.3% to 28.8%" (Geena Davis Institute 2017a, 3). This research also notes nonwhite leading characters are featured in only about 17 percent of the films studied (about 83% of lead characters are white), and of the nonwhite leading characters, 26 percent are female. Additionally, LGBTQ+ characters and characters with disabilities are rarely present as lead characters in family films, something the organization finds problematic because "when the lion's share of the stories we tell revolve around the lives of straight, white men without disabilities, children learn that people of marginalized identities simply matter less in our culture" (Geena Davis Institute 2017a, 2).

Acknowledging that profits are central to the film industry business, the report also points out that in recent years, family films with female leads and leads of color have made similar or, in some cases, more money than films with white male leads; profit concerns, in the institute's view, is not an excuse for inequitable representation.

Women in Scripted Television

In comparison to the film industry, the television industry looks a little bit different. The rise of streaming services, offering both original television and films, has resulted in more opportunities in the form of huge waves of new programming. This expansion of the industry, coupled with increased recognition of historical shortcomings in presentations of women and minorities, has resulted in storytelling that prioritizes women across all scripted television platforms—broadcast, cable, and streaming. Broadcast television executives in particular have made concerted efforts to increase diversity in roles behind and in front of the camera, giving showrunners directives to diversify writers' rooms, ensure casts are diverse, and track internal progress toward better inclusionary structures (Aurthur 2018). Writer and producer Shonda Rhimes's *Grey's Anatomy* (2005–present) and *Scandal* (2012–2018) gave ABC an early start in producing profitable, popular programming featuring diverse casts (Meyer and Griffin 2018). ABC became a broadcast television diversity leader that aimed to make sure showrunners, creators, and casts were diverse enough to tell authentic stories; programs such as *Black-ish* (2014–present) and *Fresh Off the Boat* (2015–present) have been successful (Lynch 2015). By 2018, however, all five broadcast networks had debuted slates of diverse programming. That year, "shows with actors of color in lead roles outnumber[ed] predominantly white casts" for the first time in television history (Aurthur 2018). Networks continue to prioritize funding more diverse story lines and projects (Brown and Carlson 2020).

Nina Shaw of Time's Up suggests that in the streaming realm, women are directing more television episodes, and the demand for women directors exceeds the supply (Sperling 2020). Recent data collected on the participation of women in all areas of the television industry also points to some gains. For example, according to the Women's Media Center (WMC), a nonpartisan nonprofit organization founded by Jane Fonda, Robin Morgan, and Gloria Steinem in 2005 to raise "the visibility, viability and decision-making power of women and girls in media and, thereby, ensuring that their stories get told and their voices are heard," record numbers of women and people of color directed television entertainment programs during the years 2016–2018, although few of them employed Black writers. Additionally, the Gay & Lesbian Alliance Against Defamation (GLAAD) notes that although LGBTQ women have historically been underrepresented in media, for the first time, "regular and reoccurring" female LGBTQ characters outnumbered LGBTQ male characters on prime-time broadcast television during the 2019 season, 53 percent to 47 percent, respectively (Townsend et al. 2019, 14).

The GLAAD report also demonstrates an overall increase in the presence of LGBTQ+ characters across broadcast, cable, and streaming television. To document the sexual orientation of LGBTQ+ characters on television, GLAAD examined how many characters fall in the following categories: lesbian, gay, bisexual, straight, asexual, and undetermined. The researchers also noted the number of trans men, trans women and nonbinary characters. In 2019, it found that 33 percent of regular or reoccurring LGBTQ+ characters on broadcast television were lesbians, and 30 percent of LGBTQ+ characters were lesbians on cable and streaming services. These findings confirmed that across all television platforms, gay male characters outnumber lesbian women characters.

The GLAAD study also notes few trans women on broadcast (two characters) and streaming television (five characters) but fourteen trans women characters on cable programming. When looking at bisexual character representation, the analysis indicates 26 percent of all LGBTQ+ characters across all television platforms are bisexual, with more of these being women (ninety characters) than men (thirty-six characters). The report calls attention to the drop in bisexual representation on broadcast television, noting research indicates "bi+ people actually make up 52% of LGB people," but "on broadcast television, this group experienced the most significant drop in percentage of representation year over year" (Townsend et al. 2019, 8).

Scholar Martha Lauzen's research on women in the television industry during 2018–2019 shows that 44 percent of women were characters on broadcast television programs, and 45 percent of characters on both cable television programs and streaming programs were women, a "historic high" (Lauzen 2019, 2). Additionally, during this time period, on all platforms, 45 percent of major television characters were women. The study further documents that in regard to those with speaking roles, 70 percent of female characters were white, 17 percent were Black, 7 percent were Asian, 6 percent were Latina, and 1 percent were of another race or ethnicity (12). The data for major characters was similar; 71 percent of women in major roles were white, 17 percent were Black, 6 percent were Latina, 6 percent were Asian, and 1 percent were of another race or ethnicity (12). Other research shows differences between white LGBTQ+ characters and nonwhite LGBTQ+ characters. An examination of the 2019 television lineup identifies that LGBTQ+ characters of color are relatively close in percentage to their white counterparts on broadcast and cable television. An analysis of the 120 LGBTQ+ characters on broadcast television, 215 LGBTQ+ characters on cable, and 153 LGBTQ+ characters on streaming reports that people of color comprise 52 percent, 48 percent, and 43 percent of these groups, respectively (Townsend et al. 2019).

Lauzen also documents a "historic high" in the percentage of women filling key behind-the-scenes positions in television; 31 percent of people working as creators, directors, writers, executive producers, producers, editors, and directors of photography were women across all platforms (31% in broadcast, 31%

in cable, 30% in streaming; Lauzen 2019, 2). Though these gains are notable, men are still twice as likely as women to hold these positions. For example, 52 percent of programs employed five or fewer women in behind-the-scenes positions, while only 17 percent of programs employed five or fewer men (Lauzen 2019, 3). The employment of women in key leadership positions seemed to result in increased opportunities for women in other industry roles. The research suggests that across all platforms, programs with female creators or executive producers were more likely than their male counterparts to employ women in production capacities. They were also more likely than men to be involved with projects that gave women significant roles in front of the camera (Lauzen 2019).

Lauzen's most recent analysis looks at women's participation in broadcast and streaming television during 2020–2021, when some television operations were impacted by the pandemic. This research shows female characters were featured in 45 percent of both broadcast and streaming programming but that streaming services "represented 52% of major characters on streaming programs versus 45% on broadcast network programs" (Lauzen 2021, 3). When looking at behind-the-scenes participation, Lauzen noted decreases in the percentage of women creators in both broadcast and streaming arenas. In broadcast, the number of creators decreased from "26% in 2019–20 to 22% in 2020–21," and on streaming the number of creators "declined from 33% in 2019–20 to 30% in 2020–21" (5). The report also details slight increases from the previous year in diverse women characters on streaming and broadcast programs and numerous increases and decreases in women's participation behind the scenes in both broadcast and streaming programming.

Portrayals of Women Characters

There certainly have been positive shifts in the ways women have been represented on screens in recent years. Observers agree that diverse and expansive portrayals of women are on the rise in both television and film. However, long-standing gender stereotypes persist in scripted film and television. For example, one 2020 study found that men in films are more likely to be portrayed in leadership roles than their female counterparts, with only 26 percent of such roles filled by women. Recent films may also not equitably type roles for women and men. The same study claims that 40 percent of female characters are primarily seen in "work-related roles" (compared to 60% of male characters) and that 52 percent of female characters are primarily depicted in "personal life–related roles" (compared to 34% of males) (Lauzen 2020b, 5). Similarly, across all television platforms, 53 percent of women are more likely to be identified by their "personal life role," for example, as wives and mothers, whereas only 39 percent of male adult characters on television are primarily defined as husbands and dads (Lauzen 2019).

Additionally, in film and television, a focus remains on the importance of women being attractive, and although certainly attractiveness comes into play for men, it is a less important characteristic in many male roles. As *Vulture*'s Pilot Viruet points out, "the TV attractiveness gap," often seen via "hot girl/ugly guy pairings," is "a reflection of the culture: women must be conventionally physically attractive, while men aren't held to the same standards" (Viruet 2016). Across television platforms, women characters are also younger than men characters, resulting in decreased representations of older women (Lauzen 2019). Older women are also rarely seen in films, and when they are, portrayals devalue them with demeaning jokes and stereotypical portrayals that show little understanding of (or respect for) the complex lives of older adults (Kitazawa 2017).

A 2020 study by the Geena Davis Institute on Gender in Media, the USC Viterbi School of Engineering, and TENA looked at the representation of women older than fifty years old in top-grossing films from four different countries, including the United States. It found women over fifty make up only one out of four characters over fifty years old, and older female characters are more likely to be shown as senile, homebound, feeble, and frumpy as compared to their male counterparts. According to the findings, "the vast majority of popular films in this study failed to depict even one prominent, humanized, older female character. A large majority of films (71%) have at least one female character who is 50 or older, but most of these films depicted their older female characters in stereotypical ways" (Geena Davis Institute, USC Viterbi School of Engineering, and TENA 2020, 6). This practice of ignoring older women or placing them in a negative light is unhealthy. Caroline Cicero, an assistant professor at the USC Leonard Davis School of Gerontology, explains, "If we portray older people in ways that make them look bad, or make them feel like they need to act younger than they are, we're not validating people just on the basic core of who they are. . . . We need more positive images of healthy [older] people and healthy interpersonal relationships on screen" (Kitazawa 2017).

Social Media, Gender, and the Entertainment Industry

The emergence of social media has given women's advocates a formidable tool to highlight sexist practices in the entertainment industry. For example, the London-based blog *Casting Call Woe* and the @proresting Twitter account, both written by the anonymous Miss L, call attention to sexist language in television and film casting calls for women. For example, a March 2, 2018, @proresting tweet posted the following actual description of a role that was being cast: "the only female on staff. She is beautiful and she knows her stuff, while all the guys notice her at work. She is successful professionally, but longs to start a family. She struggles with balancing them both." Miss L's comment about the post was that "one day they'll write a female character who just knows her stuff and beauty won't come into it."

Miss L, who writes anonymously because she is concerned that revealing her identity will impact her ability to get work as an actor, said that she wants to highlight the routine misogyny in the industry and the emphasis on female characters' appearances, noting that male characters are more often described in casting calls by what they do or by their personality (Birro 2016). She argues that while there are growing numbers of television shows and movies that are women-centric, like *Orange Is the New Black* and *Ghostbusters*, these remain the exception rather than the rule (Birro 2016).

Similarly, in 2016, Hollywood producer Ross Putnam started the Twitter account @femscriptintros, where he shares text from film and television scripts where female characters are introduced. Putnam, who substitutes all character names to "JANE" in his tweets, provides evidence such descriptions of women are "startingly ageist, sexist and objectifying" (Dockterman 2016). The @femscriptintros feed includes examples from scripts, such as "JANE, 26, a freckled hottie in a powder blue skirt-suit" (April 7, 2019); "JANE, forties, looks thirty-five" (January 13, 2019); "JANE, 50s, still very attractive" (June 28, 2018); and "JANE, 30s, is cute but could be hot if she made the effort" (May 6, 2018).

These examples, and many others, demonstrate an emphasis on women's appearances that is often not prioritized with male characters (Martinetti 2016; Dockterman 2016). Putnam's examples demonstrate the tendency for writers to link female characters' jobs to their looks given the number of examples where the stated profession is linked with being "hot" or "having cleavage" (Martinetti 2016). Critics of these practices, such as SYFY writer Cher Martinetti, assert that these practices need to change because "seeing strong female characters who have goals that are based on their jobs or are portrayed doing their jobs in a capable manner contributes to young female audiences considering the possibility that they, too, can hold these jobs" (Martinetti 2016).

Although social media has been effectively used to raise awareness about contemporary issues of women in media, it is also routinely used to harass women. Online "trolls"—people who antagonize, provoke, or hack and vandalize content on the internet—often choose prominent women in media as their targets. Many of the comments focus on body shaming, while others are misogynistic or racist. These ugly attacks have resulted in trolling victims dealing with anxiety and depression, and in some cases, targets of these attacks have had to disable their social media accounts (Patil 2014).

For example, after the movie trailers for a *Ghostbusters* remake starring a female cast debuted in March 2016, the film and its stars were subjected to a torrent of misogynistic reaction, including a campaign to rack up as many "dislikes" on the trailer as possible. Online trolls took special aim at African American actor and comedian Leslie Jones, one of the film's stars. Over the course of a few months, her personal website was hacked, a fake Twitter account was established in her name, and she was verbally abused on Twitter with sexist and racist comments (Silman 2016).

Similarly, Kelly Marie Tran, the first woman of color to be cast as a leading character in a *Star Wars* film, *Star Wars: The Last Jedi* (2017), became the target of a racially abusive campaign by social media trolls on Twitter and Instagram. Additionally, the entry for her character, Rose Tico, on the Wookieepedia wiki site was changed to include racist language, prompting the site's owner to ban the user and not allow anyone further to contribute to the wiki page (Moye 2017). Tran eventually disabled her social media, but she also wrote an op-ed piece in the *New York Times* in 2018 in which she vowed not to become "marginalized by online harassment. . . . I want to live in a world where children of color don't spend their entire adolescence wishing to be white. I want to live in a world where women are not subjected to scrutiny for their appearance, or their actions, or their general existence. I want to live in a world where people of all races, religions, socioeconomic classes, sexual orientations, gender identities and abilities are seen as what they have always been: human beings" (Tran 2018).

Changing Dynamics and Positive Trends

Despite lingering issues and challenges, an evolution has taken place in mainstream Hollywood's support of films featuring women's stories. Since it has been demonstrated that so-called female-oriented movies can be profitable, there is less resistance to advancing projects with female leads and casts (Barnes 2014). As Brooks Barnes writes in the *New York Times*, "Female ticket buyers—finally given the opportunity—have shown studios the big money, producers say. Women have finally proved to Hollywood's satisfaction that they can power not just a single film (with the occasional sequel) but an entire world-dominating film series" (Barnes 2014). Such films as *Bridesmaids* (2011), *Gravity* (2013), *The Hunger Games* trilogy (2012–2015), *Hidden Figures* (2016), *Wonder Woman* (2017), and *Captain Marvel* (2019) have been critically celebrated and financially successful.

These shifts can also be seen in the action genre, which has traditionally been dominated by male figures. In addition to *The Hunger Games* trilogy, *Wonder Woman*, and *Captain Marvel*, the *Star Wars* franchise features female story leads in *Star Wars: The Force Awakens* (2015) and *Rogue One: A Star Wars Story* (2016). Other examples of strong action heroines include characters in such films as *Mad Max: Fury Road* (2015) and *Haywire* (2011). Eliana Dockterman of *Time* magazine points out that different types of female heroes have emerged in Hollywood films; "they brawl" for different reasons and lead the film rather than being a "team player," as seen in such films as *The Avengers* (2012) and *Guardians of the Galaxy* (2014), or as the sexualized characters present in such films as *Charlie's Angels* (2000) and *Catwoman* (2004; Dockterman 2016).

Twenty-first-century depictions of women in scripted television also feature an expanding list of main and lead characters who are educated professionals. Woman detectives, lawyers, doctors, nurses, CIA agents, politicians, therapists, and other professionals lead story narratives on such popular shows as *The Closer* (2005–2012), *How to Get Away with*

Murder (2014–present), *Grey's Anatomy* (2005–present), *The Mindy Project* (2012–2016), *The Good Fight* (2017–present), *Homeland* (2011–2020), *Quantico* (2015–2018), and *Billions* (2016–present). Unique, complex, educated, and diverse female protagonists also drive such programs as *The Handmaid's Tale* (2017–present), *Insecure* (2016–present), *Grace and Frankie* (2016–present), and *Broad City* (2014–present). Scholars point to the evolution of roles for women in popular mainstream television, noting a shift in female lead representation and an increase in rich and complex roles (Brown 2017; Damico and Quay 2016).

While many argue the list is not long enough, an increasing number of television programs and films weave elements of diverse experiences of women into their narratives. Such filmmakers as Ava DuVernay make a point of producing diverse stories and employing inclusive production teams. Some film studios, like Paramount, publicly committed to inclusion initiatives, while other studios have committed to supporting all women filmmakers, even while they may hesitate in hiring women to direct film genres traditionally associated with men, such as horror, action, and comedy (Barnes and Buckley 2019). Positively reviewed films as *Hidden Figures* (2016), *Harriet* (2019), *Crazy Rich Asians* (2018), *Queen and Shim* (2019), and *If Beale Street Could Talk* (2018), among others, feature interesting women characters and are celebrated for their quality and diverse storytelling.

Referred to as "television's diversity queen," producer Shonda Rhimes brought numerous successful programs to ABC from 2005 until 2018, when she signed a deal with Netflix (Meyer and Griffin 2018, 2). Rhimes and the team at her production company, Shondaland, tell their shows' stories via diverse sets of characters with various life experiences that often connect to contemporary social issues. Shondaland programs such as *Grey's Anatomy* (2005–present), *Private Practice* (2007–2013), *Scandal* (2012–2018), *How to Get Away with Murder* (2014–present), and *The Catch* (2015–2017) feature "storylines that center, for example, on interracial friendships and relationships, LGBTIQ (lesbian, gay, bisexual, transgender, intersex, queer) relationships and parenting, the impact of disability on familial and work dynamics, and complex representations of womanhood" (Meyer and Griffin 2018, 2).

Popular programs from other production companies are additionally recognized for their diverse casts of women and story lines. For example, *Jane the Virgin* (2014–2019), a dramedy that centers around a multigenerational Latina family, addresses issues of immigration and presents varied representations of Latinas, showing diversity within this demographic group. *Orange Is the New Black* (2013–2019) highlights prison system practices, confronts the issue of white privilege, features a trans woman character, and overall has been recognized for "bringing to life a diverse group of women, representing backgrounds, body types and sexualities rarely seen on television" (Itzkoff 2014).

Casting Controversies

While Hollywood in general may be more aware of elements of its history of racist portrayals and exclusion, some recent casting choices have been controversial. One criticism levied at Hollywood has to do with "whitewashing" and "racial erasure," where white culture is prioritized, often at the expense of other cultures, their practices, and peoples. This practice is also criticized because it presents another roadblock for actors of color and, notably, women of color being cast in films. For example, the Media Action Network for Asian Americans (MANAA) criticized the film *Aloha* (2015) for whitewashing Hawaii, a state whose population is composed of 60 percent Asian Americans and Pacific Islanders, by featuring mostly white actors. The organization argues *Aloha* is the latest in a long list of films set in Hawaii that fails to acknowledge the diversity of the population. Others point out that casting Emma Stone as a character of Hawaiian, Chinese, and Swedish descent was especially problematic given there are many mixed-race actors who could have been selected (Singh 2015).

Whitewashing may also occur when nonwhite characters are featured in the original source material, but when the material (e.g., book, graphic novel) is adapted for a film or television program, the characters are played by white actors (a practice seen with men as well as with women). For example, the film *Pan* (2015) cast Rooney Mara as the originally conceived Native American character Tiger Lily in the book *Peter and Wendy* by J. M. Barrie—a job Mara later indicated she regretted taking because she understood her casting was problematic (Jones 2016). Additionally, *Dr. Strange* (2016) and *Ghost in the Shell* (2017) were criticized for casting white actors Tilda Swinton and Scarlett Johansson, respectively, to play roles originally conceived as Asian characters (Schacht 2019). Other examples of this practice include *Drive*'s (2011) casting of Carey Mulligan as an initially conceived Latina woman, and *Wanted*'s (2008) casting of Angelina Jolie as an initially conceived African American character (IndieWire 2017).

These choices are sometimes justified by suggesting that decision makers are adhering to colorblind casting, choosing the best person for the role regardless of one's demographic profile when they make hiring decisions. However, given that the facts demonstrate the continued underrepresentation of nonwhite actors in film, *New York Times* writer Maya Phillips argues, "Though egalitarian in theory, colorblind casting in practice is more often used to exclude performers of color. It's a high-minded-sounding concept that producers and creators use to free themselves of any social responsibility they may feel toward representing a diverse set of performers" (Phillips 2020).

At the same time, while there are examples of white actresses playing characters who in the original source material are not white, there are also examples of characters who were originally white played by women of color. For example, the British actor Gemma Chan, who is of Chinese descent, was cast as Bess of Hardwick in *Mary Queen of Scots* (2018). White comic book characters Josie (of *Josie and the Pussycats*) and Iris West were played by Black actors Ashleigh Murray on TV's *Riverdale* (2017–present) and Candace Patton on TV's *The Flash* (2014–present), respectively. Disney also announced Black actor Halle Bailey will play Ariel in the upcoming live-action remake of *The Little Mermaid*. While these and other similar casting decisions have sometimes resulted in assertions of casting hypocrisy and racist backlash, such choices may contribute to diversifying an area of the entertainment industry that has historically marginalized, erased, or problematically depicted nondominant groups. *The Guardian*'s Steve Rose suggests that when white actors are cast in nonwhite character roles, it perpetuates the historic "imbalance" of Hollywood, but when people of color are cast in white character roles, it "helps to correct a systematic imbalance" (Rose 2019).

News Coverage and Women

Women in News

Numerous outlets for news and information populate the twenty-first-century media landscape, providing audiences with a seemingly endless list of choices for content. While many of these sources provide for diverse reporting about and by women, other options may not. Scholars and organizations examine how often women are covered in mainstream news reporting, look at who is doing the reporting on women and women's issues, and consider how women and women's issues are covered. These organizations and scholars usually argue diverse groups of content producers result in expansive, higher-quality news media coverage of women that ultimately better represents the complexities of our world. If news stories are largely produced by one demographic group, such reporting might be limited in perspective and scope. As scholar Tracy Everbach observes, "News reporting, while assumed and purported to be objective, is actually highly subjective, reflecting the biases of those who run the media" (Everbach 2013, 19).

Current analyses of news coverage of women reveal a number of trends. Researchers have documented a long history of men as dominant reporters, experts, and sources for news; more contemporary studies reveal similar inequities in the present, implying women are not as important or knowledgeable as men (Everbach 2013; Women's Media Center 2019). These findings extend to both digital and traditional news platforms. In an examination of visually oriented Facebook posts from news outlets, a Pew Research study found that "across several different types of news content on Facebook, women appear in images at a consistently lower rate than men. In posts related to the economy, 9% of images that show people exclusively show women, compared with 69% of images which exclusively showed men. A total of 22% of individuals shown in stories about the economy were women, while 78% were men. For posts about entertainment, women made up 40% of depicted individuals and 27% of news photos exclusively showed women, compared with 42% for photos that showed exclusively men" (Lam et al. 2019).

Other studies have found similar imbalances in gender representation. For example, a big data study of online newspapers shows women are more likely to appear in photographs and less likely to be present in written article text (Jia et al. 2016). Here the authors interpret their findings by noting the association of "linking women to bodies and the private sphere, and men to mind and the public sphere. More importantly, [the finding] lends support to the longstanding claim by feminist scholars that women's voices are marginalised in the media, a fact that has significant implications for democracy" (Jia et al. 2016). The WMC and other advocacy groups for women contend that these studies prove that more needs to be done to include more women's voices as subjects, experts, and reporters in news content (Women's Media Center 2019).

Scholars also argue that a news industry dominated by white male faces and perspectives contributes to news coverage that privileges white and male perspectives, underreports on nonwhite communities, and advances stereotypes of women in general—and nonwhite women in particular (Moody, Dorries and Blackman 2009). The demographics of who is producing and reporting on news influences the nature of the news itself. Female reporters, for example, are more likely to include women and female sources in their stories than male reporters (Armstrong 2004). When there is a gender imbalance in news reporting, the sourcing of stories may also reflect gender disparities. While some journalists are reflective about whom they reach out to for comment, gender bias persists in news reporting (LaFrance 2016).

Without a diverse news workforce, the potential to default to harmful stereotypes and incomplete information is high when reporting on news in nonwhite communities is being delivered from a white journalist's vantage point (Larson 2006). This tendency results in problematic trends. For example, "missing white woman syndrome" or "missing pretty girl syndrome" is a research-supported phenomenon that documents how missing white women are positively described and given more media attention—particularly if they are conventionally attractive—than nonwhite missing women who, if covered at all by the news media, are more likely to be discussed with commentary about their challenging life circumstances (Moody, Dorries, and Blackman 2009).

Additionally, research shows traditional mainstream news organizations do not adequately represent different racial and ethnic groups and their stories, which may contribute to the public's lack of understanding of diverse women's stories, communities, and issues (Castañeda, Fuentes-Bautista, and Baruch 2015). For example, diverse experiences of American-born Latinas are not as prevalent in mainstream news reporting as narratives about immigration. Challenges facing women who are low-income earners, particularly women of color, are not given much attention either. Some ongoing issues that are prevalent in regions of the country with large Native American populations see little mainstream news coverage (Abbady

2017; Gray 2019). Further, examinations of mainstream media coverage of Native American and Indigenous women prompted Native American journalist Jenni Monet (2019) to argue, "Native Americans suffer from chronic misrepresentation and erasure by an established press, which continually fails to acknowledge the Indigenous timeline." But while problems related to equitable representation of different demographic and identity groups of women in news coverage persist (Ordway 2016; Women's Media Center 2019), growing awareness of these issues has perhaps led to some progress in achieving more inclusive reporting. For example, "positive" coverage of Latinx culture, communities, and achievement increased in newspaper reporting in the late 2010s (Bleich et al. 2018).

#SayHerName

A contemporary example of a challenge posed to news media to better report on women is the #SayHerName movement. In late 2014, the African American Policy Forum (AAPF) and the Center for Intersectionality and Social Policy Studies launched this campaign to raise awareness about the number of Black women and girls who have been "victimized by racist police violence" (African American Policy Forum n.d.). Scholar Kimberlé Crenshaw, a cofounder of the AAPF, asserts that while the names of Black men who have died by police action and are referenced in Black Lives Matter protests are recognizable, the "Black women who were also killed are generally missing from Americans' collective memories" (Kelly and Glenn 2020). AAPF emphasizes that the intention of the movement is not to establish any sort of competition between Black victims but instead to ensure Black women's stories are also heard.

Public media writer Jewell Jackson suggests the Say Her Name campaign is still needed today, pointing out the summer of 2020's Black Lives Matter protests were prompted by the widely publicized death of George Floyd in Minneapolis at the hands of a white police officer. Jackson explains that although an African American medical worker named Breonna Taylor was killed by police in her Louisville, Kentucky, home two months earlier, her story was not given prominent media attention until after Floyd's death, when the efforts of the Say Her Name campaign finally gained traction. "While stories of male Black victims like Eric Garner or Michael Brown have received mass attention," said Jackson, "the campaign sought to bring the same attention to Black women like Sandra Bland, Rekia Boyd, Atatiana Jefferson, and now, Breonna Taylor" (Jackson 2020).

Persistent Gender Disparities in the Newsroom

Several organizations track the presence of women in news organizations and the positions they hold, documenting their participation as journalists, editors, and producers. Other scholars and organizations study the frequency with which women's voices are heard on the news as sources, leaders, and experts. The WMC reports summarize and synthesize available data from media organizations and their own original research to identify how present women are across media industries. For example, a 2018 WMC report summarizes data from the 40 percent of U.S. newsrooms that responded to the American Society of News Editors' annual newsroom employment survey. According to WMC tabulations, 52 percent of newsroom staff among survey respondents are white men, while 31 percent are white women. Among those who occupy positions giving them authority to make choices about what news to cover, called *newsroom leaders*, 54 percent are white men, and 33 percent are white women.

The 2018 WMC report also summarizes the Radio Television Digital News Association's demographic data on professionals working in local television news. The WMC found that the industry was composed of 44 percent white men, 31 percent white women, 12 percent nonwhite men, and 13 percent nonwhite women. Other research efforts additionally document gender disparities across the news industry. The *Columbia Journalism Review* noted in 2018, for example, that 75 percent of the editors of the 135 largest newspapers in the United States are men (Allsop, Ables, and Southwood 2018). A Pew Research study reveals that compared to all workers in the United States, newsroom employees are more likely to be white and male; 61 percent of newsroom workers are male, whereas 53 percent of all workers are men (Grieco 2018). Additionally, non-Hispanic white workers comprise 74 percent of eighteen-to-forty-nine-year-olds and 85 percent of those fifty and over who work in the newsroom (Grieco 2018).

Some argue that changes in newsroom practices need to be addressed more broadly because it is unfair to place the responsibility of diversifying news coverage on underrepresented groups such as women and, in particular, nonwhite professionals (Abbady 2017). In interviews with National Public Radio, several scholars and reporters highlighted the complex nature of this issue. For example, journalists of color do not want to be assigned stories based on their race, even though they often cover such stories well. Another factor is that while mentoring relationships in news organizations are often a source of strength and professional growth for younger journalists, the majority of seasoned professionals are male and white and may have a limited understanding of the experiences of nonwhite and women professionals. Despite calls for diversifying news organizations across all departments, women of color in the news industry are laid off more frequently than any other demographic group (Abbady 2017).

WMC's *Status of Women in the U.S. Media 2019*, a report that draws from ninety-four studies, found that "across all media platforms men received 63% of bylines and credits and women received 37%" (Women's Media Center 2019, 13). Specific data informing this overall statistic includes findings that 69 percent of newswire bylines from the Associated Press and Reuters are men, 60 percent of online news is written by men, and 59 percent of print news is written by men. While some individual news outlets, like MSNBC, Vox, and the *HuffPost*, credit an evenly split number of bylines between men and women, this is not the case for the majority of organizations examined. The researchers additionally note what categories of news are reported on most often by men and women. At the Associated Press and Reuters, men and women cover lifestyle and leisure news equally, but in every other category—from business news to health coverage to politics to technology—men report on these topics more than women. In online news, women cover health and lifestyle and leisure news more than men, but men report more often in every other category.

There are positive indications, however, that parts of the news landscape are gravitating toward a more equitable breakdown along gender lines. The 2019 WMC study found that although the gender gap persists in network television news, all three of the broadcast networks have begun to close this gap since the last WMC study in 2018. At ABC, 65 percent of all byline, on-air, and producer credits were attributed to male journalists (down from 88%), and at both CBS and NBC, 62 percent of credits were attributed to male journalists (down from 68% at both networks). In newsrooms, a Pew study found that gender disparity among younger workers (ages eighteen to twenty-nine) did not exist; employees in that age group were evenly split between women and men. However, such employees are still more likely to be white; where gender parity is present among younger news professionals, racial parity is not (Grieco 2018).

At the same time, local television news employee demographics are becoming more diverse. Surveys of newsrooms indicate increased hiring of women and women of color, moving the local television industry toward more equitable representation (Papper 2019). Consideration of gender and racial equity in news includes attention to the demographics of sources being used in news reports. Advocating for more diversity in these sources, The *Columbia Journalism Review* makes available a database of diverse media experts and points to other organizations that compile lists of women, gender nonbinary, and women of color who can be contacted for story sourcing (Neason 2018).

Harassment of Female Journalism Professionals

Finally, women journalists working today face higher levels of online harassment than their male colleagues. A 2018 study from Amnesty International's Troll Project looked at the Twitter accounts of 778 women journalists and politicians from the United States and the United Kingdom. The results revealed "that 7.1% of tweets sent to women in the study were problematic or abusive. This amounts to 1.1 million problematic or abusive mentions of these 778 women across the year, or one every 30 seconds on average" (Amnesty International 2018). The research also found that online abuse against women was not aligned with any political party orientations and that women of color, particularly Black women, were more likely to be targeted than white women journalists or politicians. The Coalition for Women in Journalism "follows any case of violation that women journalists face around the world," and as such documents the unique challenges women face in this profession. The group's 2020 report confirms that women journalists in North America often face both virtual and physical sexual harassment and threats (Gurcan 2020).

In addition to the obvious problems that abusing and targeting women online poses for individuals, news organizations, and society as a whole, Twitter trolling and attacks complicate attempts to use the platform professionally. Twitter is a tool used by journalists to promote their work, connect with other journalists, and connect with underrepresented communities. It is also a platform that allows for establishing connections and sharing and commenting on reporting about diverse populations, which is necessary in a predominately white mainstream news media landscape. Frustrations with the platform, which include trolling and user debate tactics, have resulted in some journalists choosing to cut back on their Twitter use (Lieberman 2021). Amnesty International, like many other Twitter critics, asserts that the social media platform needs to be more proactive in enforcing its rules against harassment and to aggressively investigate reports of violence and abuse, arguing that Twitter's failures to do so have "a chilling effect on freedom of expression online and undermines women's mobilization for equality and justice—particularly groups of women who already face discrimination and marginalization" (Amnesty International 2018).

Media Coverage of Female Political Candidates

The news (and other) media coverage of any candidate running for office is incredibly important. Given the vast majority of voters will only get to "know" the candidates via media coverage of them, the tone and content of media coverage can have tremendous influence over how voters perceive candidates and make decisions about whom to vote for. Examinations of such news "framing" focus on what information and elements are emphasized in presenting a story to viewers or readers (Bennett 2016).

A common category of women political candidate news frames is one that references gender norms, gender expectations, and gender stereotypes (Burnette 2012; Finneman 2015; Minnesota Public Radio 2016). In her discussion of female candidates for office dating back to the 1870s, scholar Teri Ann Finneman observes that media coverage of these women has often been informed by cultural ideas about gender. She writes that "media discourse not only mirrors the social expectation of women at a particular historical time, but also helps construct an image of women politicians as novelties who are defined and confined by their gender" (Finneman 2015, 178). While not all media framing is problematic, Finneman points out gendered frames are usually central in media reporting on women.

Noted communications scholar Kathleen Hall Jamieson's (1995) book *Beyond the Double Bind: Women and Leadership* presents an argument that women in leadership positions ranging from corporations to politics must contend with a "double bind" in which they cannot be seen as too aggressive or confident, but if they are not aggressive or confident, they are dismissed as too meek to be effective leaders. As more women began to run for political office, seeking roles from congressional seats to the presidency, Jamieson and others have tracked and highlighted the ways female candidates are framed and discussed in news and other media. Analyses of media representations of national candidates—from Geraldine Ferraro to Pat Schroeder to Elizabeth Dole to Nancy Pelosi to Sarah Palin to Hillary Clinton—demonstrate particular trends in how media presents and discusses female politicians. A common thread in these analyses is that news media professionals use gendered frames to present women and their candidacies in ways not applied to male politicians and their campaigns (Jamieson 1995; Montalbano-Phelps 2005; Burnette 2012; Tippett 2019).

Even with increasing numbers of women running for and winning political office, some problematic trends in how these candidates are represented in news media persist. Scholar Lori Montalbano-Phelps describes three categories of female candidate media coverage. The first category advances the ideal of a woman as a traditional wife and mother. The second category positions the female candidate as a "man"; she is "no different from her male counterpart, except of course, for her style and appearance," suggesting that women running for office do not differ from men except in regard to how they look. The third category positions the woman as part of a "marginalized group," where her exception status is noted (Montalbano-Phelps 2005, 195).

Others point out that gender stereotyping often informs coverage of female candidates. For example, news reports more often note "women's appearance, family relationships and emotional states than they do when covering men," perhaps emphasizing cultural gender expectations associated with women (Burnette 2012, 182). Additional long-running stereotypes of women as emotionally frail or high-strung, or "disloyal" to their family responsibilities if they seek public office, can also taint news media coverage of female candidates and officeholders (Minnesota Public Radio 2016). In a conversation on Minnesota Public Radio in 2016, Kathleen Hall Jamieson explained that problematic media framing relies on assumptions about gender, not about Democrats or Republicans. She called attention to a speech that then vice presidential candidate Sarah Palin made wherein political commenters drew attention to the fact that her older daughter held Palin's baby while Palin spoke. Jamieson argued that if a father was giving a speech, a family member holding his baby would not have been regarded as noteworthy by the news media (Minnesota Public Radio 2016).

From the late twentieth century through the early twenty-first century, the media framing of female candidates for political office has improved in significant ways. In 2006, Dianne Bystrom, a scholar of women in politics, pointed out that news media coverage of male and female candidates was mostly equitable "in terms of quantity as well as quality, e.g., assessments of their viability, positive vs. negative slant, and mentions of their appearance" (Bystrom 2006, 175). However, she reported that "women candidates are more often than men described by the media in terms of their sex, children and marital status, which can affect how voters view their ability to hold political office by stirring up stereotypical images of their responsibilities of wives and mothers" (Bystrom 2006, 175). At the same time, though, the candidates themselves also influence the ways they are framed in such media products, as their own campaign advertising and websites often try to strike a balance between image traits perceived as "feminine" and "masculine" in the culture.

Jamieson points out that during the 2016 presidential campaign between Donald Trump and Hillary Clinton, the fact Trump had sent his children to boarding school had not really been spoken about in the media (Minnesota Public Radio 2016). She asserts that news media would have made that fact a major point of discussion if it had been Clinton sending her daughter to boarding school. As Jamieson notes, cultural expectations of female candidates who are mothers still differ from cultural expectations of male candidates who are fathers. Additionally, Jamieson explains how different words are used in news outlets when talking about women—for example, "shrill" and "strident"—that are virtually never used to describe men, and she called attention to Clinton's laugh being described as a "cackle." Similarly, Elizabeth Tippett (2019) notes that Fox News compared Clinton to a "nagging" wife, while CNN used the term "scolding mother." In addition, Tippett explains, the gender-based tropes of being "calculating" and "power hungry" were used to frame her. Clinton also had "token status" as the only woman running and the first woman to earn a major party's nomination for the presidency (Tippett 2019).

Gender and Presidential Politics

Common stereotypes of women are also present in the misinformation and disinformation that was connected to the 2016 presidential election. Some content framed Clinton as a villain, connecting to a media phenomenon wherein women seeking to advance their careers are disparaged or punished for being power hungry (Stabile et al. 2019). Other disinformation played upon the gender stereotype that women are frail. Doctored videos and photos were widely publicized by conservative news broadcasts and websites to raise doubts about Clinton's health and stamina (Stabile et al. 2019; Krieg 2016). In response to the distribution of this information on social media, conservative commentators raised alarms about her health, adding to an already long history of such made up or exaggerated stories being circulated in the information sphere (Krieg 2016).

During the 2020 primary season, many women sought the Democratic party's presidential nomination. Given the gender disparities in newsrooms and what stories women and men tend to report on, more male journalists reported on election news than women. One study indicates just over 67 percent of national online stories about the election were written by men (Heckman 2019). However, when media coverage of the 2020 primary race featured more women, candidates were more likely to be portrayed as individuals, different from both men and one another (Tippett 2019). As professor Nichola Gutgold explains, while gender frames were used in some reporting on women seeking the Democratic nomination for president, other frames were present as well. For example, Tulsi Gabbard's military experience, Kirsten Gillibrand's support of the #MeToo movement, Kamala Harris's former career as a prosecutor, and Elizabeth Warren's "nerdy professor" reputation were all used in media framing of their campaigns. However, Gutgold asserts that the female candidates were not completely free from problematic gendered coverage. For example, Amy Klobuchar was criticized in a series of articles for being a horrible boss. Without making a case about whether those accusations had any merit, Gutgold argues that "insofar as no man running for president has been characterized as 'mean' or a tough boss, this characterization seems to be gendered" (Gutgold 2020, 9–10).

Gender equity expert Lucina Di Meco's comprehensive 2019 report, *#ShePersisted: Women, Politics & Power in the New Media World*, highlights social media as a "double-edged sword" for women candidates; although social media allows candidates for office to easily and directly communicate with voters, the platforms also make them more vulnerable to gender-based attacks from internet trolls and bots. Di Meco's research includes interviews with eighty-eight women leaders from thirty countries, an analysis of material in over 100 publications, and an artificial intelligence–informed analysis of social media pertaining to the U.S. 2020 Democratic presidential primaries (Di Meco 2019a, 6). Her specific analysis of the Twitter and news coverage of the Democratic primary candidates between December 2018 and April 2019 reveals that women candidates are attacked more frequently than men candidates, and social media narratives about women candidates concerned their character more so than their policy positions. Di Meco explains that while male candidates are subject to similar characterizations, "they seem to be the norm for female candidates and the exception for male ones" (Di Meco 2019a, 35).

Women running for office are also subject to harassment on social media platforms. In summarizing the main takeaways from her research, Di Meco emphasizes how social media platforms can be especially challenging for women:

> Social media offers fertile ground for the spread of gendered disinformation, to be understood as the spread of deceptive or inaccurate information and images against women political leaders, journalists and female public figures, following story lines that often draw on misogyny, as well as gender stereotypes around the role of women. Women in politics in particular are the targets of overwhelming volumes of online attacks, fake stories, humiliating or sexually charged images, including photomontages, often aimed at framing them as untrustworthy, unintelligent, emotional/angry/crazy, or sexual. This type of disinformation is designed to alter public understanding of female politicians' track records for immediate political gain, as well as to discourage women seeking political careers, and it deserves specific attention because of its nature, volume and impact on democratic processes. (Di Meco 2019b)

In advance of presidential candidate Joseph Biden's announcement of Senator Kamala Harris as his vice presidential running mate, Democratic women leaders distributed an open letter to news outlets calling them out for "sexist coverage of female Democratic vice presidential contenders" and challenging them to "actively work to be anti-racist and anti-sexist in your coverage" moving forward (Duffy 2020). Sexist tropes about whether Harris and other female candidates for vice president are likable enough or too ambitious permeated the news coverage prior to Biden's eventual announcement, echoing the sexist coverage of the Democrats' presidential primary

(Duffy 2020). Critics of this coverage point out that male politicians are rarely measured by such criteria.

At the same time, Harris—like the female vice presidential candidates who preceded her—also has the task of negotiating her public persona, which in turn influences media coverage of her as a candidate. Gender reporter Alisha Haridasani Gupta points out Harris chose to identify her role in the domestic sphere as a stepmother as the one that meant the most to her. Harris's tenure as a prosecutor, senator, and Black and Indian woman is potentially softened by this framing. "At the highest point in her career," writes Gupta, "Ms. Harris was inserting herself into a persistent mold that powerful women have long been expected to fit: the warm, maternal, likeable figure" (Gupta 2020).

Women in Sports Media

In 2021, the Associated Press Sports Editors (APSE) Racial and Gender Report Card, the most recent evaluation of sports reporting hiring practices along race and gender lines, graded APSE newspapers and websites with a B+ in racial hiring, an F in gender hiring, and an overall grade of a C (Lapchick 2021). Among the findings in this report is that although gains are being made in diversifying some roles in reporting, columnist, and editorial staffs, the same is not true in regard to increasing gender equality. The report documents just 17.8 percent of APSE sports columnists are women, and only 14.4 percent of APSE sports reporters are women. The vast majority of these women are white. Similarly, a 2019 WMC report found that just 10 percent of sports articles in their sample of newspapers are written by women, 14 percent of sports stories at newswire services are attributed to women, and 21 percent of sports stories are credited to women at online news sites.

While the demographic data showing lack of diversity among those covering sports in general is one issue, the nature of media coverage of women's sports specifically is another. Media coverage of women's sports is often discussed in two categories: (1) the amount of media attention given to women's sports, which may or may not be related to the lack of gender diversity in sports reporting, and (2) the ways female athletes are portrayed or represented in the sports media coverage they do receive. Essentially, research consistently shows the media attention paid to women's sports is only a small fraction of the coverage that men's sports receive.

According to the documentary *Media Coverage & Female Athletes*, although nationwide 40 percent of athletes are women and 43 percent of athletic college scholarships are given to women, about 4 percent of media coverage focuses on women's sport (Lamke 2013). In this documentary, scholar Cheryl Cooky asserts that over the previous twenty years, the amount of media coverage of women's sports had actually declined, even as interest in women's sports, both in regard to participation and sports-related programming, was increasing.

The implementation of Title IX legislation in the 1970s making it illegal to discriminate against gender in educational settings resulted in over twenty-five years of tremendous growth of school athletic programs for female athletes, resulting in millions of girls and women playing sports. This shift continues to inform women's interest and participation in collegiate, national, and Olympic teams and sports, but sports media coverage has not caught up (Kane, LaVoi, and Fink 2013). In her discussion of the way media has portrayed female athletes over twenty-five years, Toni Bruce argues, "Mediasport is an overwhelmingly male and hegemonically masculine domain that produces coverage by men, for men and about men" (Bruce 2012, 128). As a result, women's sports and their athletes are sidelined and often marginalized. Scholars argue this approach to sports coverage needs to be addressed to fairly and equitably report on women's athletics.

Gender Disparities in Media Production

In recent years, there have been some positive changes and moves toward more equity. For example, while the quality of the broadcasts may not always be as high as sports coverage of male athletes, women's NCAA basketball and many professional and collegiate women's sports, from tennis to volleyball to gymnastics to WNBA games, are covered to some extent (Cooky, Messner, and Musto 2015). At the same time, women's sports coverage is not necessarily prominent or easy to find. As *Forbes* writer David Berri points out, in May 2018, there were many top women's competitions happening in women's basketball, softball, tennis, soccer, and golf, but the reporting on those events in the most popular sports outlets was slim. Berri promotes outlets where fans can find coverage of women's sport: "Such an initiative is necessary because these leagues do not receive very much coverage from the leading sports media entities. But although coverage remains scarce on the larger platforms, coverage does exist. At least, if you are willing to put in some work to find this coverage" (Berri 2018).

Some argue that media coverage of women's sports is lacking in comparison to coverage of men's sports because sports media outlets do not think large audiences for women's sports coverage exist (Lamke 2013). Others point out that shrinking newspaper budgets and staff result in sports coverage being directed toward men's professional teams with huge fan bases (Springer 2019). However, experts challenge the notion of minimal interest in women's competitions given the number of fans who attend events and participate in women's athletics themselves. For example, scholar Mary Jo Kane argues that because interest in women's sports is well documented, the response "nobody is interested" really refers to the sports writers and editors who choose what sports to cover, and scholar Cheryl Cooky points out choices around what sports stories to feature and how such stories are covered contributes to how audiences are built for all sports reporting (Lamke 2013).

A large and growing area of research documents the way female athletes are portrayed in sports media coverage. One common and historically consistent trend in such representations is that female athletes are more likely to be depicted in images placing them off the court or playing field, out of uniform, and/or in sexualized poses or attire. None of these settings convey their athletic competence or focus on their sport achievement (Lamke 2013).

While sexualizing and objectifying female athletes invites criticism from feminists and others seeking gender equality, sports scholars also acknowledge contemporary thinking around visual representation of athletes is complicated. While women featured by these media organizations are proud of their athleticism, strengths, and talents, some athletes also willingly participate in presentations that emphasize their attractiveness and traditionally feminine qualities, so long as they are not hypersexualized or demeaned (Kane, LaVoi, and Fink 2013). Other trends in media representations of women's sport include emphasizing the heterosexual roles female athletes serve (as girlfriends, wives, mothers), highlighting women's so-called feminine qualities (emotions, physiological differences from men), referring to adult female athletes as "girls," and providing ambivalent sports coverage that alternates between messages of legitimacy and trivialization (Bruce 2012). Toni Bruce points out the media still "views femininity as incompatible with physical strength" and advances problematic ideas about nontraditional conceptions of gender and contradictory ideas about achievement in sport and sexualized images (Hunt 2018).

Key differences have been documented between coverage of women's sporting events and men's sporting events. Research demonstrates coverage of both Olympic and professional men's sports is produced to be more exciting than women's sports; varied production techniques, including camera angle and shot variety, special effects, and graphic use, are more present in men's coverage than women's (Greer, Harden, and Homen 2009; Cooky, Messner, and Musto 2015). A 2017 study comparing coverage of men's and women's sports identifies four approaches used to cover men's sports: "high production values and techniques; fast-paced humorous, action-packed language; dominant descriptors; and lavish compliments" (Musto, Cooky, and Messner 2017, 581). Study authors Michela Musto, Cheryl Cooky, and Michael Messner argue that since these approaches and investments are not made when covering women's sports, the result is a "gender-bland sexism," whereby the "matter-of-fact, monotonous, lackluster delivery style of women's sports coverage" essentially "normalizes a hierarchy between men's and women's sports" (Musto, Cooky, and Messner 2017, 581). Coupled with slim coverage of women's sports to begin with, these contrasting styles of sports reporting communicate the message that men's sports are inherently superior to women's sports.

After years of critiques and hundreds of studies highlighting problematic ways women are reported on in news and sports media, current research documents some emerging positive trends. Though media coverage of women's sports still highlight athlete's personal lives and appearances, and commentators evaluate women athletes by referencing men's sports and male athletes (e.g., "She's the female Usain Bolt"), these characteristics of media coverage are decreasing (Hunt 2018). Images of female athleticism have increased, and there is more reporting on women as serious athletes and role models (Hunt 2018). Additionally, some elements of sports media coverage showcase women's sports and present competitors as talented, competent athletes, de-emphasizing or discarding stereotypical images of women that focus on their appearance. For example, a longitudinal content analysis of images over eight years produced by espnW, a segment of the ESPN network that is dedicated to women's sports, documented meaningful progress in reducing stereotypical representations of female athletes: "Most photographs and articles highlight female athletes as the college or professional level in ways that emphasize athleticism (photographs of athletes in uniform, in action and on the playing surface) and perseverance (athletic prowess/strength and positive skill levels)" (Wolter 2021, 16).

Calls for more gender-equitable coverage by scholars, activists, and athletes have prompted changes to elements of women's sport visibilities. For example, in response to criticism on social media, some sports publications, such as *The Athletic*, are reconsidering how to provide more equitable coverage of women's sports (Springer 2019). Additionally, some crowd funded and grassroots initiatives are "showing how women's sports and women's perspectives on sports can be entertaining, compelling and potentially money making" (Springer 2019). Sports networks may not always equitably present women athletes on their social media platforms. An analysis of Instagram posts from ESPN, Fox Sports, NBC Sports and CBS Sports reveals women athletes are hugely underrepresented compared to men athletes and are more likely to be seen passively in images (Romney and Johnson 2020). However, in using social media themselves, individuals are free to produce or share diverse representations of athletes. Scholars explain that in contrast to traditional media's social media feeds, individual social media feeds present images of female athletes that challenge gender stereotypes and present women as tremendous athletes in their own right (Staurowsky et al. 2020).

Women in Advertising and on Social Media

Persistent Stereotypes

Advertising messages in the twenty-first century continue to perpetuate long-running gender stereotypes and ideas about gender roles. For example, despite their increased education levels and participation in a variety of professions, women are often portrayed in stereotypical occupations in advertisements (Eisend 2010). An analysis of women's fashion and home magazines and men's magazines found that the women featured in the ads are portrayed flawlessly and in passive positions, and home magazines tend to feature women in traditional gender roles (Conley and Ramsey 2011).

Research also reveals that men and women are not equally represented in advertising. A 2017 report on gender bias in advertising by the Geena Davis Institute on Gender in Media indicates that despite renewed cultural movements calling for gender equality and gender equality in media representations, disparities still exist. The report documents that in 2016, only 36.9 percent of characters in commercials—spanning thirty-three different product categories—were women, noting a small increase from the 33.9 percent of female commercial characters counted in 2006. The research also reports men in commercials had "three times as much dialogue as women" and that "25% of ads feature men only on screen compared to 5% of ads that feature women only on screen" (Geena Davis Institute 2017b, 7). The organization calls for bringing more women into the process of creating advertising campaigns.

Another Geena Davis Institute study from 2020 examines 251 Cannes Lions Film and Film Craft advertisements from 2019, looking at representations of the following identity groups: gender, race/ethnicity, LGBTQ+, disability, age over sixty, and body size. Key findings include documentation that only 38.4 percent of characters in the studied ads are women, 7 percent are over sixty years old, 38 percent are characters of color, 1.7 percent are LGBTQ+ characters, 2.2 percent are characters with disabilities, and 7.2 percent are characters with large body types. Additionally, male characters are more likely to be shown working than female characters. The research also records the perpetuation of the woman-as-sex-object stereotype. In the ads studied, female characters are more likely shown in revealing clothing, partially nude, as visually objectified, and as verbally objectified than their male counterparts (Geena Davis Institute 2020, 4).

While advertising's adherence to some traditional gender constructions persists, other advertising messages offer alternatives. Research indicates that consumers have become more likely to respond negatively to stereotypical ads, and to advertising in general, when they encounter such portrayals

(Huhmann and Limbu 2016). Perhaps in response to these findings about problematic aspects of portrayals of women in advertising, the industry and its clients have become more sensitive to embracing gender equity, avoiding gender stereotypes in their approaches, and broadening its portrayals of nontraditional gender roles (Eisend 2010; Mager and Helgeson 2011).

Advertising's promotion of unattainable beauty standards for women has long been a topic of heavy criticism. Numerous studies document potentially problematic health outcomes, from poor self-esteem to eating disorders, that may be associated with the "thin ideal"—an image of a thin woman with flawless skin (often constructed using digital technology and other image alteration tools). In recent years, consumers pushed back against these practices. As a result, the industry made some changes, refraining from digitally altering some imagery and hiring models with diverse body types. Companies that have stopped airbrushing or digitally altering photos include CVS, American Eagle's Aerie (a lingerie brand), *Seventeen* magazine, Target, and Dove. Additionally, recent research demonstrates these changes can lead to positive outcomes, such as increased sales, increased consumer satisfaction with their own appearance, and increased feelings of comfort among the models themselves (Shoenberger, Kim, Johnson 2020).

Pro-Female Advertising/Femvertising

A number of advertising campaigns reflect more contemporary ideas about gender equality and use portrayals that more accurately reflect the perspectives and views of their target audiences. The digital media company SheKnows Media (now called SHE Media), surveyed female consumers about their perspectives on what they call "pro-female" advertising. The results show that 94 percent of the women surveyed described depicting women as sex objects in advertising as problematic, 52 percent indicated they have bought a product because they like the pro-female ad approach in the product's promotion, and 62 percent believed any brand can enter the "pro-female space" (SheKnows Living Editors 2014). Numerous ads and corresponding hashtag campaigns offer messages and approaches that can be categorized as pro-female. For example, the feminine product company Always rolled out a #LikeAGirl campaign that redefines the insulting connotations of the phrase "like a girl" to emphasize that doing things "like a girl" means having strength and confidence. The follow-up to the #LikeAGirl campaign, #Unstoppable, specifically tackles confidence. Some beauty companies shifted their tactics to emphasize confidence, self-worth, and gender barrier breaking. For example, Pantene's #ShineStrong film called "Sorry, Not Sorry" addresses women's tendency to apologize, and CoverGirl's #GirlsCan campaign addresses female empowerment.

In 2020, SHE Media awarded #Femvertising awards for the fifth consecutive year to six 2019 campaigns. *Femvertising*, a term popularized by the organization, is a word that shortens the descriptor "female empowerment advertising" (Åkestam, Rosengren, and Dahlen 2017). The use of feminist-oriented ideas to promote products and services is certainly not new, but scholars have noted that this approach "can be considered novel in that it focuses on questioning female stereotypes acknowledged to be (at least partially) created by advertising" (Åkestam, Rosengren, and Dahlen 2017, 796). According to the Femvertising Awards website, the recognitions were established to "honor brands that are challenging gender norms by building stereotype-busting, pro-female messages and images into ads that target women and girls." The organization's 2019 campaign winners included "RITAS Spritz–Subtle Notes," a campaign from Bud Light that sought to reach female audiences by humorously depicting three cocktail-drinking, vibrantly dressed women, and Secret's "Cheer for Each Other," a new ad in its "All Strength No Sweat" campaign (developed in partnership with the U.S. Women's National Soccer Team) to promote the message of women working together and supporting one another.

Some academic research suggests pro-female promotional advertising and femvertising is positively received by consumers, particularly by those who self-identify as feminists or support women's rights (Sternadori and Abitol 2019). Other research suggests femvertising is a worthy promotional strategy that results in positive reactions among consumers and potentially increased sales (Yang, Chen, and He 2019). However, scholars point out that some of the companies that have rolled out femvertising campaigns have not historically treated women well. They advise consumers who respond to the emotional appeal of the ads to also interrogate whether the sponsoring company is standing by its own feminist messaging (Sternadori and Abitol 2019).

Criticisms of Femvertising

While these shifts in advertising are largely acknowledged as positive, some scholars consider the use of feminist ideals in advertising as potentially problematic. In their review of published research and essays addressing female empowerment in advertising campaigns, a team of scholars highlight ways such advertising is critiqued (Windels et al. 2020). They point out messages in "femvertisements" might, in contrast to the ideals of feminism that advocate for equitable gender rights and structural equality, falsely imply that consuming the product advertised can lead to achievement of female empowerment.

The scholars also suggest some femvertising encourages women to engage in "self surveillance," whereby they are encouraged to monitor their bodies, clothes, and roles as mothers, friends, and sexual partners rather than considering (or monitoring) progress around gender equality. The scholars argue that some femvertising messages, while affirming, also tell women how to think, instructing them to be confident and body positive: "While previous generations saw advertisements that encouraged women to discipline their bodies through diets, exercise and makeup, today's women must also have only positive thoughts about themselves" (Windels et al. 2020, 21).

Appearance-Focused Social Media Use

The documented issues around mainstream media constructions of traditional ideas about femininity, idealized bodies, and attractiveness persist in the social media realm. However, concerns about mediated images of women and their potential negative influence on individual body image, body satisfaction, and self-objectification are also present, even when the content is produced by users themselves rather than a corporate entity. Users often use software to present curated or edited versions of themselves, inherently suggesting their unmodified photographs are not sufficient. Photos can be easily altered to present a more "ideal" presentation of attractiveness using a range of apps (Bosker 2013). Some observers have expressed concerns that user-generated imagery may perpetuate idealized images of beauty that can have problematic health outcomes (such as eating disorders or depression) for individuals who feel they fall short in terms of conventional attractiveness.

A review of twenty empirical studies focused on social media and body image suggests social media use is associated with body image concerns and disordered eating behaviors (Holland and Tiggemann 2016). Research suggests certain practices in which users engage, like uploading appearance-based photos and viewing status updates about such photos, are particularly problematic (Holland and Tiggemann 2016). Other research explores how the types of social media women engage with can have a big impact on one's body image. Use of "appearance-focused" social networking sites, like Facebook and Instagram, are more likely to be associated with the tendencies for users to be focused on body concerns—internalizing the "thin ideal," engaging in self-objectification, and engaging in potential disordered eating (Cohen, Newton-John, and Slater 2017).

Because appearance-oriented social media often features sexualized images, engagement on these platforms may inform users' perceptions of others, of sex, and of their own sexuality (Daniels 2016; van Oosten, Peter, and Vandenbosch 2017).

Sexualized social media content, once posted, is available for others to comment on or copy, alter, and share in some way, which might lead to users objectifying others (Davis 2018). And yet, these platforms additionally provide women with agency and the ability to create their own versions of themselves they wish to share, arguably an empowering practice. "Women can use social media to become important creators of cultural content and self-construct their own gendered and sexual identities," writes social media scholar Stefanie Davis. "In many ways, social media can serve as a unique site of resistance [a place where ideas can be challenged] not available via traditional media platforms. However, these sites can also serve to exclude certain groups and allow for the objectification of women. Women may post sexually-explicit photos online for their own empowerment, but through male commenting, editing and redistributing, this content can be transformed into degrading and objectifying material" (Davis 2018, 3).

Thinspiration, Fitspiration, and the Body Positive Movement

Some users of social media use online communities and resources to think about their bodies. *Thinspiration* communities (#thinspiration) on social networking sites focus on strategies for weight loss, inspiring others to achieve wellness and a thinner physique. Similarly, *fitspiration* communities (#fitspiration) provide encouragement to members to be more physically fit, often while looking to achieve an end goal of weight loss (Tiggemann et al. 2018; Cohen, Newton-John, Slater 2021). Online posts in thinspiration communities range from weight loss tips and encouragement to dangerous and persistent messages that have been linked to eating disorders such as anorexia and bulimia. These messages, whether they convey healthy or unhealthy attitudes, are easily created, accessed and distributed on websites, blogs, and social media networks. Tumblr and Instagram, under pressure from public health organizations and physicians, have attempted to ban posts that "promote self-harm" and celebrate disordered eating, but savvy users have figured out ways to bypass these restrictions, ensuring that dangerous and unhealthy messages such as "starving for perfection" and "keep calm and the hunger will pass" remain online (Shalby 2014).

Because fitspiration suggests a goal of being physically fit, a characteristic with demonstrated positive outcomes, some of these social networking communities promote healthy behaviors and perspectives. However, an analysis of fitspiration content on social networking sites also reveals messaging that prioritizes appearance over athleticism, objectifies the body, embraces pain or suffering as part of exercising to get fit, and emphasizes that making poor choices is connected to how people may define themselves (Deighton-Smith and Bell 2018). Scholars who have examined these social media posts report that the "overwhelming majority" of images tagged with thinspiration and fitspiration hashtags "feature sexual objectification" (Cohen, Newton-John, and Slater 2021, 3). Research also suggests that fitspiration posts may contribute to body image issues, negatively impact one's mental health, and promote compulsive exercise (Alberga, Withnell, and von Ranson 2018).

One study comparing thinspiration posts to fitspiration posts discovered similarities between the two communities. Both groups of posts, for example, focus on appearance, feature sexual suggestiveness, and advocate for restricted eating. This research suggests that while thinspiration posts are more likely to advocate for thinness and frequent weight loss, fitspiration posts tend to advance more "messages of guilt about body shape and weight than thinspiration" (Alberga, Withnell, and von Ranson 2018).

The study confirmed that fitspiration posts often focus on people showing off their physique rather than engaging in physical activity. As with thinspiration posts, fitspiration posts also frequently advocate for dietary sacrifice. The scholars suggest these findings are concerning because "exercising for appearance-related reasons previously has been linked to disordered eating, depressive symptoms, and negative body image. These problematic similarities between thinspiration and fitspiration may reflect larger changes in social conceptualizations of health and fitness, which may include mainstreaming harmful thinspiration sensibilities such as extreme food restriction and self-discipline" (Alberga, Withnell, and von Ranson 2018).

The body positive movement, or BoPo, has also emerged as an influential force on social media. Delineated by the hashtags #bodypositive, #bopo, and #bodypositivity on social networking sites such as Twitter and Instagram, millions of users have generated posts that offer quotes, pictures, selfies, and captioned visuals designed to celebrate the "real" bodies of women who do not conform to traditional societal notions of beauty and attractiveness. Instagram posts marked as body positive include selfies where women display their average- to overweight-sized bodies, posts where "before" and "after" pictures highlight how Photoshop is used to create unattainable body ideals, and posts emphasizing what the body can do versus what the body looks like (Cohen, Irwin et al. 2019). Some recent research suggests women who engage with body positive content on social media are more likely to see improvements in their mood, self-image, and body satisfaction; however, this area of investigation is still emerging (Cohen, Fardouly et al. 2019).

Researchers who examine body positive social media content also point out that posts can sometimes advance problematic presentations of women's bodies by focusing on specific body parts and featuring sexually suggestive poses and revealing clothing (Cohen, Irwin et al. 2019). Critics of the body positive movement take issue with its focus on bodies and appearance. They argue that by once again focusing on one's appearance, even in positive ways, the movement emphasizes to women that what they look like is central to who they are.

Another movement, the body neutrality movement, advances the idea that women should not be deliberating on their bodies and feeling guilty if they do not feel body positive all of the time (Weingus 2018). "Body neutrality is rooted in acknowledging what your body does, not how it appears," according to health and wellness journalist Leigh Weingus. "Your body allows you to exercise, travel the world and experience new cultures. Your body gives you the ability to hold hands or hug someone you love. Your body gets you from point A to point B" (Weingus 2018).

Solutions

Changing Gender in the Media Landscape

Proposed solutions to some of the issues outlined in this chapter include calls for media industries to prioritize hiring of women and to ensure equitable representation of gender, racial and ethnic groups, LGBTQ+ individuals, and women with disabilities. The implication is that inclusionary hiring, especially in leadership roles, will result in a ripple effect of change that yields more diverse and gender-equitable storytelling, news coverage, sports reporting, and promotional messaging.

For example, at the end of the UCLA *Hollywood Diversity Report 2020*, the authors call for a transformation of Hollywood diversity and inclusion practices by using the acronym M.E.A.N.S. to represent the five best practices they claim research supports. First, industry power players need to "modernize" (*M*) their "worldview" to commit to diversifying their organizations given the demographics in the United States. The *E* stands for "expand the net," encouraging leaders to diversify pools of candidates for powerful industry positions. By "amplifying women, particularly women of color" (A), more inclusive workspaces may emerge. "Normalize compensation" (*N*) acknowledges that not all creative talent, particularly those from underrepresented groups, may not be able to afford to begin as unpaid interns or with entry-level salaries because they "disproportionately face economic challenges that their white counterparts often don't." Finally, *S* stands for "structure incentives" in which elements are put in place to hold leaders accountable for meeting inclusion goals (Hunt and Ramon 2020, 44).

The Annenberg Inclusion Initiative offers additional suggestions for increasing the visibility of positive portrayals of women. It called for continued expansion of opportunities for women and other underrepresented demographic groups in leading film roles, emphasizing that "overcoming the biases that limit inclusion among leading characters is essential to creating an ecosystem within stories that allows for casting changes across the spectrum of roles" (Smith, Choueiti, Pieper et al. 2019, 30). They also urge the film and television industries to "just add five" women characters to films to increase the overall percentage of female characters, to become more aware of the implicit bias present in casting small roles, and to "grasp the geographic reality" when casting so new talent from such underrepresented communities as Latinx, Native American, and Native Hawaiian/Pacific Islanders are provided with opportunities (Smith, Choueiti, Pieper et al. 2019, 31).

The report's authors also advocate for increasing gender diversity behind the camera, and they urged the entertainment industry to "uncouple the link between lead and director" so female directors are not exclusively directing films with female leads, Black directors are not exclusively directing films with Black leads, and so on. The authors assert that doing so will ensure that "directors from all backgrounds have access to *all* jobs. . . . Uncoupling the restrictive link between lead characters and director race or gender is essential to reaching equality in this industry" (Smith, Choueiti, Pieper et al. 2019, 31).

Women's rights advocate and gender equality expert Lucina Di Meco argues that addressing the multiple gender-based challenges that women candidates, journalists, and politicians face with traditional and social media requires a multipronged approach. She suggests traditional media may be able to change frames on gender and politics by ensuring their newsrooms are diverse and by providing gender-sensitive training for journalists, adopting gender-sensitive indicators to monitor reporting, establishing media awards that recognize gender-sensitive reporting, and challenging gender stereotypes that exist about women in power. She also advocates for social media companies to improve diversity; use technology to thwart bots and trolls that attack, harass, and disseminate disinformation; and provide social media training programs (Di Meco 2019a, 45, 46–48).

Di Meco also argues that political parties should be doing more to support gender equality and that policy makers should support measures to increase digital literacy among the population, promote fair coverage of women candidates in the media, and establish fines and punishments for social media companies that do not remove abusive content (Di Meco 2019a, 53).

In a 2019 *Nieman Report* focused on improving coverage of women's sports, journalist Shira Springer offers several suggestions for major mainstream media outlets. She asserts that sport news organizations should be compelled to consistently cover women's sports, both in season and out of season, in the same way that men's sports are covered. Springer urges these same media companies to focus on the accomplishments and challenges of female athletes and their teams. Given the gender imbalance in sports reporters and editors, media organizations should also try to hire more female sports reporters and change the culture of prioritizing male sports in sports departments.

Industry Responses

Under pressure from such organizations as Time's Up, members of the entertainment and media industries have promised to address long-standing and persistent shortcomings in their treatment of women, both behind and in front of the camera. For example, the groups Women in Film Los Angeles and the Sundance Institute created the ReFrame Stamp in 2018 to identify films that employ women in significant on- and off-screen roles (Buckley 2019). According to the ReFrame Stamp project's website (reframeproject.org), "Stamps are awarded to narrative features that hire female-identifying people in four out of eight key areas of their production, including: writer, director, producer, lead, co-lead, speaking parts, department heads and crew. Additional points are awarded to content that has women of color in key positions." Films released in 2019 designated with a ReFrame Stamp include *Booksmart*, *Captain Marvel*, *Frozen 2*, *Little Women*, *Long Shot*, and *Us*. While the use of the inclusion rider may not be attractive to some film production studios, some producers and directors are actively seeking ways to have their work endorsed with the ReFrame Stamp (Buckley 2019). Additionally, production companies across the Hollywood sector are requiring project leads to employ more diverse groups of writers (Sperling 2020).

Industry changes are also happening on the television front. For example, NBC launched an initiative aiming to diversify such "below-the-line" positions as production coordinators and production assistants, the National Association of Broadcasters (2020) is providing guidance around launching successful diversity programs, and CBS announced in July 2020 that the network was dedicating a quarter of its television script development budget to projects originating from those who are Black, Indigenous, and people of color (Montpeller 2019; Brown and Carlson 2020). The Writer's Guild of America has also demanded reforms, telling television and movie studios "that they need to improve their practices on diversity and inclusion" (McNary 2020).

The Academy of Motion Picture Arts and Sciences has added a diversity eligibility requirement to the Oscar race. Beginning in 2024, to be considered for best picture, films have to meet certain inclusion standards. Beginning in 2022, best picture hopefuls need to submit a confidential inclusion form to the Academy as part of a transitional process that eventually will require films seeking best picture consideration to adhere to two of the following four standards: "(1) The film must feature underrepresented groups, either in substantial roles, the overall ensemble, or in its narrative themes; (2) a certain number of key crew members must be female and/or queer, nonwhite, or disabled; (3) the film's distributor must employ apprentices or paid interns from underrepresented groups; and (4) the company must have female, queer, nonwhite, and/or disabled executives in its marketing, publicity, or distribution teams" (Jones 2020). The announcement prompted a wide range of critical and celebratory reactions. Supporters praised it as a tangible step toward making the industry more inclusive and representative of American society. Detractors criticized the decision as "anti-artist" and suggested the new rules may not result in much change (Jones 2020; Voytko 2020).

As a response to consumer support for social justice issues as evidenced by the rise of advocacy and activist movements such as the #MeToo movement and the Women's March, the advertising industry is being challenged to improve its culture as well. Time's Up Advertising, a division of Time's Up, calls for an end to gender discrimination in the advertising industry and for increasing gender equality and diversity in the workplace. The organization's executive director, Christena Pyle, suggests change is not only ethically and morally right but also necessary for business: "Gen Z places civil rights and social justice issues at the forefront. Civil rights and discrimination are rated the second and third most critical threats facing the U.S., and 41% of Gen Z adults said #MeToo has had a major impact on their worldview. These priorities impact how Gen Z views and interacts with brands. More than one-third of Gen Z adults say they've boycotted a brand for political reasons in the past year" (Pyle 2019, 15). Although some advertising agencies declare they are prioritizing gender equity and diversity initiatives, seasoned professionals suggest there is still work to be done, as many women describe the agency culture as one still driven by sexist male attitudes and practices, creative teams dominated by men, and persistent gender-based salary disparities (Hsu 2019).

On the news front, programs such as the Journalism and Women Symposium, the Online News Association's Women's

Leadership Programs, and Poynter's Leadership Academy for Women in Digital Media aim to support the professional development of women in news industries, priming and supporting career tracks in leadership roles. The organization Better News (betternews.org), sponsored by the American Press Institute and the Knight Foundation, provides resources, support, and guidance for journalists and news organizations who aim to diversify their news content. Journalists are aware that diverse sources in reporting are important, and some news organizations are using automated tools that use gender and ethnicity metrics to determine how diverse their content is (Newman 2019). In August 2020, the Gannett Company, owner of 260 local news outlets and the national paper *USA Today*, committed to making its entire workforce "as diverse as the country by 2025" and stated it is "adding or reassigning journalists to 60 newly created beats in a concerted effort to enhance coverage of topics such as criminal justice, educational inequity, the roots of racism, environmental justice, fairness in housing and employment, and LGBTQ issues" (Bomey 2020).

Increasing Media Literacy

Media literacy initiatives are designed to help people access, analyze, evaluate, and create media across all forms and platforms. The Media Education Lab (n.d.) at the University of Rhode Island advances the following key media literacy questions consumers should be asking when evaluating media texts: "Who created the message and what is the purpose? What techniques are used to attract and hold attention? What lifestyles, values and points of view are depicted? How might different people interpret this message? What is omitted?" Reflecting on these questions may help consumers thoughtfully consider the nature of the representations of women in such media messages as social media posts, films, television shows, and advertisements.

A variety of media literacy initiatives are produced and distributed by such nonprofit organizations as the Geena Davis

Institute on Gender in Media, Common Sense Media, and Girls, Inc. For decades, public and private schools across the country have engaged in primary and secondary media literacy education instruction integrated into such subject areas as English language arts, health, and technology. Teaching young women how to think critically about the messages they encounter may help mitigate the potential negative impacts of these messages.

Some research studies have indicated that media education–oriented initiatives may be particularly beneficial to young women and girls. For example, media literacy programs addressing how media images of women and girls sometimes enforce gender stereotypes increase students' understanding of these issues (Puchner, Markowitz, and Hedley 2015; Friesem and Probst 2020). Other research with a focus on advertising messages in traditional and newer forms demonstrates that girls develop more critical perspectives of stereotypical gender portrayals after engaging in a media literacy curriculum (Sekarasih et al. 2018). Other media literacy initiatives consider how girls and young women engage with media, assess their media literacy skills, and aim to determine if media literacy education assists in helping them critically evaluate messages (Riesmeyer, Hauswald, and Mergen 2019).

Media scholar Elizaveta Friesem argues that while various approaches to media education suggest positive outcomes, media literacy education that focuses on gender issues should take an interdisciplinary approach to best explore the complexities of gender representations in media texts, gender identity formation in the culture, and self-gender identity. She suggests media education approaches should use the practices of the discipline but also look at "recent literature in media studies focusing on nuances of media and gender," "on gender studies, especially on scholarship elucidating such concepts as the gender binary," and on intersectionality (Friesem 2016, 371). She further writes, "It is important to make sure that media and gender classes help students explore the complexity of their relationship with the media instead of presenting a lopsided argument about dangers of media use" (Friesem 2016, 371). Finally, increasing media literacy can be accompanied by increasing calls for change by consumers. The power of social media can be leveraged to build community among those seeking to celebrate positive mediated representations of women and challenge gendered content that is stereotypical, sexist, or otherwise problematic.

Conclusion

This chapter provides an overview of some of the controversies and issues central to the topic of women and media in the United States. Interested readers may also want to expand their exploration of this diverse, expansive subject by investigating such topics as women in the music, video game, and publishing industries; in contemporary magazines; and on social networking and video-sharing sites. Readers may also want to explore how audiences, particularly women, make sense of the media messages they engage with, challenge such messages on social networking sites, and use the technology available to them to create their own media texts.

The ways women are represented in film, television, advertising, news, and other mainstream media–produced texts will continue to evolve as new stories are written, new campaigns are conceived, and new events are reported on. The high-profile pressure on media industries to be more inclusive of underrepresented groups may result in some changes both in front of and behind the scenes. In this participatory culture, women continue to have ways of easily creating content that challenges the status quo, be it via platforms they use for personal use or professional use. Continued conversations about women's place in the American media landscape will undoubtedly continue through the twenty-first century.

Bibliography

Abbady, Tal. 2017. "The Modern Newsroom Is Stuck behind the Gender and Color Line." Code Switch, NPR, May 1, 2017. https://www.npr.org/sections/codeswitch/2017/05/01/492982066/the-modern-newsroom-is-stuck-behind-the-gender-and-color-line

African American Policy Forum. n.d. "#Sayhername Campaign." Accessed September 1, 2020. https://aapf.org/sayhername

Åkestam, Nina, Sara Rosengren, and Micael Dahlen. 2017. "Advertising 'Like a Girl': Toward a Better Understanding of 'Femvertising' and its Effects." *Psychology of Marketing* 34 (8): 795–806. https://doi.org/10.1002/mar.21023

Alberga, Angela, Samantha Withnell, and Kristin von Ranson. 2018. "Fitspiration and Thinspiration: A Comparison across Three Social Networking Sites." *Journal of Eating Disorders* 6 (39). https://doi.org/10.1186/s40337-018-0227-x

Allsop, Jon, Kelsey Ables, and Denise Southwood. 2018. "Who's the Boss?" *Columbia Journalism Review* (Spring/Summer). https://www.cjr.org/special_report/editors-by-the-numbers.php

Amnesty International. 2018. "Women Abused on Twitter Every 30 Seconds—New Study." December 18, 2018. https://www.amnesty.org.uk/press-releases/women-abused-twitter-every-30-seconds-new-study

Armstrong, Cory. 2004. "The Influence of Reporter Gender of Source Selection in Newspaper Stories." *Journalism & Mass Communication Quarterly* 81 (1): 139–154.

Armstrong, Cory. 2013. "The Next Frontier in Gender Representation." In *Media Disparity*, edited by Cory Armstrong, 217–226. Lanham, MD: Rowman & Littlefield.

Aurthur, Kate. 2018. "The Year the Networks Finally Embraced Diversity." BuzzFeed, September 28, 2018. https://www.buzzfeednews.com/article/kateaurthur/network-television-racial-diversity-2018

Barnes, Brooks. 2014. "From Now On, Women Save the World." *New York Times*, September 3, 2014. https://www.nytimes.com/2014/09/07/movies/fall-arts-preview-hollywood-has-realized-that-movies-starring-women-can-make-money.html

Barnes, Brooks, and Cara Buckley. 2019. "As Hollywood Embraces Diversity, Jobs for Female Directors Remain Sparse." *New York Times*, April 14, 2019. https://www.nytimes.com/2019/04/14/movies/hollywood-female-directors.html

Bennett, W. Lance. 2016. *News: The Politics of Illusion*. 10th ed. Chicago: University of Chicago Press.

Bernstein, Alina. 2002. "Is It Time for a Victory Lap? Changes in the Media Coverage of Women in Sport." *International Review for the Sociology of Sport* 37 (3–4): 415–428. https://doi.org/10.1177/1012690202203700301

Berri, David. 2018. "Where to Find Coverage of Women's Sports." *Forbes*, May 23, 2020. https://www.forbes.com/sites/davidberri/2018/05/23/searching-for-coverage-of-womens-sports/#1d4422e23f62

Birro, Christina Jeurling. 2016. "Episode 37: Miss L—Annoyingly Exposing the Sexism of the Acting World." *Pop Culture Confidential* [podcast], March 30, 2016. http://www.popcultureconfidential.com/home/2016/3/30/episode-37

Bleich, Erik, James P. Callison, Georgia Grace Edwards, Mia Fichman, Erin Hoynes, Razan Jabari, and A. Maurits van der Veen. 2018. "The Good, the Bad, and the Ugly: A Corpus Linguistics Analysis of US Newspaper Coverage of Latinx, 1996–2016." *Journalism: Theory, Practice &*

Criticism 22 (6): 1522–1539. https://doi.org/10.1177/1464884918818252

Bomey, Nathan. 2020. "USA TODAY Owner Gannett Commits to Make Workforce as Diverse as America, Add New Beats on Race and Social Justice." *USA Today*, August 20, 2020. https://www.usatoday.com/story/money/2020/08/20/gannett-usa-today-diversity-commitment-journalism/5604473002/

Bosker, Bianca. 2013. "New Selfie-Help Apps Are Airbrushing Us All into Fake Instagram Perfection." *HuffPost*, December 5, 2013. https://www.huffpost.com/entry/selfie-instagram_n_4391220

Brown, Gretchen. 2017. "More Women, Girls Taking Prominent Roles in TV, Movies." Wisconsin Public Radio, July 7, 2017. https://www.wpr.org/more-women-girls-taking-prominent-roles-tv-movies

Brown, Jeffery, and Frank Carlson. 2020. "Hollywood Turns Scrutiny Inward amid National Discussion on Race and Policing." *PBS NewsHour*, July 15, 2020. https://www.pbs.org/newshour/show/hollywood-turns-scrutiny-inward-amid-national-discussion-on-race-and-policing

Bruce, Toni. 2012. "Reflections on Communication and Sport: On Women and Femininities." *Communication and Sport* 1 (1/2): 125–137.

Buckley, Cara. 2019. "Inclusion Rider? What Inclusion Rider?" *New York Times*, June 19, 2029. https://www.nytimes.com/2019/06/19/movies/inclusion-rider.html

Buckley, Cara, and Daniel Victor. 2018. "What Did Frances McDormand Mean by an 'Inclusion Rider' at the Oscars?" *New York Times*, March 5, 2018. https://www.nytimes.com/2018/03/05/movies/inclusion-rider-frances-mcdormand-oscars.html

Burnette, Ann. 2012. "Who's Framing Whom? Michelle Bachmann and the (Primary) Politics of Motherhood."

In *Media Depictions of Brides, Wives and Mothers*, edited by Alena Amato Ruggerio, 181–193. Lanham, MD: Lexington Books.

Bystrom, Dianne. 2006. "Advertising, Web Sites, and Media Coverage: Gender and Communication along the Campaign Trail." In *Gender and Elections: Shaping the Future of American Politics*, edited by Susan Carroll and Richard Logan Fox, 169–188. Cambridge, UK: Cambridge University Press.

Castañeda, Mari, Martha Fuentes-Bautista, and Felicitas Baruch. 2015. "Racial and Ethnic Inclusion in the Digital Era: Shifting Discourses in Communications Public Policy." *Journal of Social Issues* 71 (1): 139–154. https://doi.org/10.1111/josi.12101

Cohen, Rachel, Jasmine Fardouly, Toby Newton-John, and Amy Slater. 2019. "#BoPo on Instagram: An Experimental Investigation of the Effects of Viewing Body Positive Content on Young Women's Mood and Body Image." *New Media & Society* 21 (7): 1546–1564. https://doi.org/10.1177/1461444819826530

Cohen, Rachel, Lauren Irwin, Toby Newton-John, and Amy Slater. 2019. "#Bodypositivity: A Content Analysis of Body Positive Accounts on Instagram." *Body Image* 29: 47–57. https://doi.org/10.1016/j.bodyim.2019.02.007

Cohen, Rachel, Toby Newton-John, and Amy Slater. 2017. "The Relationship between Facebook and Instagram Appearance-Focused Activities and Body Image Concerns in Young Women." *Body Image* 23: 183–187. https://doi.org/10.1016/j.bodyim.2017.10.002

Cohen, Rachel, Toby Newton-John, and Amy Slater. 2021. "The Case for Body Positivity on Social Media: Perspectives on Current Advances and Future Directions." *Journal of Health Psychology* 26 (13): 2365–2373. https://doi.org/10.1177/1359105320912450

Conley, Terri, and Laura Ramsey. 2011. "Killing Us Softly? Investigating Portrayals of Women and Men in Contemporary Magazine Advertisements." *Psychology of Women Quarterly* 35 (3): 469–478. https://doi.org/10.1177/0361684311413383

Cooky, Cheryl, Michael Messner, and Michela Musto. 2015. "'It's Dude Time!': A Quarter Century of Excluding Women's Sports in Televised News and Highlight Shows." *Communication & Sport* 3 (3): 261–287. https://doi.org/10.1177/2167479515588761

Copeland, Libby. 2014. "Sony Pictures Hack Reveals Stark Gender Pay Gap." Slate, December 5, 2014. https://slate.com/human-interest/2014/12/sony-pictures-hack-reveals-gender-pay-gap-at-the-entertainment-company-and-deloitte.html

Damico, Amy, and Sara Quay. 2016. *21st Century TV Dramas: Exploring the New Golden Age*. Santa Barbara, CA: Praeger.

Daniels, Elizabeth A. 2016. "Sexiness on Social Media: The Social Costs of Using a Sexy Profile Photo." *Sexualization, Media, & Society* 2 (4): 1–10. https://doi.org/10.1177/2374623816683522

Davis, Stefanie. 2018. "Objectification, Sexualization, and Misrepresentation: Social Media and the College Experience." *Social Media + Society*, 1–9. https://doi.org/10.1177/2056305118786727

Deighton-Smith, Nova, and Beth T. Bell. 2018. "Objectifying Fitness: A Content and Thematic Analysis of #Fitspiration Images on Social Media." *Psychology of Popular Media Culture* 7 (4): 467–483. https://doi.org/10.1037/ppm0000143

Di Meco, Lucina. 2019a. *#ShePersisted: Women, Politics & Power in the New Media World*. #ShePersisted. https://static1.squarespace.com/static/5dba105f102367021c44b63f/t/5dc431aac6bd4e7913c45f7d/1573138953986/191106+SHEPERSISTED_Final.pdf

Di Meco, Lucina. 2019b. "Women in Politics & Social Media." #ShePersisted. https://www.she-persisted.org/

Dockterman, Eliana. 2016. "Read All the Sexist Ways Female Characters Are Introduced in Scripts." *Time*, February 2, 2016. https://time.com/4215743/femscriptintros-twitter-account-hollywood-sexism/

Duffy, Clare. 2020. "Democratic Leaders Call Out Sexist News Coverage of Female Vice Presidential Candidates." CNN, August 10, 2020. https://www.cnn.com/2020/08/09/media/media-vice-president-women-coverage-reliable/index.html

Eisend, Martin. 2010. "A Meta-Analysis of Gender Roles in Advertising." *Journal of the Academy of Marketing Science* 38 (4): 418–440. https://doi.org/10.1007/s11747-009-0181-x

Everbach, Tracy. 2013. "Women's (Mis) Representation in News Media." In *Media Disparity*, edited by Cory Armstrong, 15–26. Lanham, MD: Rowman & Littlefield.

Finneman, Teri Ann. 2015. *Press Portrayals of Women Politicians, 1870s–2000s: From "Lunatic" Woodhull to "Polarizing" Palin*. Lanham, MD: Lexington Books.

Friesem, Elizaveta. 2016. "Drawing on Media Studies, Gender Studies, and Media Literacy Education to Develop an Interdisciplinary Approach to Media and Gender Classes." *Journal of Communication Inquiry* 40 (4): 370–390. https://doi.org/10.1177/0196859916656837

Friesem, Elizaveta, and Donnell Probst. 2020. "Teaching about Intersections of Disability, Gender, and Sexuality through Media Literacy Education." *Journal of Literacy & Technology* 21 (1): 2–29.

Gajanan, Mahita. 2020. "Issa Rae Saying 'Congratulations to Those Men' Sums Up Plenty of Feelings about the All-Male Best Director Oscar Nominations." *Time*, January 13, 2020. https://time.com/5763729/issa-rae-oscar-nominations-2020/

Geena Davis Institute on Gender in Media. 2017a. "The Geena Benchmark Report: 2007–2017." https://seejane

.org/research-informs-empowers/the-geena-benchmark-report-2007-2017/

Geena Davis Institute on Gender in Media. 2017b. "Gender Bias in Advertising." https://seejane.org/research-informs-empowers/gender-bias-advertising/

Geena Davis Institute on Gender in Media. 2020. "Bias and Inclusion in Advertising: An Analysis of 2019 Cannes Lions Work." https://seejane.org/wp-content/uploads/bias-and-inclusion-in-advertising-cannes-lions.pdf

Geena Davis Institute on Gender in Media, USC Viterbi School of Engineering, and TENA. 2020. "Frail, Frumpy and Forgotten: A Report on the Movie Roles of Women of Age." https://seejane.org/wp-content/uploads/frail-frumpy-and-forgotten-report.pdf

Gonzalez, Sandra. 2020. "Issa Rae's 'Congratulations to Those Men' Quip Sums Up Oscars Frustration." CNN, January 13, 2020. https://www.cnn.com/2020/01/13/entertainment/oscars-women-directing/index.html

Gray, Lucy Anna. 2019. "Forgotten Women: The Conversation of Murdered and Missing Nation Women Is Not One North America Wants to Have—but It Must." *Independent*, February 26, 2019. https://www.independent.co.uk/news/long_reads/native-american-women-missing-murder-mmiw-inquiry-canada-us-violence-indigenous-a8487976.html

Greer, Jennifer, Marie Harden, and Casey Homen. 2009. "'Naturally' Less Exciting? Visual Production of Men's and Women's Track and Field Coverage during the 2004 Olympics." *Journal of Broadcasting & Electronic Media* 53 (2): 173–189. https://doi.org/10.1080/08838150902907595

Grieco, Elizabeth. 2018. "Newsroom Employees Are Less Diverse Than U.S. Workers Overall." Pew Research Center, November 2, 2018. https://www.pewresearch.org/fact-tank

/2018/11/02/newsroom-employees-are-less-diverse-than-u-s-workers-overall/

Gupta, Alisha Haridasani. 2020. "The Suffragists Fought to Redefine Femininity. The Debate Isn't Over." *New York Times*, August 26, 2020. https://www.nytimes.com/2020/08/26/us/womens-suffrage-femininity.html

Gurcan, Zeynep. 2020. "Outcome Report: #ThreatsToWIJ Global Campaign." Coalition for Women in Journalism, September 22, 2020. https://www.womeninjournalism.org/reports-all/outcome-report-threatstowij-global-campaign

Gutgold, Nichola. 2020. "Six Women for President in 2020: Rising above a Gendered Tradition." *Media Report to Women* (Winter): 6–12.

Heckman, Meg. 2019. "Men Are Writing Two-Thirds of National Stories about the 2020 Presidential Race." Storybench, June 6, 2019. https://www.storybench.org/men-are-writing-two-thirds-of-national-stories-about-the-2020-presidential-race/

Holland, Grace, and Marika Tiggemann. 2016. "A Systematic Review of the Impact of the Use of Social Networking Sites on Body Image and Disordered Eating Outcomes." *Body Image* 17 (June): 100–110. https://doi.org/10.1016/j.bodyim.2016.02.008

Hsu, Tiffany. 2019. "#MeToo Clashes with 'Bro-Culture' at Ad Agencies." *New York Times*, December 22, 2019. https://www.nytimes.com/2019/12/22/business/media/ad-industry-sexism.html

Huhmann, Bruce, and Yam Limbu. 2016. "Influence of Gender Stereotypes of Advertising Offensiveness and Attitude toward Advertising in General." *International Journal of Advertising* 35 (5): 846–863. https://doi.org/10.1080/02650487.2016.1157912

Hunt, Darnell, and Ana-Christina Ramon. 2020. *Hollywood Diversity Report 2020. A Tale of Two Hollywoods*. UCLA

College of Social Sciences. https://socialsciences.ucla.edu/wp-content/uploads/2020/02/UCLA-Hollywood-Diversity-Report-2020-Film-2-6-2020.pdf

Hunt, Paul. 2018. "The 15 Rules of Sports Media Representation of Female Athletes." Sportanddev.org, May 19, 2008. https://www.sportanddev.org/en/article/news/15-rules-sports-media-representation-female-athletes

IndieWire. 2017. "25 Worst Cases of Hollywood Whitewashing since 2000." August 29, 2017. https://www.indiewire.com/gallery/hollywood-whitewashing-25-roles-emma-stone-jake-gyllenhaal-scarlett-johansson/screen-shot-2017-08-29-at-12-21-38-pm/

Itzkoff, Dave. 2014. "Jailhouse Blues." *New York Times*, May 28, 2014. https://www.nytimes.com/2014/06/01/arts/television/stars-and-creators-of-orange-is-the-new-black-talk-shop.html

Jackson, Jewél. 2020. "Why Black Women Like Breonna Tayler Still Need 'Say Her Name' Movement." WFPL, July 6, 2020. https://wfpl.org/why-black-women-like-breonna-taylor-still-need-say-her-name-movement/

Jamieson, Kathleen Hall. 1995. *Beyond the Double Bind: Women and Leadership*. New York: Oxford University Press.

Jia, Sen, Thomas Lansdall-Welfare, Saatviga Sudhahar, Cynthia Carter, and Nello Cristianini. 2016. "Women Are Seen More Than Heard in Online Newspapers." *PloS One* 11 (2): e0148434. https://doi.org/10.1371/journal.pone.0148434

Jones, Jaleesa M. 2016. "Rooney Mara Regrets Her 'Whitewashed' Role as Tiger Lily in 'Pan.'" *USA Today*, February 23, 2016. https://www.usatoday.com/story/life/entertainthis/2016/02/23/rooney-mara-tiger-lily-pan-hollywood-whitewashing/80792024/

Jones, Nate. 2020. "What the Oscars' New Diversity Initiative Does—and Doesn't—Do." *Vulture*, September 9, 2020. https://www.vulture.com/2020/09/the-oscars-new-diversity-rules-explained.html

Kane, Mary Jo, Nicole M. LaVoi, and Janet S. Fink. 2013. "Exploring Elite Female Athletes' Interpretations of Sport Media Images: A Window into the Construction of Social Identity and 'Selling Sex' in Women's Sports." *Communication & Sport* 1 (3): 269–298. https://doi.org/10.1177/2167479512473585

Kantor, Jodi, Arya Sundaram, Melena Ryzik, and Cara Buckley. 2021. "Turmoil Was Brewing at Time's Up Long before Cuomo." *New York Times*, August 21, 2021. https://www.nytimes.com/2021/08/21/us/times-up-metoo-sexual-harassment.html

Kelly, Mary Louise, and Heidi Glenn. 2020. "Say Her Name: How the Fight for Racial Justice Can Be More Inclusive of Black Women." National Public Radio, July 7, 2020. https://www.npr.org/sections/live-updates-protests-for-racial-justice/2020/07/07/888498009/say-her-name-how-the-fight-for-racial-justice-can-be-more-inclusive-of-black-wom

Kitazawa, Yosuke. 2017. "Health and Entertainment Experts Discuss Hollywood's On-Screen Portrayal of Aging." USC Annenberg News Event Recaps, February 22, 2017. https://annenberg.usc.edu/news/event-recaps/health-and-entertainment-experts-discuss-hollywoods-screen-portrayal-aging

Krieg, Gregory. 2016. "The New Birthers: Debunking Hillary Clinton Health Conspiracies." CNN, August 24, 2016. https://www.cnn.com/2016/08/22/politics/hillary-clinton-health-conspiracy-theory-explained/index.html

LaFrance, Adrienne. 2016. "I Analyzed a Year of My Reporting for Gender Bias (Again)." *The Atlantic*, February 17, 2016. https://www.theatlantic.com/technology/archive/2016/02/gender-diversity-journalism/463023/

Lam, Onyi, Stefan Wojcik, Adam Hughes, and Brian Broderick. 2019. "Men Appear Twice as Often as Women in News Photos on Facebook." Pew Research Center, May 23, 2019. https://www.journalism.org/2019/05/23

/men-appear-twice-as-often-as-women-in-news-photos-on-facebook/

Lamke, Sheree, prod. 2013. *Media Coverage & Female Athletes.* University of Minnesota Tucker Center and Twin Cities Public Television, December 1, 2013. https://video.tpt.org/video/tpt-co-productions-media-coverage-female-athletes/

Langone, Alix. 2018. "#MeToo and Time's Up Founders Explain the Difference between the 2 Movements—And How They're Alike." *Time*, March 8, 2018. https://time.com/5189945/whats-the-difference-between-the-metoo-and-times-up-movements/

Lapchick, Richard. 2021. *The 2021 Associated Press Editors Racial and Gender Report Card.* Institute for Diversity and Ethics in Sport at the University of Central Florida, September 22, 2021. https://www.tidesport.org/associated-press-sports-editors

Larson, Stephanie. 2006. *Media & Minorities: The Politics of Race in News and Entertainment.* Lanham, MD: Rowman & Littlefield.

Lauzen, Martha. 2019. *Boxed In 2018–19: Women on Screen and behind the Scenes in Television.* Center for the Study of Women in Television & Film at San Diego State University. https://womenintvfilm.sdsu.edu/wp-content/uploads/2019/09/2018-19_Boxed_In_Report.pdf

Lauzen, Martha. 2020a. *The Celluloid Ceiling: Behind-the-Scenes Employment of Women on the Top 100, 250 and 500 films of 2019.* Center for the Study of Women in Television & Film at San Diego State University. https://womenintvfilm.sdsu.edu/wp-content/uploads/2020/01/2019_Celluloid_Ceiling_Report.pdf

Lauzen, Martha. 2020b. *It's a Man's (Celluloid) World: Portrayals of Female Characters in the Top Grossing Films of 2019.* Center for the Study of Women in Television & Film at San Diego State University. https://womenintvfilm

.sdsu.edu/wp-content/uploads/2020/01/2019_Its_a_Mans_Celluloid_World_Report_REV.pdf

Lauzen, Martha. 2021. *Boxed In: Women on Screen and behind the Scenes on Broadcast and Streaming Television in 2020-21*. Center for the Study of Women in Television & Film at San Diego State University. https://womenintvfilm.sdsu.edu/wp-content/uploads/2021/09/2020-21_Boxed_In_Report.pdf

Lauzen, Martha. 2022. *It's a Man's (Celluloid) World, Even in a Pandemic Year: Portrayals of Female Characters in the Top Grossing Films of 2021*. Center for the Study of Women in Television & Film at San Diego State University. https://womenintvfilm.sdsu.edu/wp-content/uploads/2022/03/2021-Its-a-Mans-Celluloid-World-Report.pdf

Lieberman, Mark. 2021. "A Growing Group of Journalists Has Cut Back on Twitter or Abandoned It Entirely." Poynter, November 16, 2021. https://www.poynter.org/reporting-editing/2021/a-growing-group-of-journalists-has-cut-back-on-twitter-or-abandoned-it-entirely/

Lynch, Jason. 2015. "ABC's Success with Diversity Comes from Focusing on Creators, Not Just Stars." *AdWeek*, January 15, 2015. https://www.adweek.com/tv-video/abcs-success-diversity-comes-focusing-creators-not-just-stars-162384/

Maddaus, Gene. 2018. "'Weinstein Effect' Leads to Jump in Sexual Harassment Complaints." *Variety*, June 18, 2018. https://variety.com/2018/biz/news/weinstein-effect-sexual-harassment-california-1202849718/

Mager, John, and James Helgeson. 2011. "Fifty Years of Advertising Images: Some Changing Perspectives on Role Portrayals along with Enduring Consistencies." *Sex Roles* 64 (3–4): 238–252. https://doi.org/10.1007/s11199-010-9782-6

Martinetti, Cher. 2016. "Women's Work: Why the Jobs of Female Film Characters Matter." SYFY, February 17, 2016.

https://www.syfy.com/syfywire/womens-work-why-jobs-female-film-characters-matter

McNary, Dave. 2020. "WGA Leaders Demand Studios Deliver More Data on Diversity and Inclusion." *Variety*, May 29, 2020. https://variety.com/2020/film/news/wga-leaders-studios-improve-diversity-inclusion-1234620588/

Media Action Network for Asian Americans (MANAA). 2015. "MANAA Condemns Sony Pictures and Cameron Crowe for Continuing to Erase Asian/Pacific Islanders in 'Aloha' Film." May 28, 2015. http://manaa.org/?p=1544

Media Education Lab. n.d. "What Is Media Literacy?" Media Education Lab, Harrington School of Communication and Media, University of Rhode Island. https://mediaeducationlab.com/what-media-literacy-0

Meyer, Michaela, and Rachel Griffin. 2018. "Riding Shondaland's Roller Coasters: Critical Cultural Television Studies in the 21st Century." In *Adventures in Shondaland*, edited by Rachel Griffin and Michaela Meyer, 1–19. New Brunswick, NJ: Rutgers University Press.

Minnesota Public Radio. 2016. "Just Can't Win: Women Seen as too Meek or too Aggressive as Leaders." MPR News, September 14, 2016. https://www.mprnews.org/story/2016/09/14/double-blind

Monet, Jenni. 2019. "The Crisis in Covering Indian Country." *Columbia Journalism Review*, March 19, 2019. https://www.cjr.org/opinion/indigenous-journalism-erasure.php

Montalbano-Phelps, Lori. 2005. "Performing Politics: Media Aesthetics for Women in Political Campaigns." In *Women and the Media: Diverse Perspectives*, edited by Theresa Carelli and Jane Campbell, 184–198. Lanham, MD: University Press of America.

Montpeller, Rachel. 2019. "NBC Introduces Its First Below-the-Line Diversity Initiatives." Women and Hollywood,

June 3, 2019. https://womenandhollywood.com/nbc-introduces-its-first-below-the-line-diversity-initiatives/

Moody, Mia, Bruce Dorries, and Harriet Blackwell. 2009. "How National Media Framed Coverage of Missing Black and White Women." *Media Report to Women*, 37 (4): 12–18.

Moye, David. 2017. "Kelly Marie Tran of 'Last Jedi' Facing Racist, Sexist Comments Online." *HuffPost*, December 27, 2017. https://www.huffpost.com/entry/kelly-marie-tran-racists-last-jedi_n_5a4400fee4b06d1621b6b2bb

Musto, Michela, Cheryl Cooky, and Michael Messner. 2017. "'From Fizzle to Sizzle!' Televised Sports News and the Production of Gender-Bland Sexism." *Gender & Society* 31 (5): 573–596. https://doi.org/10.1177/0891243217726056

National Association of Broadcasters. 2020. "Creating Diversity Initiatives in the Broadcast Industry." NABshow. https://nabshow.com/2020/thought-gallery/creating-diversity-initiatives-broadcast-industry/

Neason, Alexandria. 2018. "You Are Probably Not Quoting Enough Women. Let Us Help You." *Columbia Journalism Review*, June 1, 2018. https://www.cjr.org/analysis/women-sources.php

Newman, Nic. 2019. *Journalism, Media and Technology Trends and Predictions 2019.* Reuters Institute for the Study of Journalism, January 2019. https://reutersinstitute.politics.ox.ac.uk/our-research/journalism-media-and-technology-trends-and-predictions-2019

Ordway, Denise-Marie. 2016. "Are Women Underrepresented in News Coverage?" Journalist's Resource, January 4, 2016. https://journalistsresource.org/studies/society/gender-society/women-gender-disparity-news-coverage/

Papper, Bob. 2019. "Local Newsroom Diversity." RTDNA/Lawrence Herbert School of Communication at Hofstra University Newsroom Survey, June 13, 2019. https://www.rtdna.org/article/2019_research_local_newsroom_diversity

Patil, Sayali Bedekar. 2014. "10 Celebs Who Were Victims of Cyber Bullying & Web Trolling." TheRichest, August 2, 2014. https://www.therichest.com/nation/10-celebrities-who-were-victims-of-cyber-bullying-web-trolling/

Pedace, Roberto. 2019. "Exploring the Data on Hollywood's Gender Pay Gap." The Conversation, December 20, 2019. https://theconversation.com/exploring-the-data-on-hollywoods-gender-pay-gap-127414

Phillips, Maya. 2020. "'Hamilton,' 'The Simpsons,' and the Problem with Colorblind Casting." *New York Times*, July 8, 2020. https://www.nytimes.com/2020/07/08/arts/television/hamilton-colorblind-casting.html

Puchner, Laurel, Linda Markowitz, and M. Mark Hedley. 2015. "Critical Media Literacy and Gender: Teaching Middle School Students about Gender Stereotypes and Occupations." *Journal of Media Literacy Education* 7 (2): 23–34. https://digitalcommons.uri.edu/jmle/vol7/iss2/3

Pyle, Christena J. 2019. "Time's Up for Discrimination in Advertising." *Adweek* 60 (32): 15.

Riesmeyer, Claudia, Julia Hauswald, and Marina Mergen. 2019. "(Un)Healthy Behavior? The Relationship between Media Literacy, Nutritional Behavior, and Self-Representation on Instagram." *Media & Communication* 7 (2): 160–168. https://doi.org/10.17645/mac.v7i2.1871

Romney, Miles, and Rich G. Johnson. 2020. "The Ball Game Is for the Boys: The Visual Framing of Female Athletes on National Sports Networks' Instagram Accounts." *Communication & Sport* 8 (6): 738–756. https://doi.org/10.1177/2167479519836731

Rose, Steve. 2019. "How Casting across Racial Lines Exposes Hollywood's Power Imbalance." *The Guardian*, April 1, 2019. https://www.theguardian.com/film/2019/apr/01/how-casting-across-racial-lines-exposes-hollywoods-power-imbalance

Sampson, Mike. 2016. "Why the 'Ghostbusters' Trailer Is the Most 'Disliked' Movie Trailer in YouTube History." Screencrush, April 29, 2016. https://screencrush.com/ghostbusters-trailer-most-disliked-movie-trailer-in-history/

Schacht, Kira. 2019. "What Hollywood Movies Do to Perpetuate Racial Stereotypes." DW, February 21, 2019. https://www.dw.com/en/hollywood-movies-stereotypes-prejudice-data-analysis/a-47561660

Sekarasih, Laras, Erica Scharrer, Christine Olson, Gamze Onut, and Kylie Lanthorn. 2018. "Effectiveness of a School-Based Media Literacy Curriculum in Encouraging Critical Attitudes about Advertising Content and Forms among Boys and Girls." *Journal of Advertising* 47 (4): 362–377. https://doi.org/10.1080/00913367.2018.1545269

Shalby, Colleen. 2014. "Fighting Social Media 'Thinspiration' with Messages of Self-Acceptance." PBS, March 1, 2014. https://www.pbs.org/newshour/health/thinspiration-ban-social-media-doesnt-prevent-eating-disorders

SheKnows Living Editors. 2014. "SheKnows Unveils Results of Its Femvertising Survey (Infographic)." SheKnows, October 30, 2014. https://www.sheknows.com/living/articles/1056821/sheknows-unveils-results-of-its-fem-vertising-survey-infographic/

Shoenberger, Heather, Eunjin (Anna) Kim, and Erika K. Johnson. 2020. "#BeingReal about Instagram Ad Models: The Effects of Perceived Authenticity." *Journal of Advertising Research* 60 (2): 197–207. https://doi.org/10.2501/JAR-2019-035

Silman, Hannah. 2016. "A Timeline of Leslie Jones's Horrific Abuse." *The Cut, New York*, August 24, 2016. https://www.thecut.com/2016/08/a-timeline-of-leslie-joness-horrific-online-abuse.html

Singers, Claire. 2018. "How the U.K. and U.S. Both Can Shrink the Pay Gap at Entertainment Companies." *Variety*,

April 11, 2018. https://variety.com/2018/biz/columns/gender-pay-parity-uk-us-hollywood-guest-column-1202749763/

Singh, Maanvi. 2015. "Here's What People Are Saying about Racial Weirdness in *Aloha*." Code Switch, National Public Radio, June 2, 2015. https://www.npr.org/sections/codeswitch/2015/06/02/411264817/heres-what-people-are-saying-about-racial-wierdness-in-aloha

Smith, Stacy, Marc Choueiti, Ariana Case, Katherine Pieper, Hannah Clark, Karla Hernandez, Jacqueline Martinez, Benjamin Lopez, and Mauricio Mota. 2019. *Latinos in Film: Erasure On Screen & behind the Camera across 1,200 Popular Movies*. Annenberg Inclusion Initiative at USC Annenberg's School for Communication and Journalism. http://assets.uscannenberg.org/docs/aii-study-latinos-in-film-2019.pdf

Smith, Stacy, Marc Choueiti, Katherine Pieper, Kevin Yao, Ariana Case and Angel Choi. 2019. *Inequality in 1,200 Popular Films: Examining Portrayals of Gender, Race/Ethnicity, LGBTQ & Disability from 2017 to 2018*. Annenberg Inclusion Initiative at USC Annenberg's School for Communication and Journalism. http://assets.uscannenberg.org/docs/aii-inequality-report-2019-09-03.pdf

Sperling, Nicole. 2020. "Harvey Weinstein Is Gone but Hollywood Is Still a Man's World." *New York Times*, February 24, 2020. https://www.nytimes.com/2020/02/24/business/media/harvey-weinstein-hollywood.html

Springer, Shira. 2019. "7 Ways to Improve Coverage of Women's Sports." *Nieman Reports*, January 7, 2019. https://nieman.harvard.edu/articles/covering-womens-sports/

Stabile, Bonnie, Aubrey Grant, Hemant Purohit, and Kelsey Harris. 2019. "Sex, Lies and Stereotypes: Gendered Implications of Fake News for Women in Politics." *Public Integrity* 21 (5): 491–502. https://doi.org/10.1080/10999922.2019.1626695

Staurowsky, Ellen J., Nicholas Watanabe, Joseph Cooper, Cheryl Cooky, Nancy Lough, Amanda Paule-Koba, Jennifer Pharr, Sarah Williams, Sarah Cummings, Karen Issokson-Silver, and Marjorie Snyder. 2020. *Chasing Equity: The Triumphs, Challenges, and Opportunities in Sports for Girls and Women*. New York: Women's Sports Foundation. https://www.womenssportsfoundation.org/articles_and_report/chasing-equity-the-triumphs-challenges-and-opportunities-in-sports-for-girls-and-women/

Sternadori, Miglena, and Alan Abitbol. 2019. "Support for Women's Rights and Feminist Self-Identification as Antecedents of Attitude toward Femvertising." *Journal of Consumer Marketing* 36 (6): 740–750. https://doi.org/10.1108/JCM-05-2018-2661

Tiggemann, Marika, Owen Churches, Lewis Mitchell, and Zoe Brown. 2018. "Tweeting Weight Loss: A Comparison of #Thinspiration and #Fitspiration Communities on Twitter." *Body Image* 25 (June): 133–138. https://doi.org/10.1016/j.bodyim.2018.03.002

Time's Up. n.d. "Time's Up Was Born When Women Said 'Enough Is Enough.'" Accessed July 1, 2020. https://timesupnow.org/about/our-story/

Tippett, Elizabeth. 2019. "2020 Campaign Shows the More Women Run, the More They Are Treated Like Candidates—Not Tokens." The Conversation, November 25, 2019. https://theconversation.com/2020-campaign-shows-the-more-women-run-the-more-they-are-treated-like-candidates-not-tokens-127563

Townsend, Megan, Raina Deerwater, Nick Adams, and Monica Trasandes. 2019. *Where We Are on TV 2019–2020*. GLAAD Media Institute Report. https://www.glaad.org/sites/default/files/GLAAD%20WHERE%20WE%20ARE%20ON%20TV%202019%202020.pdf

Tran, Kelly Marie. 2018. "Kelly Marie Tran: I Will Not Be Marginalized by Online Harassment." *New York Times*,

August 21, 2018. https://www.nytimes.com/2018/08/21/movies/kelly-marie-tran.html

Ugwu, Reggie. 2020. "The Hashtag That Changed the Oscars: An Oral History." *New York Times*, February 6, 2020. https://www.nytimes.com/2020/02/06/movies/oscarssowhite-history.html

van Oosten, Johanna, Jochan Peter, and Laura Vandenbosch. 2017. "Adolescents' Sexual Media Use and Willingness to Engage in Casual Sex: Differential Relations and Underlying Processes." *Human Communication Research* 43 (1): 127–147. https://doi.org/10.1111/hcre.12098

Viruet, Pilot. 2016. "*Love* and the History of TV's Attractiveness Gap." *Vulture*, February 22, 2016. https://www.vulture.com/2016/02/love-tv-attractiveness-gap.html

Voytko, Lisette. 2020. "'Not Messing Around': Oscars' New Diversity Rules Draw Praise and Criticism." *Forbes*, September 9, 2020. https://www.forbes.com/sites/lisettevoytko/2020/09/09/not-messing-around-oscars-new-diversity-rules-draw-praise-and-criticism/#6219863b1b38

Weingus, Leigh. 2018. "Body Neutrality Is a Body Image Movement That Doesn't Focus on Your Appearance." *HuffPost*, August 15, 2018. https://www.huffpost.com/entry/what-is-body-neutrality_n_5b61d8f9e4b0de86f49d31b4

Whitten, Sarah. 2020. "The 2020 Oscar Nominations Show the Academy Is Still a White Man's Game." CNBC, January 18, 2020. https://www.cnbc.com/2020/01/17/2020-oscar-nominations-show-the-academy-has-an-issue-with-diversity.html

Windels, Kasey, Sara Champlin, Summer Shelton, Yvette Sterbenk, and Maddison Poteet. 2020. "Selling Feminism: How Female Empowerment Campaigns Employ Postfeminist Discourses." *Journal of Advertising* 49 (1): 18–33. https://doi.org/10.1080/00913367.2019.1681035

Wolter, Sarah. 2021. "A Longitudinal Analysis of espnW: Almost 10 Years of Challenging Hegemonic Masculinity." *Communication & Sport* 9 (5): 718–741. https://doi.org/10.1177/2167479519895479

Women and Hollywood. 2016. "Producer Reveals the Incredibly Terrible Ways Screenwriters See Female Characters—and Women." February 11, 2016. https://womenandhollywood.com/producer-reveals-the-incredibly-terrible-ways-screenwriters-see-female-characters-and-women-de9af55f48e5/

Women's Media Center. 2018. *The Status of Women of Color in the U.S. Media 2018*. http://www.womensmediacenter.com/assets/site/reports/the-status-of-women-of-color-in-the-u-s-media-2018-full-report/Women-of-Color-Report-FINAL-WEB.pdf

Women's Media Center. 2019. *The Status of Women in the U.S. Media 2019*. https://womensmediacenter.com/reports/the-status-of-women-in-u-s-media-2019

Yang Feng, Huan Chen, and Li He. 2019. "Consumer Responses to Femvertising: A Data-Mining Case of Dove's 'Campaign for Real Beauty' on YouTube." *Journal of Advertising* 48 (3): 292–301. https://doi.org/10.1080/00913367.2019.1602858

NBC
GOLDEN
GLOBE
AWARDS

Introduction

In this chapter, several scholars and writers offer their perspectives on a variety of topics related to how women are portrayed in American media and how they are treated professionally in the worlds of entertainment, advertising, and other media-oriented industries. To begin, Sara E. Quay proposes popular television programs continue to implicitly advance and challenge feminist ideals, a pattern identified in television programs of the late 1960s. In her analysis of teen television, Lori Bindig Yousman argues young women on these shows often advance similar constructions of femininity, leaving little room for explorations of diverse characters and narratives.

Two essays that provide important perspectives on representations of different demographic groups follow. Virginia McLaurin overviews the patterns of filmic representations of Native American women in film, noting long-standing tropes, while Melissa Yang summarizes the representation of Asian women in American media, pointing out why some contemporary representations are important to celebrate. Next, Nora Hickey offers a personal perspective on the rise of the woman in contemporary superhero films, particularly within the DC and Marvel comic book universes, and explains why this trend

---

At the 2020 Golden Globes, Nora Lum, known professionally as Awkwafina, won Best Actress in a musical or comedy role for her character in *The Farewell.* This was the first time an Asian American won this award at the Globes. (Featureflash/Dreamstime.com)

is important. Referencing a different type of comic-informed media, Amaris Feland Ketcham describes how women comic creators are using the social media platform Instagram to share their perspectives, advance stories of underrepresented women, and contribute to comics journalism.

While reminding readers that equitable representation in Hollywood is an issue, Susan X Jane celebrates the work of director and filmmaker Ava DuVernay and her commitment to providing directing and producing opportunities to professionals from underrepresented groups, particularly Black women. Dunja Antunovic and Nicole LaVoi provide a useful overview of the representation of women in sports media, demonstrating that although women's sports are popular with audiences and athletes, this is not reflected in mainstream sports coverage. Finally, Julie Frechette argues that newsrooms need to continue to change to appropriately cover women's stories in ways that are meaningful and representative of their experiences.

Magical and Difficult Women: Resisting the Waves of Feminism in Popular Television

Sara E. Quay, PhD

In her 1995 landmark publication *Where the Girls Are: Growing Up Female with the Mass Media*, Susan J. Douglas devotes a chapter to the appearance, in the 1960s and early 1970s, of unusual female characters who "were capable of magic" (Douglas 1995, 126). Specifically, the female leads in *Bewitched* (1964–1972), *I Dream of Jeannie* (1965–1970), and *The Flying Nun* (1967–1970) had magical abilities that—with the twitch of a nose, the blink of an eye, or a sudden gust of wind, respectively—allowed them to move beyond the private domestic sphere of the home into the public male-dominated realm of work and industry. These moves registered contemporary feminist debates around the confinement of women to the sole roles of wife and mother and "conjured up the promise of women's liberation and the unleashing of female power that was to come" (Tally 2016). Some fifty years later, another unusual female character—the anti-heroine—appeared on the television screen, who, like her predecessors, had traits that positioned her to engage with current questions around gender. In both instances, the magical women of the twentieth century and the difficult women of the twenty-first reflected potential changes in women's empowerment. Also, in both instances, that empowerment was ultimately neutralized, suggesting that television representations of women both support and resist cultural change.

In *Where the Girls Are*, Douglas grounds her argument in the historical context of the 1960s and the lead-up to second-wave feminism, a time during which women's roles in American culture were being redefined (Grady 2018). Citing President John F. Kennedy's 1961 Presidential Commission on the Status of Women, the 1963 Equal Pay Act, and the publication of Betty Friedan's best-selling *The Feminine Mystique* (1963), along with a plethora of articles in magazines like *Reader's Digest* and *U.S. News and World Report*, Douglas argues that the period during which the series' aired was one of "prefeminist agitation" against limited roles and rights for women (Douglas 1995, 125). In *Bewitched*, *I Dream of Jeannie*, and *The Flying Nun*, these issues were registered when the lead female characters' magic allowed them to move beyond the domestic spaces traditionally defined as female. While those representations can be viewed as supportive of second-wave feminist values, they were not without complexity. Despite the magic that allowed the female leads to engage in the public male world of work, doing so inevitably led to disastrous results. As Douglas writes, when Samantha, Jeannie, or Sister Bertrille used their "powers outside the home, in the public sphere, the male world was turned completely upside down" (Douglas 1995, 126). That chaos, and the neat return of the characters to their domestic spaces at the end of each episode, suggested that a woman's place actually is in the home. In the end, Douglas writes, these series acknowledged "the impending release of female sexual and political energy [of the second wave of feminism] . . . while keeping it all safely in a straitjacket" (Douglas 1995, 126), like Jeannie closed away in her bottle.

This pattern of simultaneously empowering and containing feminist agendas through unique female characters recurs decades later in the early twenty-first century. The 2016 presidential election of Donald Trump and defeat of Hillary Clinton, who was expected by many to be the first female president, led to national marches and social media movements like #MeToo and Time's Up. Such activism was been defined as part of the fourth wave of feminism, a predominantly digital, inclusive movement with at least one goal being to "hold our culture's most powerful men accountable for their behavior . . . [that has] begun a radical critique of the systems of power that allow predators to target women with impunity" (Grady 2018). Into this moment appears the television anti-heroine who, as Laura Bogart writes, "arrive[s] at a time where women are increasingly encouraged to tap into the anger that we've been told to smile through and tamp down for generations" (Bogart 2018). Whereas the witches and genies of the twentieth century used magic to challenge gender stereotypes around home and work, the anti-heroine uses "difficult behavior" to challenge gender stereotypes around "acceptable" female traits and to push back against systemic male abuse and harassment. Elizabeth Jennings on *The Americans* (2013–2018), Claire Underwood on *House of Cards* (2013–2018), and Annalise Keating on *How to Get Away with Murder* (2014–2020) are among the anti-heroines whose alienating, difficult, and even amoral behavior transgresses "traditional female attributes that include the injunction that female characters should be likable" (Tally 2016, 8). This break with gendered expectations around behavior can be seen as positive because anti-heroines "bestow women with full personhood, in all its ugliness and contradiction" (Joho 2018), and "despite some of their dubious actions, are still exemplary of the complexities of the human condition" (IndieWire 2017).

While the anti-heroine has been touted as a positive step in television's representation of women because she exercises power and ambition akin to her male anti-hero counterparts, that power of being difficult, similar to the power of being magical, ultimately fails to truly advance the goals of fourth-wave feminism. As Laura Bogart (2018) writes, "At its shallowest, TV's trend of unlikeable women appropriates structures we'd rightfully call 'toxic masculinity' in men without interrogating those structures or asking its heroine to move beyond them." Whereas the magic women of the twentieth century could only effectively use their power in the private sphere, the anti-heroines of the twenty-first century simply reproduce the negative characteristics of the men against which fourth-wave feminism fights. And just as the genies, witches, and flying nuns of the second wave of feminism became cautionary tales about women stepping into the male world of work and industry, the anti-heroine is a "cautionary tale warning women that going full tilt toward your own desires will only lead to self-destruction or soul-crushing loneliness. Until modern television pushes the antiheroine's characterization beyond trauma, it's doomed to inadvertently ascribe to the same troubling myths about women it wants to subvert" (Bastién 2017).

Bibliography

Bastién, Angelica Jade. 2017. "America Is Afraid of Ambitious Women, Even on TV." The Outline, January 26, 2017. https://theoutline.com/post/958/tv-antiheroines-america-fears-ambitious-women

Bogart, Laura. 2018. "Are TV's Strongest Women Anti-Heroines or Just Assholes?" Dame, December 10, 2018. https://www.damemagazine.com/2018/12/10/are-tvs-strongest-women-anti-heroines-or-just-assholes/

Douglas, Susan. 1995. *Where the Girls Are: Growing Up Female with the Mass Media*. New York: Three Rivers Press.

Grady, Constance. 2018. "The Waves of Feminism, and Why People Keep Fighting over Them, Explained." Vox, July 20, 2018. https://www.vox.com/2018/3/20/16955588/feminism-waves-explained-first-second-third-fourth

IndieWire. 2017. "10 Unforgettable TV Anti-Heroines." December 11, 2017. https://www.indiewire.com/gallery/10-unforgettable-tv-anti-heroines/tv-anti-heroines/

Joho, Jess. 2018. "The Female Characters of 2018 Wielded Femininity as a Weapon." Mashable, December 21, 2018. https://mashable.com/article/2018-women-weaponized-sexism-antiheroines/

Robinson, Penelope. 2010. "Super Women and the Changing Face of Feminism." *Pondering Postfeminism* (blog), February 17, 2010. https://postfeminist.wordpress.com

Tally, Margaret. 2016. *The Rise of the Anti-Heroine in TV's Third Golden Age*. Newcastle upon Tyne, UK: Cambridge Scholars Publishing.

Sara E. Quay, PhD, is dean of the School of Education and director of the Endicott Scholars Program at Endicott College. She is the author and coauthor of numerous articles and books, including 21st-Century TV dramas: Exploring the New Golden Age *(2016),* September 11 in Popular Culture: A Guide *(2010), and* The Cultural History of Reading in America *(2008).*

Same Girl, Different Show: Representations of Young Femininity in Teen TV

Lori Bindig Yousman, PhD

In 1990, the Fox network debuted *Beverly Hills, 90210*, a prime-time soap opera about a group of wealthy, attractive teenage friends. The show soon became a global sensation and launched a new genre: teen television. Over the next thirty years, programs like *Dawson's Creek* (1999–2003); *One Tree Hill* (2003–2012); *The O.C.* (2003–2007); *Gossip Girl* (2007–2012); *Pretty Little Liars* (2010–2017); and *Riverdale* (2017–present) followed suit, appealing to twelve-to-thirty-four-year-old female viewers, a sought-after demographic that networks and advertisers had previously struggled to reach (Kaklamaniduou and Tally 2014).

Although women have been historically underrepresented on television (Lauzen 2018), teen TV features young women more centrally and seriously than other genres (Nash 2006). As such, teen television has played a significant role in how young femininity is portrayed. However, a look at the genre reveals that these representations are eerily similar.

Though there are exceptions, teen TV's female protagonists tend to be cis, white, middle- to upper-class, and heterosexual. When the genre does include other types of young female characters, their differences are largely ignored. For instance, while Andrea from *Beverly Hills, 90210*, and Joey from *Dawson's Creek* experienced economic hardship, their struggles rarely differentiated them from their affluent peers. Similarly, although Emily from *Pretty Little Liars* was the first lead female of color in a teen television show, the series only acknowledged her ethnicity a handful of times throughout its 160 episodes. Likewise, *Riverdale* diversified its leading ladies by casting a Brazilian American actress to play Veronica Lodge, but the primary marker of the character's Latinx heritage is her parents use of "*mija*" (or "daughter" in Spanish). *Riverdale* also features two Black female characters, Josie and Toni, but they both take secondary roles to other white (or white-passing) characters.

To be fair, *Pretty Little Liars* was unique in its sensitive portrayal of Emily's coming-out narrative, her romantic relationships with other women, and the prejudice that she and her partners encountered. Showrunner I. Marlene King's own sexual identity has been credited for this portrayal, which supports GLAAD's (2020) findings that employing diverse creators and producers behind the scenes can lead to more inclusive and nuanced representations on-screen. Unfortunately, the show's portrayal of CeCe, Ali's transgender sibling, as a mentally deranged villain simply replicated a dangerous stereotype that has plagued the LGBTQ community for decades (Gross 2001). Entirely missing from the genre are nonbinary and gender-fluid characters despite the overall increase in nonbinary representation on prime-time television during the

2019–2020 season (the 2019–2020 season also featured the most LGBTQ characters to date; GLAAD 2020). The absence, marginalization, and demonization of diverse female leads in teen TV ultimately suggest that only certain kinds of young women (i.e., cis, straight, white, well-off) are worthy of having their stories told.

Regardless of class, race, or sexuality, teen television's female leads are unwaveringly uniform in appearance. While there are superficial aesthetic differences in their hair, eye color, skin tone, and height, all of the young women are incredibly thin and are conventionally beautiful. The strict adherence to Western ideals and continued lack of body diversity in teen TV perpetuates long-standing concerns over media's promotion of unhealthy beauty standards. While several shows reference characters' struggles with eating disorders and body image (issues known to afflict the genre's target demographic), teen television fails to address these unrealistic norms through casting or meaningful ongoing story lines.

Hypersexuality is also pervasive in representations of young femininity in teen TV. Female characters often appear in provocative attire and are regularly objectified by "camera work that takes on the perspective of a heterosexual male as it focuses in on sexualized female body parts . . . or slowly pans up the length of a woman's body" (Yousman and Bindig Yousman 2020, 21). Increasingly, teen television depicts female leads as consciously inviting the male gaze as a form of empowerment—a choice that young women freely make as illustrated by Blair's burlesque striptease in *Gossip Girl* or Betty's "serpent dance" in *Riverdale*. Even female characters who are uninterested in male partners, such as *Pretty Little Liar*'s Emily and *Riverdale*'s Cheryl and Toni, still conform to the hypersexual feminine ideal and are viewed through the male gaze. Thus, for young women, the genre appears to conflate being desirable and empowered with hypersexuality.

On the surface, teen TV heroines challenge media stereotypes of passivity and frivolity that have long been associated with femininity (Gauntlett 2002). After all, they use their seemingly disparate talents to solve mysteries (*Pretty Little Liars* and *Riverdale*), attend Ivy League universities (*The O.C.* and *Gossip Girl*), and establish successful companies (*Beverly Hills, 90210*, and *One Tree Hill*), all while celebrating the bonds of sisterhood. Yet, when that same drive and ambition is used to undercut and backstab "frenemies" in their quest for popularity and love, the genre reproduces the same age-old tropes of young women as catty, emotional, competitive, and untrustworthy. Furthermore, teen TV repeatedly shows young women privileging their romantic relationships above all else—from Joey choosing Dawson over a trip to France on *Dawson's Creek* to Spencer pursuing her sister's fiancé on *Pretty Little Liars*. This romantic imperative is reinforced in series finales that conclude with female protagonists becoming wives and mothers. While marriage and motherhood can be rewarding, the genre regularly frames them as the ultimate goal for young women rather than just one facet of a full and satisfying life.

Despite thirty years of female characters and story lines, teen television fails to offer varied and authentic representations of young women. Instead, the genre continues to reproduce traditional notions of femininity rooted in gender stereotypes. Research shows that female viewers look to teen TV for guidance on their behavior, relationships, and identity (McKinley 2003). Unfortunately, all they find is same homogenized version of young femininity, devoid of any real alternatives, which provides a skewed version of what young women should aspire to be.

Bibliography

Gauntlett, David. 2002. *Media, Gender, and Identity*. London: Routledge.

GLAAD. 2020. *Where We Are on TV 2019–2020*. GLAAD Media Institute. https://www.glaad.org/whereweareontv19

Gross, Larry. 2001. *Up from Invisibility*. New York: Columbia Publishers.

Kaklamaniduou, Betty, and Margaret Tally. 2014. *The Millennials on Film and Television*. Jefferson, NC: McFarland.

Lauzen, Martha. 2018. *Boxed In 2017–18: Women on Screen and behind the Scenes in Television*. San Diego State University Center for the Study of Women in Television and Film. https://www.nywift.org/boxed-in-study-2018/

McKinley, E. Graham. 2003. "Floating with the Current: Hegemony in Young Women's Talk about *Dawson's Creek*." Paper presented at the annual Eastern Communication Association Convention, Boston, MA, April 2003.

Nash, Ilana. 2006. *American Sweethearts*. Bloomington: Indiana University Press.

Yousman, Bill, and Lori Bindig Yousman. 2020. *Critical Media Literacy and Cultural Autonomy in a Mediated World*. Culture Reframed. https://www.cultureframed.org/wp-content/uploads/2020/02/CR_Critical_Media_Literacy_Report_2020.pdf

Lori Bindig Yousman, PhD, is an associate professor and chair of the Department of Communication Studies in the School of Communication, Media, and the Arts at Sacred Heart University. Her research is grounded in gender, media literacy, and popular culture. Most recently, she coedited the award-winning fifth and newly released sixth editions of Gender, Race, and Class in Media *published by SAGE Publications.*

Defined by Desire and Dispossession: A Cautionary Tale about Early Film Representations of Native American Women

Virginia McLaurin

In the 1910 film *Indian Squaw's Sacrifice*, viewers observed a Native woman saving a white man's life, marrying him, and bearing his child, only to discover that he was in love with a white woman all along. Rather than take offense to this, she graciously kills herself so that he can fulfill his desire to marry the white woman and allows her child to be raised by this new couple.

The theme of Native women desiring white men only to die after consummating the relationship was a repeated theme across early cinema history. The 1914 film *The Squaw Man*, remade in 1918 and 1931, tells a nearly identical story to *Indian Squaw's Sacrifice* except that the man in question is from England. In 1908's *The Kentuckian*, a Native woman kills herself so that her white husband can claim his family inheritance; 1912's *At Old Fort Dearborn* has a Native woman killed by her tribe as she aids her white lover; in 1915's *The Sealed Valley*, a Native woman seals herself into a ravine so that her white paramour can pursue a white woman; and 1925's *Scarlet and Gold* depicts a Native woman killing herself so that her Mountie husband can marry a white woman.

The repeated imagery of white men dominating passive Native women through sexual conquest mirrors the ideas of European populations entering and subduing the landscape of North America. The North American lands themselves were often referred to as "virgin lands," with the implication that it would be the responsibility, even the moral imperative, for Europeans to come and properly fertilize these lands (Locke 1952).

In the early age of cinema, the late nineteenth and early twentieth centuries, the conquest of Native lands was still recent history. Some of the militaristic tactics used in the West received negative press in eastern states, where people mistakenly believed that their own Native population had already disappeared. Cinema could provide a palatable alternative version of this history, one where Native people and lands willingly opened themselves to white Americans only to tragically die, through no fault of those same Americans. During the late 1800s, cinema was largely centered on the East Coast in areas like New Jersey, and the idea of the tragic, noble Native demise became the standard for depictions of colonization (Hanlon 1964).

Native male sidekicks also frequently assist white heroes and often die at the conclusion of their helpfulness. But one major difference between Native male and female characters is that Native men who love white women are generally rejected in early cinema (e.g., *The Call of the Wild*, 1908; *A Red Man's Love*, 1909; *Chief White Eagle*, 1912; *Early Days in the West*, 1912; *From Out of the Big Snows*, 1915; *Dawn Maker*, 1916; *The Danger Trail*, 1917; *The Savage*, 1917; *Red Clay*, 1927). It is the Native female characters in particular who are sexually conquered, bear children, and die in service to white Americans, exhibiting Western ideas about the roles of men as dominant and women as submissive as well as the "inevitability" of American colonial actions.

The fact that the children produced by mixed marriages in film are almost always raised by white couples signifies several intellectual trends in how Native Americans should be approached. In the late 1800s, two ideas were in competition: the eradication of all Native Americans or their "reeducation." The second idea gained prominence on the East Coast, and the result of this ideology was a boarding school system where Native American children were forcibly separated from their families and subjected to extreme abuses. This process was justified by the idea that Native cultures were savage and that Native people could only "belong" in American society if they were raised by white people within "civilized" American culture.

Early cinema presented a romanticized version of an incredibly traumatic and brutal period of colonization. The films of the late 1800s and early 1900s portray Native people, and women in particular, as desiring the conquest that white people bring to them. They are doomed to die in these story lines, reinforcing the idea that they have no place in the future of the United States; yet, the films repeatedly absolve the white characters (and perhaps viewers) of any blame or guilt over Native deaths. And finally, the idea that Native children should be raised by white families is normalized and even seen as a "happy ending" in these films.

American Western films would continue to perpetuate the idea of Indigenous women desiring white frontiersmen. In

Broken Arrow (1950), Apache woman Sonseeahray marries white protagonist Tom Jeffords, and her later death brings peace to the land; in *Drum Beat* (1954), the sister of the peaceful, "good" Modoc chief offers to marry Johnny MacKay and later dies protecting him; in *Far Horizons* (1955), Sacagawea consistently protects Lewis and Clark and forms a romance with Clark, but she later sacrifices their relationship so that he can marry his white fiancée; and in the revisionist Western *Little Big Man* (1970), Dustin Hoffman's character has a Cheyenne wife who begs him to marry and have sexual relations with her sisters, but all of these women are later massacred.

Even modern films often exhibit the trend of Native women desiring white men. Disney's *Pocahontas* (1995) and *The New World* (2005) both made Pocahontas older to portray her relationship with John Smith as a romantic one. In *Legends of the Fall* (1994), Brad Pitt's character marries a part-Native woman who is later shot due to his actions. *Night at the Museum* (2006) has Sacagawea fall in love with Teddy Roosevelt, who is arguably symbolic of the American frontier. And *Avatar* (2009) has an Indigenous woman from Pandora fall in love with soldier Jake Sully, though she is fortunate enough to live through the ensuing invasion.

Animated children's films show similar pairings. *The Road to El Dorado* (2000) portrays the only significant Indigenous female character as overtly sexual and interested in relations with the Spanish male characters. *Atlantis: The Lost Empire* (2001) has Kida, a "princess" character from Atlantis who exhibits traits of Indigenous societies, fall for the white male American lead, Milo, who understands the Atlanteans' written language better than they themselves do.

When Native women are included in non-Indigenous films, they are often love interests for white men. But in films made by Indigenous creators or with significant Indigenous feedback, Native American women are more likely to be main characters. They also more frequently have Indigenous romantic partners (e.g., *Dance Me Outside*, 1994; *Naturally Native*, 1998; *Older*

Than America, 2008; *Christmas in the Clouds*, 2001; *Barking Water*, 2009), and many are not shown as romantic partners at all but have other interests and goals (e.g., *Smoke Signals*, 1998; *Rhymes for Young Ghouls*, 2013).

Films contribute to the way we view history, how we feel about ourselves, and our responses to other people. While an individual portrayal may have limited impact on a culture, repeated patterns certainly do. Even today, most films struggle with the idea that Native people and cultures have a role to play in the future. In addition to analyzing the media of the past, we may rightly question what colonialist messages we may still be receiving from films today.

Bibliography

Hanlon, Thomas, dir. 1964. *Before Hollywood There Was Fort Lee, N.J.: Early Movie Making in New Jersey*; Image Entertainment, 2003. DVD.

Hilger, Michael. 1986. *The American Indian in Film*. Metuchen, NJ: Scarecrow Press.

Locke, John. 1952. *The Second Treatise of Government*. Indianapolis: Bobbs-Merrill.

Virginia McLaurin is a cultural anthropologist specializing in Indigenous-created media and stereotypical representations of Indigenous people.

No More Dragons, Lotuses, and Tigers? The Evolution of Asian American Women in the Media

Melissa Yang, PhD

Introduction

Ask any Asian American woman to name a recent pop culture moment that made her proud to be an Asian American woman. She will probably tell you about the night when Sandra Oh hosted the 2019 Golden Globe Awards and won the Best Actress award for her role in "Killing Eve" or when Awkwafina won the 2020 Golden Globe's Best Actress award for her role in "The Farewell." Such prideful moments are particularly cherished by Asian Americans females like myself because there has been a dearth of Asian representation in the media (Chin et al. 2017).

Sadly, this sense of pride bolstered by few and far between moments is often overshadowed by events such as the recent increase of anti-Asian racism due to COVID-19. History has shown that anti-Asian sentiments existed as early as 1882 when the U.S. Supreme Court voted to uphold the Chinese Exclusion Act, the first law ever to legalize xenophobia. Oftentimes, when our country experiences social or economic uncertainties, immigrants and their American-born families get blamed for stealing American jobs or, in the case of COVID-19, bringing the virus over from China. Such mentalities stem from seeing Asian Americans as foreigners and a source of threat, which is reinforced regularly in the media. Specifically, Asian females have long been stereotyped as hypersexualized and exotic "orientals" who are either the submissive "lotus blossom" or the conniving "dragon lady" (Sun 2003). More recently, the "tiger mom" trope paints a picture of the overbearing and borderline abusive Chinese parenting style. All of these negative stereotypes perpetuate otherness among Asian females.

It is against this backdrop of social hostility and media misrepresentation that beckons the need to understand how the Asian American female images in the media have evolved over the past century. "Asian American" is a catch-all phrase that encompasses many identities ranging from East Asian (e.g., Chinese, Korean, Japanese), Southeast Asian (e.g., Filipino, Vietnamese), and South Asian (e.g., Indian) to Pacific Islanders. This article will mainly discuss East Asians using examples predominantly played by Chinese American actresses to summarize their onscreen stereotypes into three progressional categories.

Unidimensional Stereotypes

The Asian female media presence started as early as the silent film era (the 1920s) with a couple of prominent actresses, Anna May Wong (Chinese American) and Miyoshi Umeki (Japanese American). Back then, instead of authentic stories of the immigrant struggles, most Asian females were reduced to stereotypical foreign roles. The "dragon lady" and the "lotus blossom" stereotypes are two that found their way from the screen into the consciousness of the American public.

The dragon lady stereotype characterizes Asian women as evil, dangerous, and cold. In response to the limited character options, Anna May Wong questioned, "Why is it that the screen Chinese is nearly always the villain of the piece, and so cruel a villain—murderous, treacherous, a snake in the grass. We are not like that. . . . We have our rigid code of behavior, of honor. Why do they never show these on the screen?" (Sakamoto 1987). The dragon lady epitomized by Wong's character in *Daughter of the Dragon* (1931) schemes alongside a white man to cause harm. She is also portrayed as "eye candy" dressed in exotic and revealing outfits or form-fitting Manchu gowns, also known as *quibao* in Mandarin and *cheongsam* in Cantonese, to reinforce her otherness and invite the male gaze. Through demeaning roles such as a prostitute (*Shanghai Express*, 1932) and a slave girl (*The Thief of Bagdad*, 1924), audiences have come to define an Asian female's identity by her physical traits rather than her intellect. Years later, we can still find similar exoticized and hyperfeminized stereotypes circulating in the media, such as Lucy Liu's dominatrix prostitute role in *Payback* (1999; Hai and Dong 2019).

As for the lotus blossom stereotype, it sexualizes an Asian woman as a passive, docile, and fragile China doll. For example, in *Flower Drum Song* (1961), Miyoshi Umeki plays a subservient showgirl who illegally emigrated from Hong Kong. This stereotype often defines a woman's self-worth based on her romantic relationship with her white male counterpart. As seen in *The World of Suzie Wong* (1961), the protagonist, Suzie

Wong, gives up her life in Hong Kong to pursue her love for the white male lead. Similarly, Ariane Koizumi's reporter role in *Year of the Dragon* (1985) falls in love with the white male policeman and assists him in fighting a gang leader in Chinatown (Rajgopal 2010).

Paradoxical Portrayals

Moving into the latter half of the twentieth century, Asian female representation entered a paradoxical phase. On the one hand, Asian females were better integrated into contemporary settings with more diverse roles. On the other hand, they were still sexualized and stereotyped.

Stories like *The Joy Luck Club* (1993) and *All-American Girl* (1994) moved Asian women from a foreign backdrop into American society. *The Joy Luck Club* successfully depicted the complicated relationship between first-generation immigrant mothers and their second-generation Chinese American daughters. Despite the film's authentic portrayals, Asian females still struggled for consistent visibility and validation on TV. This is best illustrated by Margaret Cho's sitcom, *All-American Girl* (1994). As suggested by the title, Asian females were accepted as "all-American." However, in reality, its one-season appearance implies a time of volatility for the Asian presence in the media.

Besides the all-Asian casts in both stories mentioned above, Asian females were predominantly cast as the token Asian in supporting roles. They included a wider repertoire of occupations, such as Julie, a paleontologist, on the second season of *Friends* (1995); Dr. Jing-Mei "Deb" Chen on *ER* (2000–2004); and the private detective Alex Munday on *Charlie's Angels* (2000), but many were still hypersexualized. For example, there is a famous scene of Alex Munday, played by Lucy Liu, where she wears a tight black leather skirt suit with a whip in hand, which resembles a dominatrix derived from the dragon lady stereotype.

This period of paradoxical portrayal can be summed up by another Lucy Liu character, Ling Woo, on *Ally McBeal*

(1997–2002). Contrary to the lotus blossom, she is a capable and independent lawyer. Instead of being docile and passive, she is outspoken and exerts agency over her sexuality. As captured in one popular viral meme, Ling Woo talks about sex explicitly and in a tantalizing way by saying, "If I made love to you, you'd go blind. . . . Yes, I'm amazing in bed." At the same time, she is still subject to hypersexualization and stereotypical portrayal as one who uses her sex appeal to advance her career.

Multiplicity of Roles

If the baby boomers and Gen Xers grew up seeing dragon ladies and lotus blossoms on-screen while the millennials saw a mixture of contradictory Asian female roles, Gen Zers are on the brink of changes that offer a multiplicity of Asian female images. Parallel to the existence of stereotypical portrayals is an array of roles with more depth and complexity.

The emergence of Asian American female writers and producers brought more authenticity to stories featuring Asian female leads. For instance, Lulu Wang wrote and directed *The Farewell* (2019), and Adele Lim cowrote the screenplay for *Crazy Rich Asians* (2018). Both were mainstream box office successes that set the precedence that films featuring Asians are financially viable.

These shows and films portray Asian females as funny, powerful, and quirky individuals with their unique struggles rather than as decorative ornaments. For example, in her recent show, *Awkwafina Is Nora in Queens* (2020), Awkwafina plays herself as a jobless young adult who lives with her grandmother and father. She smokes marijuana and appears in a baggy rapper's outfit, both of which debunk the model minority and hypersexualized stereotypes. Ali Wong cowrote the screenplay for *Always Be My Maybe* (2019), a Netflix rom-com that features a rare on-screen romantic relationship between the lead Asian couples. Wong's character, a powerful restaurant owner, counters the long-standing stereotypes of the dragon lady and lotus blossom.

Stereotypes still exist in these contemporary all-Asian cast stories, but they are less likely to be the butt of a joke than to help advance a complex story line. For example, take Constance Wu's role as Jessica on *Fresh Off the Boat* (2015–2020). Her character may be derived from the tiger-mom trope who is domineering, but she is not rigid and overly focused on her children's academics. Instead, the show gives her space to be humorous and show her sense of pride in her Chinese heritage.

Moving away from these exemplary cases, token Asian stereotypes still exist. For instance, Ali Wong's role as Doris on ABC's *American Housewife* (2016–present) was typecast in the first season with the tiger-mom narrative as someone who is feared even by her friend's kids. She is unapologetically authoritarian and takes pride in it as a way to manipulate her children into being perfect overachievers. The increase of diverse roles, together with typical stereotypes, sums up the contemporary portrayal of Asian females in media.

We have come a long way from *Flower Drum Song* to *Joy Luck Club* to *Crazy Rich Asians*, but these milestones are not without resistance. For instance, Kelly Marie Tran was the first Asian female lead to appear in a *Star Wars* film, *Star Wars: The Last Jedi* (2017), but she was bullied off of Instagram by a small but vocal group of fans calling to "bring back the straight white male hero" (Feldman 2018). Real-world stories like this speak to the work that is left for our society to improve in the areas of sexism and racism.

Bibliography

Chin, Christina, Meera Deo, Faustina DuCros, Jenny Jong-Hwa Lee, Noriko Milman, and Nancy Wang Yuan. 2017. "Tokens on the Small Screen: Asian American and Pacific Islanders in Prime Time and Streaming Television." https://www.aapisontv.com/uploads/3/8/1/3/38136681/aapisontv.2017.pdf

Feldman, Kate. 2018. "Pro-'Straight White Male Hero' Group Takes Credit for Running 'Star Wars' Actress Kelly Marie Tran Off Instagram." *Chicago Tribune*, June 11, 2018. https://www.chicagotribune.com/ny-ent-star-wars-kelly-marie-tran-20180611-story.html

Hai, Yan, and Haibin Dong. 2019. "Asian American Women Cinematic Image: The Exotic Beauty and/or Perpetual Foreigner." *China Media Research* 15 (1): 85–92.

Rajgopal, Shoba Sharad. 2010. "'The Daughter of Fu Manchu': The Pedagogy of Deconstructing the Representation of Asian Women in Film and Fiction." *Meridians: Feminism, Race, Transnationalism* 10 (2): 141–162. https://doi.org/10.2979/meridians.2010.10.2.141

Sakamoto, Edward. 1987. "Anna May Wong and the Dragon-Lady Syndrome." *Los Angeles Times*, July 12, 1987. https://www.latimes.com/archives/la-xpm-1987-07-12-ca-3279-story.html

Sun, Chyng Feng. 2003. "Ling Woo in Historical Context: The New Face of Asian American Stereotypes on Television." In *Gender, Race, and Class in Media: A Text-Reader*, edited by Gail Dines and Jean M. Humez, 656–664. Thousand Oaks, CA: SAGE Publications.

Melissa Yang, PhD, is a professor in the School of Communication at Endicott College. She has spoken to parents and community groups about media and digital literacy. Her research interests include children and media, parental mediation, and immigrant families' media use.

Women Discovered as Super

Nora Hickey

How does one interpret a grave? How does one decipher any artifact?

Bj 581, an ancient burial plot, was uncovered in 1878. Here, in a former Viking town in present-day Sweden, one skeleton was laid to rest in the tenth century. The bones were accompanied by a sword, arrows, horses, strategy gameboards, and other items that marked the site as one inhabited by a war leader. For more than 100 years, people assumed the skeleton buried with accoutrements of battle was a man—only, it was not. In 2017, the unexpected was revealed: this Viking warrior was no male. Here lay a female skeleton (Solly 2019), a celebrated female leader.

For so many years, this particular grave was interpreted as male because accepted opinion on Viking culture was that it was hierarchical and populated with male fighters and female homemakers. The DNA tests that revealed the female genes forced the question: how many female heroes have we missed?

This startling reversal of established truth reflected my experiences in watching superhero films of the twenty-first century. I was taught through the films that came before—the Batmans and Supermans, the patriots and the shape-shifters, the outsiders and misfits, the cool and the candid—that superheroes were men. Sure, there were the outliers, such as *Red Sonja* (1985) and *Tank Girl* (1995), but these were mere drops in an ever-growing flood of films dedicated to the fights and plights of the superpowered. For years, men of the superhero variety had the marquee roles, and I had gotten so accustomed to their names, their faces, and their stories that I did not think there was a real possibility for women to get the same star treatment. Where were those female warriors?

I knew they occasionally existed on TV and most fully in the vibrant pages of comics, but the superhero movie wave that swept society beginning in the early 1990s was bereft of the kaleidoscope of female heroes that DC, Marvel, and other comics had been creating since the 1940s.

Women were poised to take a prominent role in the early 2000s, but *Catwoman* (2004) and *Elektra* (2005), two movies to put the spotlight on women, were, upsettingly, big flops. And women were increasingly seen as supporting players in group films.

Ensemble movies have become very popular in the comics-to-movie universe and do feature female characters, but often in less impactful ways. *X-Men* (2000), *The Avengers* (2012), *Guardians of the Galaxy* (2014), *Justice League* (2017), and *Black Panther* (2018) all include female players, some more completely than others. *Guardians of the Galaxy* and *Black Panther* stand out as films that let their female superheroes do more, and it is perhaps no coincidence that these females are women of color in a fairly white space. So, when Wonder Woman, one of the first major superheroes born in 1941, appeared in huge relief in front of me, I was knocked dizzy.

On one scorching summer afternoon in 2017, I entered a cool and dimly lit auditorium, alone but for my buttered popcorn. *Wonder Woman* had come out earlier in the summer, and I was determined to see it before it left theaters. The movie was big news in my world. I taught a class that included a unit on Wonder Woman (focusing on her unusual creator and comics), and that spring we had discussed the importance of her finally getting her own movie. I had to see it on the big screen for myself.

With the propelling music, striking visuals, and well-rounded protagonists and antagonists, I was near tears. Here was a movie where a woman was finally getting her due as a bona fide superhero. When Diana/Wonder Woman chooses to go across No Man's Land, "where no man can cross," she chooses to be a superhero for good, fighting in ways that males have not (Jenkins 2017). She is uniquely female but not in expected ways—not soft or overly accommodating. She uses love, not to support her man but to get stronger and defeat true evil.

It was not until the *Wonder Woman* movie that women began to get top billing more frequently. That trailblazing movie was followed by *Ant Man and the Wasp* (2018), which partly tells the story of the female Hope van Dyne/Wasp. *Dark Phoenix* (2019) infamously bombed at the box office, but *Captain Marvel*, released the same year, did stupendously well. And in the villain realm, *Birds of Prey* (2020) features Harley Quinn, an increasingly popular figure in the superhero world.

The ensemble entries continue to be a sign of growing industry awareness of the importance of women superheroes in these long male-dominated worlds, but the blockbusters with the female headliners are what blow open the old graves for me—that show just how well women can be warriors, too.

Captain Marvel was Marvel's entry into female-driven films, and she came a bit later than her DC equivalent. In some ways, I could feel that passage of time; the evolution of women in society seemed reflected in Captain Marvel's story. She, like Wonder Woman, was extremely talented as a fighter, a rising star in her world. And she too chooses to help those who are truly helpless (the Skrulls who are subjugated by the Kree—of whom Captain Marvel is a member). She fights and makes friends with sarcasm and strong emotion, even as she is often told by the males around her that she must learn to control it. But unlike Wonder Woman, Captain Marvel's emotions do not venture into romance. She is seen with friends and mentors but no romantic love. *Captain Marvel* has shown that women's stories can exist without the desirous male gaze.

Of course, the female superhero machine is just as driven by the demands of the genre—the attractive and fit fighters are the epitome of conventional good looks, and the CGI pyrotechnics are a bit overused. However, there are signs in *Wonder Woman* and *Captain Marvel* of how a female-focused film might be different, how the feminine could offer a vital, lesser-told story. Indeed, I do not believe it is any coincidence that these distinctive stories are told by female directors—Patty Jenkins for *Wonder Woman* and Anna Boden (with codirector Ryan Fleck) for *Captain Marvel.*

Ultimately, what I am talking about here is our culture finally recognizing women as superheroes, and, like the discovery of the Viking female warrior proves, she was, in fact, always a warrior. It is only now that she is being recognized as such.

No longer do we assume the next superhero blockbuster will be centered around a man—finally, women can be super, too.

Bibliography

Jenkins, Patty, dir. 2017. *Wonder Woman*. Burbank, CA: Warner Bros. Pictures. Screenplay by Allan Heinberg. On Demand TNT, 2020.

Solly, Meilan. 2019. "Researchers Reaffirm Remains in Viking Warrior Tomb Belonged to a Woman." *Smithsonian Magazine*, February 21, 2019. https://www.smithsonianmag.com/smart-news/researchers-reaffirm-famed-ancient-viking-warrior-was-biologically-female-180971541/

Nora Hickey is a teacher and writer in northern Colorado. Her work has appeared in Guernica, Narrative, Edible New Mexico, *and other publications.*

From Panel to Platform: Women Comics Creators on Instagram

Amaris Feland Ketcham

The publishing industry and distribution have long complicated women's ability to print and spread their comics work widely. Social media is changing that, as more women are able to take publishing, building an audience, and distributing their work into their own hands.

According to founding contributor Trina Robbins, the comic *Wimmen's Comix* was born in the Bay Area in the 1970s, when "98% of the cartoonists were male, and they all seemed to belong to a boy's club that didn't accept women" (Robbins 2016, vii). While *Wimmen's Comix* ran until 1992, Robbins points out that distribution troubles started in the 1980s, when chain bookstores replaced independent sellers. Comics became relegated to specialty stores that were often run by men interested in DC and Marvel comics—not stories told by women, about women. These stores reinforced a selectivity of the comics canon, narrowing acceptable style and stories to only superhero comics. As comics scholar Adrienne Resha points out, these retailers acted as "cultural 'gatekeepers,' [making] people with disabilities, women, and people of color . . . feel unsafe or unwelcome" (Resha 2020, 68). In the last several years, women comics creators have responded by finding ways to use social media to share drawn nonfiction, offering stories from nondominant perspectives and even eyewitness accounts of social upheaval.

The format of the social media platform Instagram lends itself to sharing comics particularly well; this platform emphasizes visual content over written content, and the square image constraint mimics the panels' conventions of traditional comics. This "panel" also creates order, structure, and consistency to posts, allowing the images to be read sequentially and for the final panels to remain hidden from view until they have been accessed by swiping. Because the audience cannot read ahead or peek at the final panel, it can have a punch line or concluding image that lands at just the right time. Some female comics creators use these final images in surprising ways. For example, the cartoonist Lucy Knisley posts comics about her daily life, her cat, and her young son. After several drawn images, once the comic concludes, she often includes a photograph of what prompted the comic. These glimpses of her home and family help make the short comics read as true to life, and they make her social media presence seem more authentic, honest, and personal—traits valued by social media users.

Some of the comics work that women are publishing online are more akin to freewrites—exercises that help get their creativity flowing for the larger, longer projects they are working on. These low-stakes exercises allow them to test ideas, to make work that might turn into a project later, and to respond to current events more immediately. They allow creators to share a daily practice. Comics creators can post more frequently than if only promoting published work, allowing them both the sustained content and continual audience engagement that could not be maintained with the periodic posting of completed works, especially given the long turnaround times in publishing. On Instagram, the more frequently someone posts, the more likely their posts are to be seen, as the algorithm prioritizes recent posts. One such artist is Kelcey Parker Ervick, who made a personal commitment to create comics daily, posting works in progress. She often draws stories from her grandmother's immigration and women's history, such as the history of the first female boxers in Indiana. Thus, her daily practice not only keeps her skills sharp but ensures that her audience will see her posts and stay engaged with her work.

The ability to post in real time, to publish quickly without editorial oversight, allows creators to respond to current affairs and to make a space where women think about, process, internalize, and analyze societal structures and problems. Women creators are able to make themselves present in these pressing conversations. Comics creator Sarah Mirk often weighs in on contemporary issues by making zines about them and then posting photographs of these zines. Mirk's recent zines have been about monuments, white privilege, the Black Lives Matter protests in Portland, and toxic positivity. These polemics are text heavy with drawn infographics and cartoon characters to illustrate certain points. Mirk herself is frequently a character. Her captions often include what prompted the making of the zine, sources for facts and statistics included, and hashtags about the topic (e.g., #COVID19, #whiteprivilege). The use of hashtags works with the Instagram algorithm's prioritization of content people are searching for; additionally, people can follow hashtags. This opens her work up to new audiences, which she can then direct to her website to purchase zines and her other work.

Tessa Hulls, a Seattle-based cartoonist, used real-time posting to document the Capitol Hill Organized Protest in a modified zine style of comics journalism. Since Hulls did not have any affiliation with press organizations, she could freely interview people in the occupied zone, write about what she deemed worthy of sharing (not just "newsworthy events," such as shootings), and interpret and explain aspects of the protest without having to claim objectivity or impartiality. In her captions, she included links to sources and places to find additional information. Within a week, she gained 7,000 new followers. These subscriptions were not only because people were interested in this unique form of comics reportage but because a community began to develop within the comments: there, commenters found the space to debate and negotiate ideas, becoming a part of the conversation. Like many other women comics creators, Hulls personally responds to questions and many comments as well as anything she is tagged in. Instagram facilitates this level of personal interaction, which makes audience members feel like they are part of a community and keeps them engaged.

While the top hashtags that accompany #comics on a regular basis still refer to DC and Marvel superheroes, the community of women comics creators has found a place to thrive on Instagram. As they respond in real time to events in their lives and contemporary issues, their audience grows, creating a space for them in a market that has so often excluded their voices.

Bibliography

Resha, Adrienne. 2020. "The Blue Age of Comic Books." *Inks: The Journal of the Comics Studies Society* 4 (1): 66–81. https://doi.org/10.1353/ink.2020.0003

Robbins, Trina. 2016. *The Complete Wimmen's Comix*. Seattle: Fantagraphic Books.

Amaris Feland Ketcham teaches interdisciplinary liberal arts at the University of New Mexico, including courses on nonfiction and poetry comics. Her most recent book, Glitches in the FBI *(Casa Urraca, 2020), uses dialogue from* The X-Files *as source material for found poetry.*

The Ava Effect: Women Amplifying Women behind the Camera

Susan X Jane

The media plays an important role in representing the stories, experiences, and perspectives of people of different backgrounds. Seeing oneself represented in media can be validating and inspiring. Young people in particular benefit from being exposed to diverse characters and stories about different cultural backgrounds. Movies, TV, and other forms of media can help audiences learn about different cultures that they might not otherwise have access to. Yet, media representation often fails to accurately reflect the country's multicultural population.

Improving the diversity of representation is important to ensure the media continues to respond to an increasingly diverse population. In the United States, 38 percent of people are members of a racial minority group, and more than 50 percent of Americans are women. Increasingly diverse audiences are seeking the representation of different races, cultures, and backgrounds, making improved representation both a moral and business imperative for media companies to consider. Despite the import of these issues and many years of efforts to improve diversity, there is still a lack of adequate and authentic representation of women and minority groups, particularly of Black women.

Mainstream movies and TV shows have a long pattern of stereotypical representations of Black women. Characters often have stereotypical roles—servile, sassy, angry, and sexualized. These stereotypes trace their roots back to a time when Black women characters were written and produced by white creators who may have lacked the knowledge or will to create accurate portrayals. To create more authentic representations, TV and movies need directors, writers, and producers of different backgrounds who can shape a vision of characters and worlds that are imbued with the authentic voice and grounded in lived experience.

Increasing representation of racial minorities and women in media requires multiple strategies: increasing the number of on-screen roles for actors, especially in recurring or starring roles; combating race and gender stereotypes in television and movies; and increasing the opportunity behind the camera for women and racial minorities to write, direct, and produce television and movies.

Increasing the number of female and minority directors and producers is no small task. There is less diversity behind the camera than there is in front of it. In 2017, an inclusion brief from the Media Diversity and Social Change Initiative written by Stacey Smith found that in an analysis of 1,000 of the top-grossing films between 2007 and 2017, only 4 percent of all directors were female, and 80 percent of those were white (Smith et al. 2018, 1). Only six of the films were directed by a woman of color and only three of those by a Black woman. The report went on to predict that prospects for improving these numbers were bleak. A significant barrier to entry in film and television is experience. Directors and producers who do not have experience can find getting a first shot difficult.

One of these few directors of color, Ava DuVernay, has been working to increase the representation of Black women in directing and producing in Hollywood. A longtime publicist, writer, and director, DuVernay gained widespread national attention for her first major motion picture, *Selma*, for which she won a Golden Globe in 2015. Following her win, DuVernay produced the television show *Queen Sugar* for OWN, a family drama set in Louisiana about a family-owned sugar farm inherited by three siblings, based on the book by Natalie Baszile. As producer, DuVernay set out to work with directors that she knew and respected: "I wanted to make something in my own likeness . . . which meant asking can I bring in women who've never directed television before?" DuVernay did just that, setting an all-female slate of directors for the first season.

Three seasons later, twenty-five different women have directed an episode or more of *Queen Sugar*. The opportunity to direct an episode of network television and the connection to a tribe of colleagues who direct and produce has opened doors for many of those DuVernay brought on to the show. The directors that are part of this professional tribe have dubbed these opportunities "#the AvaEffect." The powerful effect of women supporting other women is evident in the work produced in film and TV by directors that DuVernay has chosen. Directors for *Queen Sugar* have continued to direct and produce major productions—Vic Mahoney directed *Star Wars: The Rise of Skywalker*, Amanda Marselis has directed *Westworld*, and DeMane Davis directed and produced *Self Made*, a fictionalized biography of famed Black entrepreneur Madam C. J. Walker—and have in turn opened doors for women and minorities on the productions they lead, amplifying the voices of those marginalized and blowing past the barriers that have so long kept the world behind the camera white and male.

The Ava Effect describes both the specific opportunities that DuVernay has offered to women she has supported and also names the powerful impact that one woman can have in opening up opportunities for others like her. Just two years later, USC Annenberg's *Inclusion in the Director's Chair* report indicated a 270 percent increase in the number of Black directors (USC Annenberg 2017, 2). In 2019, 47 percent of all TV episodes were directed by women. Instead of waiting for traditional gatekeepers in positions of power to give marginalized individuals opportunities, change can occur when women and minorities support each other, uplift each other, and—most importantly—create real opportunities for each other. Using this model of amplification, marginalized people can subvert the barriers to entry that slow change.

Bibliography

Fernandez, Maria Elena. 2016. "*Queen Sugar*'s All-Female Directors on How the Show Gave Them Their First TV Jobs." *Vulture*, November 30, 2016. https://www.vulture.com/2016/11/queen-sugar-all-women-directors-on-getting-first-tv-jobs.html

Smith, Stacy L., Marc Choueiti, Angel Choi, and Katherine Pieper. 2018. *Inclusion in the Director's Chair: Gender, Race, & Age of Directors across 1,200 Top Films from 2007 to 2018*. http://assets.uscannenberg.org/docs/inclusion-in-the-directors-chair-2019.pdf

USC Annenberg staff. 2017. *Where Are the Female Directors and Those of Color?* USC News, February 2, 2017. https://news.usc.edu/115841/where-are-the-female-directors-and-those-of-color/

Susan X Jane is a diversity educator, speaker, and trainer. She writes and talks about media, race, and culture and is the principal of Navigators Consulting.

Media Coverage of Women's Sport

Dunja Antunovic, PhD, and Nicole M. LaVoi, PhD

Sport is an important context for understanding the status of women in media. Sport participation is an integral educational experience for millions of girls and women in the United States, but the media do not reflect girls' and women's involvement in sport. This essay evaluates the patterns in media coverage of women's sport and calls on the sport industry and fans to change the culture around women's sport.

Studies conducted over the last fifty years point to persistent problems in the way sports media represent women, both in terms of quantity and quality. First, despite women's increased participation in all levels of sport (including high school, college, professional, and international), the media often dedicate minimal—if any—coverage to women's leagues and events. During a regular week, or what journalists would consider "routine media coverage," women's sport only appears in 0.6–5.2 percent of broadcast sports news, such as ESPN, Fox Sports, and local network affiliates (Billings and Young 2015; Cooky, Messner, and Musto 2015). National newspapers (such as the *New York Times* and the *Chicago Tribune*) reflect similar patterns, while medium-city and small-city papers might dedicate a slightly higher percentage (above 10%) of stories to women's sport (Kaiser 2018). High school sports coverage tends to be more equitable because local newspapers use sport to build community.

Digital media content is more difficult to measure because new platforms proliferate, but digital platforms did not lead to a substantial change in the amount of content about women's sport. Women's sports might be the focus of women-centered outlets (such as espnW, ESPN's women-focused digital platform), but they remain relegated to separate spaces, leaving the "traditional" sports media organizations intact (Wolter 2021).

Sport organizations are using digital platforms to stream games, but these are often difficult to find or require subscriptions in addition to the cable package or sport-channel-specific packages (Phillips and Antunovic 2019). In other words, fans might be able to watch women's games via digital streaming services, but the most readily available content continues to focus on more of the same: a select few men's professional and college sports, notably men's American football, men's basketball, men's baseball, and men's hockey (Billings and Young 2015; Cooky, Messner, and Musto 2015).

Researchers have also noted that when women *do* receive media attention, the stories and images are stereotypical and disrespectful. Instead of focusing on athletic accomplishments, sports media spent decades objectifying women based on the myth that sexualization is the most profitable way to sell women's sport (Kane, LaVoi, and Fink 2013). While some forms of stereotyping are more overt than others, sports media coverage trivializes women's accomplishments with subtle language clues (such as attributing their success to men) or by undermining women's achievements.

Recent findings suggest that sexist patterns might be changing. For example, women gain heightened media visibility during the Olympic Games and the FIFA Women's World Cup. The amount of media coverage of women's sport during these events has increased, and the tournaments continue to break viewership records (Lough and Geurin 2019). Journalists are now also critiquing women's exclusion from certain Olympic events, unequal working conditions, and disparities in pay (Cooky and Antunovic 2018).

In the twenty-first century, content about women's sport exists beyond mainstream sports media organizations. While some digital content and specifically unmediated comments are often derogatory, sexist, and discriminatory (LaVoi and Calhoun 2014), independent sports journalists have created collectives and newsletters that specifically focus on women's sport. For example, *PowerPlays!* offers a feminist perspective on sport, while *GIST* creates content by women for women, often about women's sport. In addition, women's sport leagues and athletes are now able to bypass media organizations and directly communicate with fans through social media. Women's sport thus gains visibility through public relations, branding, and marketing initiatives (Lough and Geurin 2019). To create lasting change, the industry needs to invest in resources, staff, and space to covering women's sport.

Sport consumers play an important role in the efforts toward gender equity in media coverage. Sports media organizations evaluate interest based on metrics on viewership, clicks, and social media engagement. Thus, fans of women's sport can contribute to the representations of women's sport by engaging with the content, demanding more content, and subscribing to platforms that are specifically dedicated to women's sport. The website and social media platforms of the Tucker Center for Research on Girls & Women in Sport at the University of Minnesota provide useful resources to do so. Data provide convincing evidence fans *are interested* in women's sport (Nielsen 2018). Creating substantial change toward gender equity in sports media representations will take a collective effort.

Bibliography

Billings, Andrew C., and Brittany D. Young. 2015. "Comparing Flagship News Programs: Women's Sport Coverage in ESPN's *SportsCenter* and FOX Sports 1's *FOX Sports Live*." *Electronic News* 9 (1): 3–16. https://doi.org/10.1177/1931243115572824

Cooky, Cheryl, and Dunja Antunovic. 2018. "The Visibility of Feminism in the Olympic Games: Narratives of Progress and Narratives of Failure in Sports Journalism." *Feminist Media Studies* 18 (5): 945–948. https://doi.org/10.1080/14680777.2018.1498100

Cooky, Cheryl, Michael A. Messner, and Michela Musto. 2015. "'It's Dude Time!': A Quarter Century of Excluding Women's Sports in Televised News and Highlight Shows." *Communication & Sport* 3 (3): 261–287. https://doi.org/10.1177/2167479515588761

Kaiser, Kent. 2018. "Women's and Men's Prominence in Sports Coverage and Changes in Large-, Medium-, and Small-City Newspapers, Pre– and Post–Title IX: A Local Play for Equality?" *Communication & Sport* 6 (6): 762–787. https://doi.org/10.1177/2167479517734852

Kane, Mary Jo, Nicole M. LaVoi, and Janet S. Fink. 2013. "Exploring Elite Female Athletes' Interpretations of Sport Media Images: A Window into the Construction of Social Identity and 'Selling Sex' in Women's Sports." *Communication & Sport* 1 (3): 269–298. https://doi.org/10.1177/2167479512473585

LaVoi, Nicole M., and Austin S. Calhoun. 2014. "Digital Media and Female Athletes." In *Handbook of Sport and New Media*, edited by Andrew Billings and Marie Hardin, 320–330. New York: Routledge.

Lough, Nancy, and Andrea N. Geurin. 2019. "Introduction." In *Routledge Handbook of the Business of Women's Sport*, edited by Nancy Lough and Andrea N. Geurin, 1–5. New York: Routledge.

Nielsen. 2018. "Global Interest in Women's Sports Is on the Rise." October 3, 2018. https://www.nielsen.com/us/en/insights/article/2018/global-interest-in-womens-sports-is-on-the-rise/

Phillips, Anji L., and Dunja Antunovic. 2019. "'Seeking a Storybook Ending': Examining the Future Distribution of Women's Sporting Events." In *ESPN and the Changing Sports Media Marketplace*, edited by Greg G. Armfield, John McGuire, and Adam Earnheardt, 269–287. New York: Peter Lang Publishing.

Wolter, Sarah. 2021. "A Longitudinal Analysis of espnW: Almost 10 Years of Challenging Hegemonic Masculinity." *Communication & Sport* 9 (5): 718–741. https://doi.org/10.1177/2167479519895479

Dunja Antunovic, PhD, is an assistant professor of sport sociology at the University of Minnesota's School of Kinesiology. Her research focuses on the intersection of sport, media, and gender.

Nicole M. LaVoi, PhD, is a senior lecturer in the area of social and behavioral sciences in the School of Kinesiology at the University of Minnesota and the director of the Tucker Center for Research on Girls & Women in Sport. Through her multidisciplinary research, she answers critical questions that can make a difference in the lives of sport stakeholders—particularly girls and women.

Exposing the "Invisible Majority"—Representations of Women in News Media

Julie Frechette, PhD

There is no doubt that women represent a sizable and significant demographic for media and that reporting on women's issues has increased over the past decade. Representing more than half of the world's population, women have challenged their exclusion and discrimination across media, with the #MeToo and #TimesUp social movements representing the latest global coalescence of women demanding equality that includes better news media coverage about them. With 1.7 million #MeToo tweets extending to eighty-five countries in its first year (Park 2017), news coverage of women's inequality in society has seeped into pop culture and politics in unprecedented ways, charting a new course for those fighting to end a legacy of women's exclusion and marginalization in media (Frechette 2021).

In 2017, increased reporting of sexual harassment cases by prominent figures and celebrities in news and entertainment helped publicize the #MeToo movement, which originated more than a decade earlier when Tarana Burke coined the phrase "Me Too" as a way to help women vocalize their experiences of sexual violence (*Chicago Tribune* 2021). At fourteen of the nation's largest newspapers, articles exploring sexual assault and harassment surged by 30 percent during the fifteen months after Hollywood mogul Harvey Weinstein's alleged sexual crime hit headlines (Women's Media Center 2019), and an astounding 115,000 news stories on #MeToo can be found in the largest online newspaper archive (Newspapers.com 2021).

In today's media environment, not all coverage about women's issues has been adequate or favorable. In fact, research findings continue to confirm that despite their social, economic, and political gains, women "continue to be persistently underrepresented and stereotyped in news media" (Vandenberghe 2019). "It seems that gender equality is still an elusive dream despite the increasingly prominent roles of women worldwide"

(Humprecht and Esser 2017; Ross et al. 2016). An in-depth literature review shows that women are still underrepresented in news contexts worldwide with a ratio of approximately three male actors for every female one (Rush, Oukrop, and Sarikakis 2005, cited in Vandenberghe 2019).

Most news stories about women, including those in powerful roles, emphasize their femininity in terms of their appearance and age, along with their marital or family status. This is certainly the case in politics, where women continue to be judged according to different standards than their male counterparts. For instance, in 2016 election coverage, presidential candidate Hillary Clinton was harshly judged for her pantsuits, age, likability, and trustworthiness. According to one study in the United States, female Democratic leaders running for office in 2020 were still frustrated by double standards and sexism in media, with news reports about how Amy Klobuchar treated her staff, why Elizabeth Warren's early poll numbers were underwhelming, and why some donors remained angry at Kirsten Gillibrand for asking former senator Al Franken to resign over accusations of sexual misconduct (Roarty and Glueck n.d.). In an analysis of 130 articles from mainstream news outlets, female presidential candidates were consistently described more negatively than their male counterparts, a disconcerting trend in the 2020 election coverage (Frandsen and Bajak 2019).

Within the news industry, women continue to struggle. According to the U.S. government's most recent report, women own a mere 7.4 percent of the nation's commercial television stations, with men still dominating every part of news, entertainment, and digital media (Women's Media Center 2019). In an interview with *Ms.* magazine entitled "Who's Telling Our Stories," outgoing CNN anchor Brooke Baldwin criticized the network for its lack of women leaders in the organization (Goodwin 2021). Despite her thirteen-year history reporting for CNN, Baldwin was taken off the air and replaced by Jake Tapper for news coverage of the 2020 election, demonstrating that internal gender biases in news organizations linger. "The most influential anchors on our network, the highest-paid, are men. My bosses, my executives are men. The person who oversees CNN Dayside is a man, and my executive producer for 10 years is a man" (Baldwin, cited in Goodwin 2021).

Similar patterns exist at all of the news divisions at Fox, NBC, CBS, ABC, and most news outlets, including cable news, online news, and social media. Additionally, if stories about women are covered at all, camera operators and producers are predominantly men, thereby affecting how stories about women are visually and editorially framed and represented. In radio, only 17.4 percent of the nation's FM and AM stations have women as general managers (Women's Media Center 2019), while sports desks continue to earn a sixth consecutive F for lack of gender equity, with males representing 90 percent of sports editors, 70 percent of assistant sports editors, 83 percent of the columnists, 89 percent of the reporters, and 80 percent of the copy editors (Lapchick 2018). At the four most widely circulated U.S.-based newspapers, women represented only 15 percent of guest writer op-eds on international issues during 1996, 2006, and 2016 (Foreign Policy Institute, cited in Women's Media Center 2019).

As Brooke Baldwin and others contend, having more women in news is necessary because women continue to fight to include stories for and about girls and women. For news media to improve their reporting and representations of women, they will need to diversify their ownership and managerial staff so that women represent at least half of the personnel, signifying gender parity in terms of overall representation in the media landscape. Only then will the "invisible majority" be fully recognized across media channels and platforms.

Bibliography

Chicago Tribune. 2021. "#MeToo: A Timeline of Events." February 4, 2021. https://www.chicagotribune.com/lifestyles/ct-me-too-timeline-20171208-htmlstory.html

Frandsen, Alexander, and Aleszu Bajak. 2019. "Women on the 2020 Campaign Trail Are Being Treated More Negatively by the Media." Storybench, March 24, 2019. https://www.storybench.org/women-on-the-2020-campaign-trail-are-being-treated-more-negatively-by-the-media/

Frechette, Julie D. 2021. "The Reverberations of #MeToo on Pop Culture and Politics: How the Movement Is Shaking Patriarchal Power Structures." In *Gender, Race, and Class in Media: A Critical Reader*, edited by Bill Yousman, Lori Bindig Yousman, Gail Dines, and Jean McMahon Humez, 623–631. Thousand Oaks, CA: SAGE Publications.

Goodwin, Michele. 2021. "29. Who's Telling Our Stories? CNN's Brooke Baldwin on Women and Media." *Ms.*, April 5, 2021. https://msmagazine.com/podcast/29-whos-telling-our-stories-cnns-brooke-baldwin-on-women-and-media/

Humprecht, Edda, and Frank Esser. 2017. "A Glass Ceiling in the Online Age? Explaining the Underrepresentation of Women in Online Political News." *European Journal of Communication* 32 (5): 439–456. https://doi.org/10.1177/0267323117720343

Lapchick, Richard. 2018. *Sports Media Racial & Gender Report Card*. TIDES, May 2, 2018. https://www.tidesport.org/associated-press-sports-editors

Newspapers.com. 2021. Search results for "#MeToo." https://go.newspapers.com/results.php?query=#MeToo&s_place=&date_field=

Park, Andrea. 2017. "#MeToo Reaches 85 Countries with 1.7M Tweets." CBS News, October 24, 2017. https://www.cbsnews.com/news/metoo-reaches-85-countries-with-1-7-million-tweets/

Roarty, Alex, and Katie Glueck. n.d. "'There's Still a Lot of Sexism': Dem Leaders Frustrated by Double Standards Facing Female Candidates." Emily's List. Accessed March 9, 2022. https://emilyslist.org/news/entry/theres-still-a-lot-of-sexism-dem-leaders-frustrated-by-double-standards-fac

Ross, Karen, Karen Boyle, Cynthia Carter, and Debbie Ging. 2016. "Women, Men and News." *Journalism Studies* 19 (6): 824–845. https://doi.org/10.1080/14616 70X.2016.1222884

Rush, Ramona R., Carol E. Oukrop, Katherine Sarikakis, Julie Andsager, Billy Wooten, and E-K Dauphin. 2005. "Junior Scholars in Search of Equity for Women and Minorities." *Journalism &and Communication Monographs* 6 (4): 151–211. https://doi.org/10.1177/152263790 500600402

Vandenberghe, Hanne. 2019. "Representation of Women in the News: Balancing between Career and Family Life." *Media and Communication* 7 (1): 4. https://doi .org/10.17645/mac.v7i1.1627

Women's Media Center. 2019. *The Status of Women in U.S. Media 2019*. February 21, 2019. https://www.womens mediacenter.com/reports/the-status-of-women-in-u-s -media-2019

Julie Frechette, PhD, is a professor and chair of the Department of Communication at Worcester State University and the president of the Action Coalition for Media Education. She has published numerous books and articles on media literacy, critical cultural studies, gender, and media.

Introduction

There are many women who have played a role in pioneering aspects of journalism, film, television, and advertising as these industries developed. While their contributions are not always recognized, women have played—and continue to play—important roles in shaping today's media landscape. Media historians have detailed the many contributions of pioneering woman filmmakers, journalists, television producers, and magazine editors, and an ever-growing body of academic scholarship, books, essays, and websites demonstrates the breadth of talent, ambition, and smarts that influential women are showcasing today across a wide range of media industries.

This chapter spotlights women who have impacted the film, television, news, or advertising industries in important and lasting ways. The women profiled here are talented pioneers, artists, writers, actors, activists, and professionals who have contributed in some way to their particular field and who may have also engaged in work that resulted in changes in the ways women have been represented in media texts or hired by media companies. Some of the women profiled here may be familiar to readers, while others may not. Some of these women made a

---

As a feminist activist and founding editor of *Ms.* magazine, Gloria Steinem has been a symbol of the women's liberation movement in the United States for more than 30 years. In 2005 Steinem was part of a team who founded the Women's Media Center, a nonprofit women's organization working to ensure that women are appropriately represented in the media. (Library of Congress)

national or international impact, while others' influences may be confined to a particular sector of a specific media industry.

This chapter also profiles some significant women-centered media creations that have influenced public attitudes about gender in some way. While this list is also short given the large number of influential films, journalistic work, landmark television programs, and other works present in U.S. media history, the profiles hopefully demonstrate the powerful significance of particular media content and its respective representations.

People

Lois Weber (1879–1939)

Born in Allegheny, Pennsylvania, Lois Weber performed as a pianist, singer, and stage actor before launching her career in the developing motion picture industry. Today, Weber is considered one of two women—the other being Alice Guy-Blaché—who contributed the most to the development of early cinema (James 2019). She is a prominent historical figure in the silent era of film.

Weber and her husband, Phillips Smalley, started working in the motion picture industry in 1907, acting together on-screen and codirecting scripts written by Weber. As scholar and biographer Shelly Stamp observed, "Their status as a married, middle class couple was often used to enhance their reputation for highbrow, quality pictures" (Stamp 2013). By 1912, they were working at the Universal Film Manufacturing Company, producing one or two one-reel (i.e., short) films a week (Stamp 2013). Weber is credited with pioneering new film techniques throughout their work, including the use of a split screen and double exposure (James 2019). A notable example of split screen use appears in the film *Suspense* (1913), a tense eleven-minute film about someone trying to break into the home of a woman (played by Weber) who calls her husband on the phone, expressing fear for her safety and that of a baby in her care (James 2019).

As the duo worked, Weber emerged as the leader in their creative partnership. She was the sole author of film scripts and became the first woman to direct an American feature film, *The Merchant of Venice*, in 1914 (Stamp 2013). In 1916, she possibly became the first woman to direct big action scenes in *The Dumb Girl of Portici*, which featured a procession of soldiers on horses, a mass demonstration, and a riot (James 2019). She engaged in all aspects of the film industry and became recognized as a film leader. Including her short films and features, Weber directed at least 138 films (Movshovitz 2019).

However, Weber earned the reputation as a film "trailblazer" not simply because of her numerous contributions to the American film library but also because of the nature of her work. Weber, wrote one film scholar, "saw movies as an alternative to journalism, a new accessible way to circulate information" (Weitzman 2019, 14). According to Stamp, Weber "considered cinema what she called 'a voiceless language.' And by that I think she meant cinema had an ability to convey ideas to anybody, regardless of their educational level, regardless of their command of English, right, at a period when there were many immigrants to the U.S. who did not speak English as a first language" (Movshovitz 2019).

Weber's popular films addressed social issues and sparked controversy and sometimes even resulted in backlashes from audiences and U.S. censorship boards (Stamp 2013; James 2019). For example, the allegorical *Hypocrites* (1915) caused a stir because it featured nudity, *The People vs. John Doe* (1916) prompted debates about capital punishment, and *Shoes* (1916) engaged audiences in thinking about poverty and the difficult choices people make to survive. Weber's film *Where Are My Children?* (1916) addressed both birth control and abortion, two practices that were illegal at the time and rarely spoken about in public (Stamp 2013; James 2019). In 1917, *The Hand That Rocks the Cradle* debuted with a narrative that advocated for legalizing birth control. The film's release (and its predecessor *Where Are My Children?*) corresponded with Margaret Sanger's campaign for "voluntary motherhood" through the development, distribution, and use of birth control (Stamp 2010).

In 1916, Weber was the first and only woman elected to the Motion Pictures Directors Association, and she remained the only women in the group for years (Stamp 2013). Recognized as a pioneer in advancing developments in film directing, she was the highest-paid studio director in the United States in 1916 (James 2019). In 1917, Weber founded her own production company, Lois Weber Productions. In trying to navigate away from what she viewed as a somewhat rote way of producing films, she shot many of her films' scenes on location (Stamp 2013). Weber crafted film narratives that focused on women's stories, providing sharp commentary on marriage, relationships between men and women, and social class (Stamp 2010). She consistently advocated for women to have complex roles in her films (Movshovitz 2019).

Weber and Smalley divorced in 1922, and Weber continued writing and directing films through the early 1930s. Eventually, however, public interest in socially conscious films began to fade, and films with sound took over the industry. Additionally, big shifts in the Hollywood film industry made it difficult for independent film companies to survive and prevented women from succeeding in the industry the way they once did (Stamp 2013). The film industry eventually became seen by men as a "big business" to which women were unsuited (Mahar 2001). This may have been the reason why Weber's career declined. She advocated for more opportunities for women in film in newspaper articles, pointing out the sexism in the industry, but her calls were unheeded (James 2019).

After her death, Weber and her films were essentially forgotten by the industry and by film historians. Many of her films have been lost as a result. Several have been recently restored, however, and Weber is now recognized for her tremendous contributions.

Lucille Ball (1911–1989)

In March 2020, *Time* magazine named Lucille Ball one of the most important and influential women of the past century. Given Ball's accomplishments as an actor, comedian, producer, and studio executive, it is not difficult to understand why. Ball holds iconic status in American culture for her starring roles in several enormously popular television programs as well as significant accomplishments on stage, in film, and on the radio.

Lucille Ball was born in Jamestown, New York, on August 6, 1911. She expressed an early interest in performing. She attended drama school and worked as a model in her late teens and early twenties; eventually a modeling job led to film work (Kanfer 2003). Ball worked in the film industry through Hollywood's Golden Age of the 1930s and 1940s, first for RKO Radio Pictures and then for Metro-Goldwyn-Mayer. Most of her acting work during this time was in so-called B movies. At the time, more prestigious films featuring known stars were accompanied by lower-cost shorter films called B movies. Ball became known as "queen of the Bs" because she often played small, witty roles or bit dramatic parts (Kanfer 2003). Sometimes actors in B movies rose in the Hollywood hierarchy and were cast in more prominent films, but this was not Ball's path to stardom.

Instead, even as she pursued her film career, Ball also began working in radio. In 1948, she starred in the radio comedy series *My Favorite Husband*, and after the series gained in popularity, CBS asked Ball to develop it for television (Stark 1997). Ball wanted her husband, Desi Arnaz, to play her husband on the television show, but CBS initially refused because Arnaz was Cuban; they did not know how the husband and wife pairing would be received by audiences (Kanfer 2003; Stark 1997). Ball refused to participate in the show without her husband, so the duo formed their own production company, Desilu Productions, and took *My Favorite Husband* on the road, essentially proving to CBS that there was an audience for their work (Stark 1997).

Eventually, the comedy was developed for television and premiered on CBS in 1951 as *I Love Lucy*. The domestic comedy focused on exaggerated conflicts in the life of Lucy and Ricky Ricardo (played by Ball and Arnaz) along with their neighbors on the show, Fred and Ethel. As television writer Steven Stark later noted, Ball and Arnaz made "legendary" contributions to television: "First sitcom to be a hit. First show to be Number 1 three years in a row. First show to reach an audience of ten million households. First major hit show to be produced in Hollywood. First show to use the innovative three-camera technique. First show to be filmed live before a studio audience" (Stark 1997, 26).

I Love Lucy ultimately became the "prototype" for the situation comedy television standard that was to follow (Murray 2005). The successful use of the three-camera setup, the use of telefilm, and the practice of selling reruns of the show, leading to a profitable syndication practice, began with *I Love Lucy* and informed the establishment and success of subsequent situation comedies (Murray 2005). Additionally, the show was novel in its portrayals, which included the interracial marriage of Lucy and Ricky, the authentic female friendship between Lucy and Ethel, and eventually, when Ball herself became pregnant, the pregnancy of Lucy Ricardo (Murray 2005).

I Love Lucy's chief draw was the comedic Ball, whose popularity eclipsed many male stars of the day (Stark 1997). "President Eisenhower changed the date for his presidential address so that it would not conflict with Lucy," wrote historian June Sochen. "Marshall Field's department store in Chicago closed early on Monday nights so everyone could go home and watch Lucy" (Sochen 2008, 154). In the 1950s postwar entertainment world, Ball became the first woman to gain significant economic power (Kanfer 2003). She redefined the situation comedy not just in setting standards for the form but also within the form's content, presenting an image of a housewife in hilarious ways that often challenged the expected conventions of what it meant to be a woman at the time and implying through various narrative comedic episodes that Lucy felt confined and unsatisfied with her role in the domestic realm (Stark 1997). For example, Lucy was consistently seen in her show's narratives seeking work outside of her role in the home.

While these initiatives were played for laughs, and often relied on self-deprecating humor, they also implied a dissatisfaction with traditional gender roles and exposed the "absurdity of the restrictions placed on women in the 1950s" (Egge 2015).

Four years after *I Love Lucy* went off the air in 1957, Ball launched another successful sitcom, *The Lucy Show*. Meanwhile, Ball and Arnaz's independent Desilu Productions produced such hits as *The Dick Van Dyke Show*, *The Untouchables*, *The Andy Griffith Show*, and *My Three Sons* (Kanfer 2003). Two years after Arnaz and Ball divorced in 1960, Ball bought Arnaz out of the company and became the first woman to head a major television and film production company. The company struggled a bit as film studios started producing television programs themselves, but Ball and her team were able to manage, producing the ultimately successful programs *Mission Impossible* and *Star Trek*. She also starred in two popular comedies, *The Lucy Show* (1961–1968) and *Here's Lucy* (1968–1974). Desilu also continued to make money from the syndication of *I Love Lucy* episodes, but for personal, professional, and financial reasons, Ball ultimately sold the company to Paramount (Kanfer 2003).

Ball is remembered for her impact on the television industry as well as her creativity and business acumen. Her performance on *I Love Lucy* is celebrated for her incredible talent and her ability to challenge male dominance in a nonthreatening, comedic way (Kanfer 2003). As the first female CEO of a major production company, she broke a glass ceiling at a time when women were not especially prominent in the business side of the industry. Ball was a pioneer who paved the way for other women performers in television comedy, and her portrayal of Lucy Ricardo is still celebrated today as *I Love Lucy* lives on in syndication.

Barbara Walters (1931–)

Born in Boston, Massachusetts, on September 25, 1931 (although some sources say 1925), Barbara Walters is a broadcast journalist whose successful work on American television contributed to the dismantling of the male-dominated broadcast news that was pervasive in the mid-twentieth century. Her work has been recognized with a Lifetime Achievement Award from the National Academy of Television Arts and Sciences, Daytime and Primetime Emmy Awards, and induction into the Television Hall of Fame. A graduate of Sarah Lawrence College, Walters donated millions to the institution, and the Barbara Walters Campus Center opened in 2019.

Walters is best known for her in-depth and exclusive television interviews, "a form of television news she perfected and personified" (Mahler 2014). Her first *Barbara Walters Special* on December 14, 1976 featured interviews with Barbra Streisand and then president-elect Jimmy Carter and his wife, Rosalynn. Years later, Walters claimed that those first guests reflected her desire to interview people from many walks of life. As her interview specials evolved, each program featured at least one celebrity and one political figure among the slate of three interviews. While the specials sometimes prioritized celebrity interviews as a response to audience's preferences, Walters also interviewed newsmakers on other programs, such as *20/20* (Walters 2008).

Over her fifty years working in television, Walters interviewed a long list of world leaders, American presidents, celebrities, and other notable figures. The list includes some notable exclusives. In 1977, Cuban president Fidel Castro agreed to his first American prime-time interview with Walters, and she also secured the first joint interview with the president of Egypt, Anwar el-Sadat, and the prime minister of Israel, Menachem Begin, on November 20, 1977 (Lipton 2001). In 1999, Monica Lewinsky agreed to speak with Walters about her relationship with President Clinton, a show watched by an estimated 48.5 million viewers (Carter 2004). Other interviews include conversations with Katherine Hepburn, Bing Crosby, Margaret Thatcher, Vladimir Putin, Christopher Reeve, Clint Eastwood, President Barack Obama, Oprah Winfrey, and Hillary Clinton. Over the years, Walters has been criticized by some who suggested her work blurs the lines between journalism and entertainment, while others celebrate her achievements as a pioneering woman journalist (Carter 2004; Williams 2013).

Walters began her career as a writer for CBS before moving into a producer role at NBC. She wrote for NBC's *Today Show*, beginning as a writer of features delivered by whomever was the current "Today Girl," an on-air personality whose job it was to engage in simple conversation and look nice. At the time, Walters later recalled, television "did not include women who were doing anything with their brains" (Walters 2008, 107). *Today Show* host Frank McGee prohibited Walters from speaking until he had asked three questions in the program's news interviews, but Walters was allowed to conduct interviews outside of the studio on her own ("Barbara Walters" 2004). This prompted her to arrange as many interviews as she could outside of the studio, to significant success. Ultimately challenging the status quo, she established herself as a talented contributor at the *Today Show*, moving from a writer to a "reporter at large," to the show's first official female cohost (McLeland 2004). Walters expanded her role as cohost from reporting on soft news features to more hard news stories, further establishing herself as a strong interviewer in the process (McLeland 2004; Walters 2008).

In 1976, she left the *Today Show* to coanchor the *ABC Evening News* with Harry Reasoner, the first woman to take on the role of a network anchor. Her lucrative contract, which earned her $1 million annually, was controversial, and her style was perceived by some as a threat to the status quo of male reporting at the time (Lipton 2001; McLeland 2004).

Many people openly wondered whether viewers would be receptive to the evening news being delivered by a woman, but Walters pointed out that many of her fans were women viewers who were pleased with the types of questions and reporting she offered (Brown 1976). While Walters made history in taking the evening news anchor position, Reasoner did not want her there and refused to collaborate with her beyond what was absolutely required ("Barbara Walters" 2004). Walters persevered in coanchoring the half hour newscast while working on developing her interview specials. She also later developed content for the ABC newsmagazine program *20/20*. In 1984, she joined *20/20* as a cohost while continuing to produce her interview specials.

In 1997, Walters and producer Bill Geddie developed a daytime talk show called *The View*, where contemporary topics would be discussed by Walters and a group of cohosts from different generations with various backgrounds and perspectives. *The View* added a new component to the morning television lineup. Before *The View*, politics was not a topic of discussion on daytime television, and it was uncommon for those in journalistic roles to share their opinions (Setoodeh 2017). Though the program's hosts have changed over the years, the program is still a staple of ABC's daytime television lineup. Walters left *20/20* in 2004 and officially retired from *The View* in 2014.

Caroline R. Jones (1942–2001)

Caroline R. Jones, a notable advertising professional, is credited with contributing to the development of advertising campaigns that both featured and addressed Black consumers. Considered a trailblazer in a white, male-dominated industry, Jones achieved many "firsts" as a Black advertising professional. She is remembered for playing lead roles in the creation of a number of popular, widely distributed advertising campaigns; holding a variety of leadership positions in the industry; and creating her own agency. In 1990, Jones was awarded the Advertising Woman of the Year Award, and in 2012, *Advertising Age* deemed Jones one of the "100 Most Influential Women in the History of Advertising."

Jones was born in Michigan in 1942 and was the oldest of ten children. The first person in her family to attend college, she graduated from the University of Michigan and was hired as a copywriter trainee and secretary at J. Walter Thompson, a leading advertising agency (Elliot 2001). She eventually became the first Black woman to be a copywriter at the agency and worked her way up in the company until she left in 1968 to co-establish Zebra Associates, one of the first advertising agencies owned by African Americans (Grant 2015; Davis 2013). As a Zebra vice president, Jones became the first Black woman vice president in the industry at large.

In 1975, Jones became the first Black woman vice president of a large mainstream advertising agency, Batten, Barton, Durstine & Osborn (BBDO), when she was hired as vice president and creative director. In 1977, she cofounded the Mingo-Jones firm with her colleague Frank Mingo, and in 1986, she founded Caroline Jones Advertising (which becames Caroline Jones Inc. in 1995), where she served as president and creative director until her death (Davis 2013).

While Jones was considered an expert in advertising to Black consumers, "she struggled against the assumption that her ads should only address African American consumers," and her perspective prevailed as her campaigns were ultimately used to appeal to broader national audiences (Grant 2015). For example, Jones's conception of promoting Campbell's soup relied on using emotion to help show how soup fit into family life; "where Campbell's traditional approach had been to depict the product and its features, Jones convinced the client that average people—Black models in this case—had to be shown enjoying the soup in loving familial settings. This approach was so successful in courting Black consumers, that Campbell's adapted the concept into its general market advertising, using white models" (Davis 2013, 317). Her work on promotions for the U.S. Post Office, Goodyear, Anheuser-Busch, and Kentucky Fried Chicken, with the memorable tagline, "We do chicken right," were other campaigns that achieved national recognition (Grant 2015).

In her biographical analysis of Jones's career, scholar Judy Foster Davis pointed out that "Caroline Jones' career coincided with several major social shifts pertaining to diversity, including the US Civil Rights movement; increased racial integration; the feminist movement, and the emergence of multiculturalism as a marketing orientation" (Davis 2013, 311). However, significant structural forces made it difficult for women, and particularly Black women, to easily succeed in the advertising business. Jones pushed back against some of these systemic roadblocks by advocating for increased inclusion of Black and other minority images in advertisements. She fought against racism in the industry at large, reached out to support minority women, and cofounded and founded her own firms (Davis 2013).

Over the years, Jones developed a research-based expertise in marketing to Black consumers in clever and sophisticated ways, and many of her appeals had crossover success, meaning they were also used in general campaigns. At the same time, however, Jones expressed frustration that her work at various agencies was sometimes seen solely as for Black consumers. "When I walk in the door to pitch an account," Jones complained, "people automatically think 'Black advertising'" (Davis 2013, 323). Outside of her agency work, Jones was active in the business community and routinely participated in the radio program *Focus on the Black Woman* and the television program *In the Black: Keys to Success* (Elliot 2001).

A collection of Caroline Jones Advertising Agency records and papers can be found at the National Museum of History. The Smithsonian Online Virtual Archives' Caroline Jones Collection includes digitized copies of advertisements she helped create for Campbell Soup, Toys "R" Us, Anheuser-Busch, and Kentucky Fried Chicken. Additional materials include some of Jones's writing, research and promotions on the Bahamas for the travel industry, and advertising agency documents.

Oprah Winfrey (1954–)

In 2018, the Smithsonian's National Museum of African American History and Culture opened an exhibit called "Watching Oprah: The Oprah Winfrey Show and American Culture," which is described as work that "considers the story and impact of Oprah Winfrey in her many roles: as host of a world-famous television show; as an actress, film producer and media mogul; as a philanthropist and educator; and as a daughter of the civil rights generation whose phenomenal story of success illustrates the struggles and achievements of African women throughout history." The existence of this exhibit points to the lasting impact the former "queen of daytime" turned "queen of all media" has had over the course of her career.

Born in Kosciusko, Mississippi, on January 29, 1954, Winfrey began her career at a Nashville, Tennessee, television station as a reporter and news anchor in the 1970s before moving to Baltimore, Maryland, to coanchor an evening news program. While there, she also hosted a local talk show before moving to Chicago in 1984 to host a morning television talk show called *AM Chicago*. Her success led to the development of an hour-long, nationally syndicated program called *The Oprah Winfrey Show* that aired from 1986 to 2011.

Winfrey initially established herself as a talk show host who embraced guests and topics that were taboo and sensational, such as nudist colonies, women's sexual satisfaction, the Ku Klux Klan, and sex crimes (Kelly 2010). Although her show sometimes replicated elements of the "trash" TV programs that were dominant at the time, Winfrey also elevated discussions of sensitive topics, such as education policy, drunk driving, the AIDS crisis, and date rape, with her direct questions, warmth, and humor (Kelly 2010). In the 1990s, Winfrey rebranded the show to adhere to a more spiritual perspective that focused on health, wellness, and self-improvement. As the show continued to prosper, Winfrey welcomed a diverse slate of guests—from experts to celebrities to politicians—to educate and engage her viewers. She launched the television careers of many of her reoccurring guests, including Dr. Phil, Rachael Ray, and Dr. Oz.

Winfrey is also a notable actor, starring in the film *The Color Purple* (1985), the television miniseries *The Women of Brewster Place* (1989), and the film *There Are No Children Here* (1993).

While critics celebrated her performance in *There Are No Children Here*, Winfrey's focus on her talk show interfered with pursuing significant acting work until her involvement in 1998's filmic adaptation of Toni Morrison's novel *Beloved* (Adewunmi 2017). Winfrey played the main character, and her production company coproduced the film. Since *Beloved*, Winfrey has performed in films that include *The Princess and the Frog* (2009), *The Butler* (2013), *Selma* (2014), *The Immortal Life of Henrietta Lacks* (2017), and *A Wrinkle in Time* (2018).

Currently, Winfrey runs her company, Harpo Inc., and oversees her *O Magazine* and cable television channel OWN: Oprah Winfrey Network. OWN's programming advances an inclusive slate of stories and issues. For example, the channel sponsors a documentary film club where particular films are highlighted and discussed, including *Miss Representation*, a documentary that explores the media's depiction of women; *No Women, No Cry*, a film about maternal mortality; and *Family Affair*, a film about abuse. Its entertainment and scripted programming targets African American audiences.

In 2016, OWN debuted the original scripted television series *Greenleaf*, in which Winfrey had a reoccurring role, about a Black megachurch and its community. The popular series ended in 2020, and a spin-off is in the works (Toby 2021). Ava DuVernay's drama *Queen Sugar* (based on the book by Natalie Baszile) also debuted on OWN in 2016, addressing sometimes polarizing cultural issues and debates (Penrice 2018). In 2021, the channel debuted *Delilah*, a drama about a lawyer who is divorced and raising two kids. Executive producer Craig Wright describes the show in this way: "Delilah wants to be the start of a conversation about Black womanhood, Black sisterhood and its immense value to the world. . . . There's no better time for a heroine like Delilah, and I just hope all the Delilahs out there can watch the show and know how important we know they are" (Toby 2021).

In 2018, Winfrey partnered with Apple, striking a deal to create original programs for the company. She also began working as a contributor to *60 Minutes* and CBS News. Her programming on Apple TV includes *The Oprah Conversation* and an upcoming biographical documentary. She has also produced or executive-produced numerous films and television series and has written several books. Winfrey's work as a philanthropist includes donating over $100 million for girls' education opportunities (Otterson 2018).

Geena Davis (1956–)

Born in Wareham, Massachusetts, on January 21, 1956, Virginia Elizabeth (Geena) Davis is an actor, producer, and activist who began her movie career with a part in *Tootsie* in 1982. Over the decades, Davis performed in numerous films, including *The Fly* (1986), *Beetlejuice* (1988), *The Accidental Tourist* (1988), *Thelma & Louise* (1991), *A League of Their Own* (1992), and *The Long Kiss Goodnight* (1996). She also starred in the television show *Commander in Chief* (2005) and played characters on *Grey's Anatomy* and *GLOW*. Davis won the Academy Award for Best Supporting Actress for her role in *The Accidental Tourist*; however, her role in *Thelma & Louise* attracted more cultural attention.

Thelma & Louise, a feminist road trip movie, explores female friendship between two women navigating a sexist world. The 1991 film was notable because of its themes, political messaging, prioritizing of women's experiences, and entertainment value. In reflecting on the movie twenty years after its release, *Atlantic* writer Raina Lipsitz described it as "revolutionary, the first film in a long time to tell the truth about women's lives. Not only did it star two women, but their friendship was the film's central subject, the story was written by a woman, and those stars were, at the time, 35 and 45—well past their prime by Hollywood's ever-narrowing standards of physical perfection. Though portrayed as sexually attractive, Davis and Sarandon had more to do than sit around looking pretty" (Lipsitz 2011). The film is still referenced today as a cinematic landmark and is part of the Library of Congress's National Film Registry.

Davis followed up the success of *Thelma & Louise* one year later with *A League of Their Own*, an entertaining box office hit about women's professional baseball during World War II directed by Penny Marshall. As Davis got older, however, it became more difficult to find work. In an interview with the *Guardian*'s Hadley Freeman, Davis explained that after she turned forty, "I fell off a cliff. I really did. . . . In the early stages of my career, I was blithely going along thinking 'Meryl Streep, Jessica Lange and Sally Field, they're all making these great female-centric movies. And I'm getting these great roles, really tippy-top roles, so things must be getting better for women.' But suddenly, the great roles were incredibly scarce. It was a big difference" (Freeman 2020).

It was Davis's experience watching television with her young daughter that prompted her to establish the Geena Davis Institute on Gender in Media, a research-driven organization that since its 2004 founding has worked to promote gender balance in family entertainment (Watson 2016). Davis was frustrated and angered by the lack of female characters on children's television and the ways girls were portrayed when they were present. Arguing that gender-oriented portrayals communicate messages to boys and girls about what they are capable of, Davis emphasizes the need for kids to be exposed to a variety of occupations and roles embodied by both men and women. Since 2004, the institute has published numerous research-based reports on gender parity and the representation of women and other underrepresented groups in television, film, and advertising. Part of the research uses artificial intelligence to identify and quantify details about character portrayals and speaking time in television programs and films and to scan manuscripts for bias ("Film Star" 2020). Results of the research are shared with those working in the industry and the public alike. In 2019, Davis was awarded an honorary Oscar, the Jean Hersholt Humanitarian Award, for her work advocating for gender parity on-screen via the Geena Davis Institute on Gender in Media.

In 2015, Davis founded the Bentonville Film Foundation to highlight work created by women and other underrepresented filmmakers. The 2020 festival featured films where "80% were directed by women, 65% by people of colour, and 40% by LGBTA people" (Freeman 2020). The foundation works with the Geena Davis Institute to pool research and collaborate with industry insiders to advocate for systemic change in the industry, changes that research indicates are profitable (BFFoundation n.d.). For example, films with women in leading roles have proven able to generate high profits, sometimes higher profits than films with men in leading roles, and yet women do not make up even half of the leads in top-grossing films (Freeman 2020). It is Davis's hope that continuing her work in this area will lead to permanent shifts in perceptions and actions in the industry at large. Both the Geena Davis Institute and the Bentonville Film Foundation work with schools and other nonprofit groups on educational initiatives addressing gender imbalance, unconscious bias, and stereotyping.

Joanelle Romero (1957–)

Joanelle Romero is a Native American film and television actor, musician, and producer. Her award-winning documentary short *American Holocaust: When It's All Over, I'll Still Be Indian* (2000) is a sobering look at the slaughter of American Indians after Europeans discovered the New World. By detailing aspects of the deaths of millions of American Indians over the centuries, the film suggests "that Americans never truly have absorbed and comprehended the enormity of what was perpetrated in the European settlement of North America between 1492 and the end of the Indian wars some 100 years ago" (Boehm 2001). The film was short-listed for an Academy Award nomination. Romero is now one of just a few Native members of the Academy of Motion Picture Arts and Sciences (Nsiah-Buadi 2018).

As the daughter of Rita Rogers, an actor who performed in Elvis Presley movies, Romero was born in Albuquerque, New Mexico, and grew up in Hollywood, ultimately pursuing an acting career herself. In 1977, Romero starred in *The Girl Called Hatter Fox*, a television movie centering on the life of a Native woman; the piece was the first television narrative of a modern Native woman in the United States (Nsiah-Buadi 2018). Since that time, however, television shows featuring Native women in lead roles have not really materialized. "It took Hollywood 42 years to produce another film where a Native actress is in a contemporary role, and that's Netflix's *Chambers*," said Romero. "In regard to episodic television, it's been 16 years and because of our call to action and meeting with the networks, we finally got a Native actress as a series regular on episodic television, which is great" (Tupica 2020b). Actor Sivan Alyra Rose starred in *Chambers*, and Tantoo Cardinal played a character in ABC's *Stumptown*. Both shows, despite some positive reviews, lasted one season.

Romero has spent much of her career providing opportunities for Native talent and advocating for more inclusion of Native women in mainstream narratives. In 1994, she founded and became CEO of the Red Nation Celebration Institute, a Native arts and cultural organization in Los Angeles, California. She also established the Red Nation International Film Festival to highlight Natives working in television and film. The success of this ongoing event led to the creation of such additional initiatives as the Native Film Market–Indigenous Filmmaker Showcase, the Native Youth Matter Film Series, and Native Women in Film & Television (Schulman 2019). In 2006, she founded the Red Nation Television Network, an online streaming company focused on distributing Native content (Tupica 2020b). The streaming channel, which launched before Netflix and Hulu, "reaches 10 million viewers in 37 countries" (Shulman 2019).

In 2018, Romero and her team at Native Women in Film & Television produced the #WhyWeWearRED campaign. This campaign describes itself as an "initiative that aims to bring awareness to murdered and missing Native women & girls and the direct link of the lack of inclusion of Native women in film & television." Noting that Native women are more likely to be victimized than any other demographic group, the initiative aims to raise awareness about the lack of media coverage of these tragedies and the absence of Native women in media more generally. "The representation of Native women in mainstream film and television is plagued by invisibility, stereotypes and whitewashing," explained one #WhyWeWearRED press release. "While the Academy of Motion Picture Arts and Sciences has reported a body that is 30 percent people of color, only 0.0026 percent of its members are Native women" (Red Nation International Film Festival n.d.). In 2020, she developed Indigenous New Media, a company that aims to support talented young Native Americans who want to develop films, television programs, and documentaries (Tupica 2020a).

Christine Brennan (1958–)

Christine Brennan is a national sports columnist for *USA Today* and a sports commentator for such media outlets as CNN, ABC News, *PBS NewsHour*, and National Public Radio's *Morning Edition*. Born March 31, 1958, in Toledo, Ohio, Brennan is the oldest of four children. In a 2006 National Public Radio interview, she reflected that her parents were supportive of her interest in sports, and her dad took her to many games. She was an athlete but did not benefit from Title IX legislation that required, among other things, for schools to provide equal opportunities for girls and boys to participate in sports. "President Nixon signed Title IX in 1972 and it had not yet begun to take effect, so equality for girls in sports was non-existent back then. The cheerleaders had better uniforms than we athletes did" (NPR 2006).

Brennan earned her undergraduate and graduate degrees at Northwestern University. From there, she began her career as a sports reporter at the *Washington Post*. She worked at the *Post* for over a decade before joining *USA Today* in 1997. In addition to her sports reporting for *USA Today*, she also became a regular commentator for national media outlets on a wide range of sports-related issues.

The Associated Press Sports Editors (APSE) has named Brennan as one of the top ten sports columnists in the country three times, and she is also recognized for her decades of experience in covering the Olympic Games and her coverage of the 2016 Olympic sex abuse scandal (Adams 2020). In addition to sports commentary, Brennan's columns often discuss social issues related to sports culture, such as sexist practices and racial discrimination. She has also authored several books, including *Best Seat in the House* (2006), a memoir documenting her relationship with her father and his support through the lens of their mutual love of sports. She has also written three different books on figure skating. One of them, *Inside Edge: A Revealing Journey into the Secret World of Figure Skating* (1997), provides readers with detailed insight into the competitive sport and was named one of the best sports books of all time by *Sports Illustrated* (McEntegart 2002).

Brennan worked as the first woman sports reporter for the *Miami Herald* in 1981, at a time when few women worked as sports journalists. Now an award-winning sports media professional, Brennan often speaks about the sexist behavior and harassment she endured working both at the *Herald* and the *Washington Post*, where she became the first woman reporter to cover Washington's NFL team in the 1980s. In a 2020 column about allegations of sexual harassment and verbal abuse of women working for the Washington NFL team, Brennan shared some of her own experiences with the team over the years, including unwanted advances, sexist comments, and repeated lies about her personal life repeated by members of the organization. "That was a very different time, a time when you didn't mention things like that to your editor, or anyone else," recalled Brennan about her experiences covering the team in the 1980s. "It was a time when you tried to ignore the harassment and the sexism and keep right on going, which is exactly what I did. Now, however, terrible behavior like that is eventually reported. Men lose their jobs. People are outraged" (Brennan 2020). As an advocate for more gender inclusivity in sports media, Brennan recounts stories about her formative years but emphasizes that in today's environment, working hard and dealing with challenges are necessary to achieve success (Waldman 2015).

Brennan has received numerous awards during her long and distinguished career, including recognitions from numerous universities, the Women of the Year award from Women in Sports Events (WISE), and the Women in Sports Foundation's Billie Award for journalism. In 2020, she received the APSE Red Smith Award, a yearly honor given to someone who has significantly contributed to sports journalism (Adams 2020). In addition to acknowledging her professional accomplishments, the APSE recognized Brennan's ongoing mentorship of young professionals and students and her commitment to funding scholarships in her hometown, fellowships at Northwestern University, and a scholarship-internship initiative she founded when she served as president of the Association for Women in Sports Media (Adams 2020).

Avis Little Eagle

Avis Little Eagle is the founder and publisher of the *Teton Times*, an independent newspaper operating out of South Dakota that serves the Standing Rock Reservation, a Native American community that straddles the border between North Dakota and South Dakota. She is also a publicly elected councilwoman for the Standing Rock Sioux Tribe and has served as councilwoman, vice chairwoman, and councilwoman-at-large for the tribe over many years. She was elected to the board of the Native American Journalists Association in 2019. Her recent advocacy as councilwoman includes opposing the Keystone pipeline, participating in getting out the vote campaigns, and helping the community manage the COVID-19 pandemic safely. She also sits on the board of trustees at Sitting Bull College in Fort Yates, North Dakota.

Little Eagle graduated from Sitting Bull College in 1987 and pursued her education at Black Hills State University, where she majored in mass communications and minored in Native studies (Little Eagle and Nienaber 2017). In 1990, she began working at the *Lakota Times*, the first newspaper to serve the Pine Ridge Reservation in South Dakota. Tim Giago, founder and editor of the *Lakota Times*, hired Little Eagle as a news reporter. During her tenure at the paper, she worked her way up from reporter to managing editor, increasing her contributions as the paper grew and changed in name to *Indian Country Today* (Giago 2007). Giago described her as a "courageous" journalist, pointing to Little Eagle's ten-part series on fake medicine men and women, which he described as "one of the major accomplishments in Indian journalism" (Giago 2007). Her additional reporting at the *Lakota Times* and *Indian Country Today* focused on tribal, social, economic, environmental, and governmental issues relevant to Natives in the region. She also wrote opinion pieces that addressed such topics as the need for more Native voices in journalism and mismanagement of tribal funds.

Little Eagle has been a consistent advocate for more diversity in journalism, noting that non-Native journalists often report on and tell stories in ways that are hurtful to Indians. She is not alone in this advocacy. For example, noted journalist and Nieman Fellow Jodi Rave has consistently argued for the need to increase the number of Native American reporters in local, regional, and national newsrooms, stating, "It largely falls on mainstream news outlets to explain what's happening on tribal lands and in urban Indian settings. That means it is often non-Natives who are telling Native stories, since only 295 self-identified Native journalists work at daily newspapers . . . and they are even more nonexistent in broadcast news divisions" (Rave 2005, 8).

Avis Little Eagle founded the *Teton Times* in 2002. The paper is published in print form weekly and maintains a Facebook site but does not publish a digital news site. "The internet is not as available on Indian reservations as it is to the rest of the America," explained Giago, "so newspapers and Indian radio are still the main sources for spreading the news" (Giago 2014).

In her commitment to ensuring the success of the *Teton Times*, Little Eagle has taken on a wide assortment of roles, including reporting and selling ads to ensure the paper survives, while committing to operating as an independent free press (Rave 2018b). The commitment to independent operation is especially important because many tribal newspapers have historically functioned as public relations vehicles for tribal leaders rather than as independent news organizations providing information and watchdog functions over tribal government (Rave 2005).

While Indian journalists and their news outlets are not always known nationally, within Indian communities, they are highly regarded and relied upon. However, the digital age has impacted the news industry in Indian Country just as it has elsewhere in the nation. A 2018 report authored by Rave noted that in 1998, there were 700 media sources serving Indian Country; by 2018, that number had decreased to 200. The report additionally documented that tribal governments own about 75 percent of Native media outlets, which compromises the ability for communities to gain access to independent reporting (Rave 2018b).

"American Indians are invisible as contemporary people or romanticized as relics of a bygone era" in mainstream media, according to Rave. "The invisibility affects how policymakers make decisions about Native people whose lives are often struck by high rates of poverty, suicide, poor health care, and missing and murdered Indigenous women" (Rave 2018a). Therefore, Native media is needed "not only to inform and engage our communities but also to lift up our stories in the broader culture." Little Eagle's commitment to publishing the *Teton Times* provides the Standing Rock community with an independent news outlet that accomplishes these goals.

Soledad O'Brien (1966–)

Maria de la Soledad Teresa O'Brien is an experienced, award-winning journalist and producer who has contributed as a reporter and producer at NBC, CNN, PBS's *NewsHour*, HBO, and Al Jazeera America. She is the current CEO of Starfish Media Group, a media production and distribution company she established in 2013. According to the Starfish Media Group's website, part of the mission of the company is to "look at often divisive issues of race, class, wealth, poverty and opportunity through personal narratives." O'Brien is also the host of the syndicated political magazine program *Matter of Fact*, a show examining such diverse topics as health care, tariffs, artificial intelligence, climate science, and elections, and she is a contributor to HBO's *Real Sports with Bryant Gumbel*. She also runs PowHERful, a nonprofit organization that supports women of color in their quest to earn an undergraduate degree, and she has toured college campuses nationwide to engage students in conversations about race (Trent 2015).

Born September 19, 1966, in St. James, New York, O'Brien began her career as a reporter for a radio medical talk show and later spent many years working for NBC in various roles. She left NBC in 2003 to work as a coanchor for CNN's *American Morning*. At CNN, O'Brien reported on stories ranging from the tsunami in Thailand to Hurricane Katrina to the 2005 terrorist attacks in London. She then moved to CNN's documentary division, where she worked on two notable projects, *Black in America* and *Latino in America* (History Makers 2014). Both documentary programs focused on the complex lives and wide range of experiences of those two demographic groups. As the daughter of a Black and Cuban mother and a father with Irish and Scottish roots who is from Australia, O'Brien describes herself as "a mixed race, first generation American" (O'Brien 2009). When discussing her work on *Latino in America*, she points out that "her ethnic roots are relevant" when considering just how few journalists are Latino despite the growing population of Latinos in the United States. O'Brien suggested that a lack of understanding about the Latino community may be a contributor to a dominant news focus on Latinos that prioritizes immigration, crime, and drugs (O'Brien 2009).

O'Brien is active on Twitter and uses the platform to weigh in on aspects of race, diversity, and politics in American culture. She made news headlines when she criticized CNN, her former employer, for its lack of diversity in senior staffing after the network pointed out the Trump administration did not have any Black senior staff members (O'Brien 2018). She regularly challenges elements of news reporting and political commentary on Twitter. In video posted on *The Root*'s YouTube channel, O'Brien states that she has "assigned herself the job of the Twitter race correspondent," pointing out racist language in news reporting. She has also urged journalists to become more honest and accountable in their reporting by more straightforwardly noting when public officials and others make racist comments rather than using euphemisms to soften the rhetoric (*The Root* 2018).

In the past few years, O'Brien has furthered her mission to call out journalists' and news organizations' reporting, especially given her large numbers of followers on Twitter and Instagram. An exploration of O'Brien's public quest to "hold people accountable" reveals she also uses social media to "elevate journalists she believes are doing good work and to share stories she thinks need to be seen" (Norlian 2021). On February 24, 2021, testifying at a House hearing on media disinformation, O'Brien stressed this need for accountability in regard to journalism at large while also pointing out problematic aspects of the news media landscape: "Stop saying you want a diverse staff and go hire one—fast. A diversity of staff is not just fair, but it helps you reach into different communities and tell an accurate story of America. The public will trust you again if you tell the truth of who lives in this country and report accurately on communities" (O'Brien 2021).

O'Brien's new miniseries, *Disrupt and Dismantle*, debuted on BET in March 2021. The program's focus is on Black and brown communities, the societal inequities people in these communities encounter, and solutions that might result in meaningful change. Topics include environmental racism, policing, and the so-called school-to-prison pipeline. *Harper's Bazaar* writer Bianca Betancourt wrote that "what O'Brien is pleading for viewers to understand is that racism can permeate our world in the subtlest of ways. It can manifest in environmental racism and discriminatory zoning laws in ethnic neighborhoods, or even affect a Dallas, Texas grandmother demanding a literal mountain of discarded rooftop shingles be removed from her backyard. It can also impact the right to inhale clean air" (Betancourt 2021). While O'Brien has always reported on marginalized communities, supporters hope that a show that explores structural racism at a time when the COVID-19 pandemic has highlighted the health disparities among different demographic groups might lead to more awareness of socioeconomic inequality in the United States and help spur necessary reforms.

Shonda Rhimes (1970–)

Award-winning writer, creator, television showrunner, and producer Shonda Rhimes has been credited with changing the landscape of television with popular, culturally relevant programming such as *Grey's Anatomy*, *Private Practice*, and *Scandal*. Her entertainment company, Shondaland, has also produced television shows, including *How to Get Away with Murder*, *The Catch*, *Station 19*, and *Bridgerton*. Shondaland.com, part of Hearst Magazines Digital Media Network, hosts Shondaland podcasts and also includes essays, interviews, and articles in the categories of "life," "health and wellness," "culture," "impact," and "change makers." Rhimes, who was inducted into the Television Academy of Arts and Sciences Hall of Fame in 2017, has also earned lifetime achievement awards from the Directors Guild of America, the Writers Guild, and the Producers Guild.

Born in Chicago on January 13, 1970, Rhimes attended Dartmouth College, where she earned her BA. From there, she earned an MFA from the University of Southern California's School of Cinema and Television. After graduating, Rhimes began her career writing film screenplays. In 2003, she pitched her idea for *Grey's Anatomy* to ABC. Though some male executives reportedly did not appreciate depictions of the female characters' sex lives or completely understand what Rhimes was trying to accomplish in creating a program that diverged from traditional medical dramas, the show was ordered at the end of 2003 and debuted in 2005 with a diverse cast of lead characters (Press 2018). The show broke viewing records and became a cultural phenomenon in part because "the success of *Grey's* took the industry's prevailing prejudice that audiences wouldn't watch shows centered on women or people of color and crushed it like a bug" (Press 2018, 116).

Years later, Rhimes described her conception of *Grey's Anatomy* as "something I felt was perfectly normal: I made the world of the show look the way the world looks. I filled it with people of all hues, genders, backgrounds and sexual orientations. And then I did the most obvious thing possible: I wrote all of them as if they were . . . people. People of color have three dimensional lives, have love stories and are not funny sidekicks, clichés or criminals. Woman are the heroes, the villains, the badasses, the big dogs. This, was told over and over, was trailblazing and brave" (Rhimes 2015, 139). In the fall of 2021, *Grey's Anatomy* entered its eighteenth season, making it the longest-running television medical drama in television history (Wagmeister 2020).

The success of *Grey's Anatomy* led to the creation of other hit shows that established Rhimes as a powerful television showrunner, someone who was able to bring high ratings to ABC at a time when traditional network television viewing was declining. Rhimes thus had an important influence on the landscape of television storytelling. "Showrunning is now television's counterpart to the film auteur," wrote scholars Michaela Meyer and Rachel Griffin. "Film auteurs are typically regarded as individuals whose influence and artistic control is so profound that they give film its personal and unique stamp" (Meyer and Griffin 2018, 5).

Rhimes's style as a producer includes colorblind casting, a focus on cultural issues, shocking story lines, and over-the-top dramatic presentations (Meyer and Griffin 2018). This style, and the resulting programming created by Rhimes and her team at Shondaland, made an impact. Before Kerry Washington was cast as the lead on *Scandal*, the last network television drama featuring a Black lead woman character had aired in 1974 (Press 2018). Another Shondaland show, *How to Get Away with Murder*, starring Viola Davis, also found a committed audience. Often both provocative and entertaining, episodes and story narratives addressed such social issues as abortion, LGBTQ parenting, woman's ambition, and work dynamics in novel ways (Meyer and Griffin 2018).

Rhimes's casting choices have been celebrated and credited with prompting change in an industry that tends to skew white and male. As a Black woman herself, Rhimes's race and gender are often pointed out. In her 2015 memoir, *Year of Yes*, Rhimes wrote that she "wishes people would stop thinking it remarkable that we can be great at what we do while Black, while Asian, while a woman, while Latino, while gay, while a paraplegic, while deaf" (Rhimes 2015, 138–139). She professes to hate the word *diversity* because it may define people too often by their demographics, and she asserts that she is "normalizing TV" so that television reflects what the world looks like: "The goal is that everyone should get to turn on the TV and see someone who looks like them and loves like them. And just as important, everyone should turn on the TV and see someone who doesn't look like them and love like them. Because perhaps then they will learn from them. Perhaps then they will not isolate them. Marginalize them. Erase them. Perhaps they will even come to recognize themselves in them. Perhaps they will even learn to love them" (Rhimes 2015, 235–236).

Despite the success of her programs, conflicts arose between Rhimes and ABC and its parent company, Disney, over program contents and budgets (Rose 2020). In August 2017, Rhimes signed a lucrative contract with Netflix that gave her more control over her projects and allowed her to develop Shondaland "into an enduring company that will live within Netflix in the same way that Marvel exists inside the Walt Disney Company" (Koblin 2018).

By 2018, Rhimes and her production company had eight series in planning phrases (Koblin 2018). Two are now available: the period romance *Bridgerton* and *Dance Dreams: Hot Chocolate Nutcracker*, a documentary on the dancer and choreographer Debbie Allen. Both of these programs debuted in late 2020. A show based on the real grifter Anna Delvey became available in February 2022, and Netflix notes other upcoming Shondaland projects include the comedy series *Sunshine Scouts*, an adaptation of Isabel Wilkerson's book *The Warmth of Other Suns*, and a series about working in Silicon Valley based on Reddit CEO Ellen K. Pao's book *Reset* (Moore 2021).

Samantha Skey (1972–)

Samantha Skey is the CEO of SHE Media, a women's lifestyle digital media company. One of the only women who is leading a media company in the United States, Skey oversees the operations of the SheKnows Partner Network, which owns the fashion and beauty website StyleCaster, the health site HelloFlo, the publishing and live events–oriented BlogHer, and the parenting website SheKnows. Skey began her career working in digital sales and marketing, eventually engaging in what the industry calls "interactive" marketing (connecting with consumers via digital platforms) in the mid-1990s (Stroud 2019). Before being hired by SHE Media—first as president in 2013 and then as CEO in 2018—Skey worked at companies such as CNET, the Walt Disney Company, Passenger, and RecycleBank. She is a graduate of Hamilton College and the recipient of numerous industry awards.

When Skey joined SHE Media (formally called SheKnows Media) in 2013, most of the company managers were men, but by 2018, 90 percent of those in management were women (Messina 2018). Skey explains that she is driven by "the triple bottom line: people, purpose and profits," and that SHE Media needed to focus on the purpose aspect of women's media that engaged with women as employees and consumers in positive ways (Stroud 2019). In an interview with *Forbes* magazine, Skey states, "Because the world is run by profit . . . it is important for women to succeed in profit-driven companies" (Stroud 2019). Additionally, she indicates that the company's profits are aligned with "people" and "purpose" by describing her commitment to transparency about the demographic composition of the company's workforce: "I've published our wage metrics around gender and race. We publish our representation of speakers onstage at #BlogHer. We have a commitment to a minimum of 50% of women of color on any stage. Composition of workforce is another published metric, ensuring that we have no wage gap based on anything other than title" (Stroud 2019).

Skey believes that the best way to secure revenue is to cultivate loyal consumers through content that is engaging and results in return visits to their site, thus providing "value" to advertisers (Stein 2014). The company does this by advancing a digital publication model where one platform integrates "users, editors and content creators" in ways that "empower women to discover, share and create" (Brandchannel 2015). The "women positive" model is supported by consumer research. The company surveyed female consumers about their perspectives on what they call "pro-female" advertising. Results show that 94 percent of the women surveyed indicate depicting women as sex objects in advertising is problematic, 52 percent indicate they have bought a product because they like the pro-female ad approach in the product's promotion, and 62 percent believe any brand can enter the "pro-female space" (SheKnows Living Editors 2014). Given these results and other indications that commercial messaging advancing female empowerment is met with positive responses from many consumers, SheKnows believes that its approach is both positive and profitable (Stampler 2014).

Successful initiatives that Skey led during her first few years at SHE Media include the #BossyIs campaign and The Pitch. The #BossyIs campaign asked nine-year-old girls to define the word *bossy*. The campaign built on Facebook's Sheryl Sandberg's #BanBossy initiative, which advocated for eliminating the use of this adjective to describe girls and women who are assertive. The campaign resulted in significant media reach and the establishment of Hatch, a company initiative focused on tweens (Stein 2014). The Pitch was created to provide a space for women entrepreneurs to pitch their products to audiences and businesses, allowing for consumer feedback and advertising revenue (Brandchannel 2015).

SHE Media also recognizes, supports, and celebrates advertising that is respectful of women and advances ideas about women's smarts, strength, and empowerment. In 2020, the company awarded #Femvertising awards for the fifth consecutive year to six 2019 campaigns. "Femvertising," a term popularized by the organization, is a word that shortens the descriptor "female empowerment advertising" (Åkestam, Rosengren, and Dahlen 2017). According to the Femvertising Awards website, the awards were established to "honor brands that are challenging gender norms by building stereotype-busting, pro-female messages and images into ads that target women and girls."

The evolving digital space provides opportunities for growth but is often associated with younger consumers. However, Skey believes that new audiences for SHE Media include parents of teenagers and "empty nesters," a demographic she thinks is underserved in terms of lifestyle content (Messina 2018). She also acknowledges that while social media is important, SHE Media is more focused on building its online presence because "if your content has true value, you can rely on search for long-term loyalty, whereas social media requires platforms and changing algorithms every few months" (Messina 2018).

Mindy Kaling (1979–)

Born Vera Mindy Chokalingam in Cambridge, Massachusetts, Mindy Kaling is an award-winning actor, director, writer, comedian, and producer. A fan of sketch comedy shows as a teenager, Kaling moved to New York after her graduation from Dartmouth College and started performing stand-up comedy while working as a production assistant on a cable television show (Sittenfeld 2011). In 2002, Kaling cowrote (with Brenda Withers) a comedic play called *Matt & Ben* that envisioned how Matt Damon and Ben Affleck wrote the screenplay for *Good Will Hunting*. Kaling played Affleck, and Withers played Damon in the stage production, which received positive reviews.

Kaling's performance impressed television writer and producer Greg Daniels, who ultimately hired her for a supporting role in NBC's *The Office* (Sittenfeld 2011). She gained mainstream recognition for starring as Kelly Kapoor on *The Office*, where she also worked as a writer and then ultimately as a director and executive producer. She stayed with the program for nine seasons and briefly returned for an appearance on the series's final episode.

Kaling has since established herself as a force in the entertainment industry with a number of successful projects. In 2012, her comedy show *The Mindy Project* debuted on Fox; it finished its run on Hulu in 2017. Kaling also acted in several movies, including *Inside Out* (2015), *A Wrinkle in Time* (2018), and *Oceans 8* (2018), and she wrote two best-selling memoirs, *Is Everyone Hanging Out without Me (and Other Concerns*; 2011) and *Why Not Me?* (2015). She also executive produced, wrote, and starred in *Late Night*, a successful film that debuted at the Sundance Film Festival in 2019 and was acquired by Amazon Studios for a record-breaking $13 million (Otterson 2019; Warner Bros. 2019).

Other projects include the coming-of-age comedy *Never Have I Ever*, a show streaming on Netflix that Kaling cocreated and is loosely based on her own experiences growing up; a Hulu television miniseries remake of the film *Four Weddings and a Funeral*; and an upcoming wedding comedy that takes place in the United States and India (McNary 2019; Otterson 2019). In 2019, Kaling and, by extension, her production company, Kaling International, signed a six-year deal with Warner Bros. Television to "develop, write and produce new television projects for all platforms, including broadcast, cable channels, and streaming" (Otterson 2019).

As with other women and women of color who are successful in the historically male-dominated entertainment industry, Kaling is often recognized for being the "only" and "the first." When she worked on *The Office*, for example, she was the only woman and the only person of color in the writer's room (Sittenfeld 2011). Her show *The Mindy Project* cemented her place in television history as the "first woman of color to create, write, and star in a primetime sitcom" (Nelson 2019).

While Kaling initially acknowledged that she once felt "frustrated" by pressure to be a "spokesperson" or "role model" for inclusive representation in the industry, she now emphasizes that she embraces this role and the power she has to make change (Nelson 2019). However, while Kaling engages in inclusive hiring practices and views "holding the door open for others" as a "responsibility," she also points out that such standards and scrutiny are unevenly applied: "I think there is a different standard for me as a show creator, as someone to provide employment, than there is for someone in a lot of these other TV shows that you see with predominantly white casts and with white writing staffs. . . . They don't get the scrutiny, and it used to frustrate me a lot when I was younger because I was the first Indian-American woman to have my own show in the States, and I was the first woman of color to get nominated for an Emmy in writing" (Blyth 2019).

Kaling's work has been praised for its representations of typically underrepresented groups. As scholar Amita Nijhawan points out, in American media, South Asian women are "often repressed, serious, concerned with work and achievement or alternatively with menial roles, with little in terms of personal or sexual life" (Nijhawan 2015). On *The Mindy Show*, however, title character Mindy Lahiri (played by Kaling) challenges stereotypes and stigmas assigned to women in general and South Asian women specifically. She does this in a character who is accomplished, sexy, and smart while also being both confident and insecure. As Nijhawan observes, Kaling's character "sees herself as American" and "avoids marking herself as a racial minority by making her quest for love and her confusion about body image something all women can identify with. . . . By not using the usual stereotypes of South Asians and Asians on American television, while at the same time acknowledging race, I suggest that she make herself a citizen of the alleged 'melting pot' as the melting pot should be, a hybrid space for hybrid identities" (Nijhawan 2015).

Kaling's acknowledgment of race and gender continues to be present in her current work. Her reimagining of the film *Four Weddings and a Funeral* as a series on Hulu focuses on a Black woman and a Pakistani man. Her film *Late Nigh*t was informed by her own experiences as a "diversity hire" for *The Office*, an experience that made her feel self-conscious but at the same time resulted in her praise of NBC for its diversity writing program (Blyth 2019). Her Netflix series *Never Have I Ever* offers a depiction of a first-generation Indian American girl who is smart and high achieving but also gets into trouble, challenging the "nerd" stereotype of Indian Americans as awkward, quiet, and solely focused on academics (Thorne 2020). The show additionally frames the protagonist Dev as an American teenager who wants to lose her virginity and her nerd status, a characterization Kaling says challenges how "we are programmed to see Asian girls in a certain way on teen shows" (Nelson 2019). Many entertainment observers expect that her

2019 deal with Warner Bros. will likely lead to further projects that inherently contribute to more inclusive and positive representations of women on television.

Chloé Zhao (1982–)

Chloé Zhao is a filmmaker, producer, and director. She was born in China, and at the age of fourteen, she left Beijing to attend a boarding school in London. She finished high school in Los Angeles, California; attended Mount Holyoke College in Massachusetts; and continued her education at New York University's film school. In interviews, Zhao reflects on her enjoyment of Western popular culture when she was growing up and her drive to explore new places (Fontoura 2021).

Despite her stated fondness for mainstream popular culture, Zhao established herself as an independent filmmaker with a number of noncommercial films that earned accolades. Her debut film, *Songs My Brothers Taught Me* (2015), takes place on South Dakota's Pine Ridge Indian Reservation. The movie tells the story of a teenage boy named Johnny who wonders whether he should leave the reservation to pursue a new path in life.

Zhao's process in creating this film relied on her commitment to spending time in the community and casting community members in the film itself. *New York* magazine writer Alison Willmore wrote that as a Chinese woman telling a story in a Native community, Zhao "felt unconstrained by both American colonial history and the legacy of guilt that comes with it. Zhao tried to make herself porous, immersing herself in life there and attempting to get past the familiar narratives offered up to expectant visitors. She filled her film with locals, guiding them through fictionalized performances that were informed by their own experiences" (Willmore 2021). This practice resulted in more than thirty drafts of the film's script. This process was important, said Zhao, because real-life status updates in the community informed the ongoing story she was crafting (Macaulay 2013).

Songs My Brothers Taught Me (2015) screened at the Cannes Film Festival and earned positive reviews and recognitions for Zhao and her team. Zhao's follow-up film, which she wrote, directed, and produced, was *The Rider* (2017), a Western shot in South Dakota's Badlands about an injured rodeo competitor. The film won the top prestigious award at the Cannes' Directors Fortnight Section, and Sony Pictures Classics picked it up for distribution, leading to further recognition and film directing offers (Kohn 2018).

Rolling Stone writer Maria Fontoura describes Zhao's films as relatively apolitical and neutral despite their focus on underrepresented and marginalized groups. Instead, Zhao's films focus on introducing viewers to the details of people's lives in the places they inhabit, without an explicit agenda (Fontoura 2021).

Zhao's independent films prioritize working with actors who have not had formal training, and she arranges for such cast members to get a share of any of the film's profits (Willmore 2021). This policy was in place with her 2021 film *Nomadland*, starring Frances McDormand. The movie was based on a nonfiction book about a subculture of Americans without traditional homes who move around the country, working seasonal jobs and primarily living out of their vans. At both the 2021 Golden Globes and Academy Awards, Zhao won the Best Director award, becoming the first Asian woman director to win these prizes. The film also won for Best Drama Motion Picture at the Golden Globes and Best Picture at the Academy Awards.

Zhao directed *Eternals* (2021), a film in the Marvel Cinematic Universe, becoming the first Asian woman to direct a Marvel film. The film itself also features a couple of firsts; characters include a gay superhero and a hearing-impaired superhero. At the time of this writing, Zhao is working on a biopic on Bass Reeves, the first Black U.S. marshal, and is slated to direct a feature from Universal Studios that is a science fiction–Western version of *Dracula* (Willmore 2021).

Influential Organizations and Representations

Ms. Magazine (1972–present)

Ms. magazine claims it "was the first U.S. magazine to feature prominent American women demanding the repeal of laws that criminalized abortion, the first to explain and advocate for the Equal Rights Amendment, to rate presidential candidates on women's issues, to put domestic violence and sexual harassment on its cover, to commission and feature a national study on date rape and to blow the whistle on the undue influence of advertising on magazine journalism" (*Ms.* n.d.). While today these types of issues—and many others—are covered from a women's perspective in a variety of magazines, blogs, television programs, and documentaries, this was not always the case. As the first magazine to ever be founded, owned, and operated by women, *Ms.* is a notable text in women's media history (Pogrebin 2011).

The origins of the magazine date back to 1970, when 100 women participated in a sit-in at the *Ladies' Home Journal* editorial offices, demanding that the magazine hire a woman as editor in chief (Pogrebin 2011). In the mid-twentieth century, the magazine industry was mainly run by men, even at publications that were primarily read by women. Woman magazine writers were limited to writing on fashion, cooking, romance, and beauty. As the women's movement gained momentum, however, these practices were challenged (Pogrebin 2011). Numerous women engaged in activist practices, advocating for women's equality and a change in cultural perceptions around what women could and should be and do.

Gloria Steinem, now recognized as a feminist icon, was a dominant voice in the twentieth-century women's movement, speaking across the country to groups, college students, and the media. As a freelance writer, she began her career writing for such publications as *Esquire*, the *New York Times*, *Ladies' Home Journal*, and *Harper* (Conkling 2020). In 1968, she was hired by the monthly magazine *New York* as a contributing editor and political columnist. There she wrote pieces on such fraught subjects as the national unrest after the assassinations of Martin Luther King Jr. and Senator Robert Kennedy and the war in Vietnam. Eventually, Steinem's activism in the women's movement gave her the idea to create a feminist magazine specifically for women (Conkling 2020). She led a team of feminist-minded publishers, including Betty Harris and Patricia Carbine, and editors and writers, including Letty Cottin Pogrebin and Joanne Edgar, to produce *Ms.* (Pogrebin 2011; Conkling 2020).

With the economic support of *New York* magazine editor Clay Felker, *Ms.* launched its "preview issue," dated Spring 1972, as an insert in the 1971 year-end issue of *New York*. The cover featured an image of a female figure with many hands juggling tasks that women were expected to accomplish in American society. Steinem noted that the cover "had a universality because it's harking back to a mythic image—the many-armed Indian God image. And it solved our problem of being racially 'multibiguous' because she is blue: not any one race" (Pogrebin 2011). The publication's debut included features and articles titled "The Housewife's Moment of Truth," "We Have Had Abortions," "On Sisterhood," "I Want a Wife," "Can Women Love Women?" and "Down with Sexist Upbringing."

The debut issue was embraced by readers. Subscription orders poured into the *Ms.* office, quickly rising to 200,000 per year, while newsstand sales matched that figure (Conkling 2020, 170). Readers responded positively to the magazine's purpose, and there were no shortages of writers or story ideas, despite skepticism from mainstream media about public reception of the publication. One documentation of the magazine's popularity was the "hundreds of phone calls a day, 1,500 unsolicited manuscripts a month, and 1,000 letters to the editor each week" (Le Rougetel 2018, 7).

However, despite the subscription-driven revenue, the magazine needed advertising to be financially solvent and to keep the subscription price at an attractive level for readers.

This was a challenge. *Ms.* adhered to an advertising policy that was essentially unheard of in the industry at the time: advertisements could not demean women and needed to present women respectfully. Additionally, advertising companies could not expect what is known as a *complementary copy*. Complementary copy is a magazine's practice of publishing articles that in some way reinforce or praise the products of advertisers. However, *Ms.* wanted to keep the editorial department and advertising departments separate and did not engage in this standard "quid pro quo" that governed the content of women's magazines (Steinem 1990, 28). Instead, the publication tried to recruit companies that traditionally advertised to men (e.g., car companies, credit cards, insurance, financial services) to also reach out to women, who were also in the market for these goods and services. Despite some eventual successes, this was mostly an uphill battle that did not yield enough revenue to keep the magazine in operation using its current business model (Steinem 1990).

In 1979, Steinem and her team incorporated *Ms.* as a nonprofit publication operating out of the Ms. Foundation for Women (Conkling 2020). In 1987, the magazine was sold to an Australian media company, Fairfax, that also founded the teen magazine *Sassy*. Two years later, *Ms.* was purchased by Dale Lang, an owner of an independent publishing company in the United States. The magazine evolved to adopt an advertising-free publication model over the subsequent decades and is currently published by the Feminist Majority Foundation—which acquired *Ms.* in 2001—four times a year.

The Color Purple (1985)

The film *The Color Purple*, based on Alice Walker's 1982 Pulitzer Prize–winning novel, tells the story of Celie Harris, a southern African American woman who over the course of her life survives horrific abuse. Spanning over decades, the narrative begins in the early 1900s and, through the depiction of Celie's story, offers a view into the violence, poverty, racism, and sexism experienced by Black women during this time. In *The Color Purple*, teenaged Celie is twice pregnant by her stepfather, who gives away their babies; is married off to a horrible, abusive man who wants to be with someone else; and is separated from her sister. The film tells the story of Celie's survival and, in so doing, spotlights her relationships with two women—one romantic and one not. Directed by Steven Spielberg, the film stars Whoopi Goldberg, Oprah Winfrey, Margaret Avery, Danny Glover, and Akosua Busia. According to the American Film Institute (2020), "Alice Walker's contract stipulated she would serve as project consultant and that 50% of the production team—aside from the cast—would be African American, female, or 'people of the Third World.'"

The film was controversial upon its release. As cultural scholar Jacqueline Bobo (1998) summarizes, many Black male reviewers criticized the film for its portrayal of Black men, arguing the depictions furthered stereotypes of Black men as brutal. In comparison, Black feminist critics noted that the film raised issues of sexual violence, physical and mental abuse, and single parenting by Black women that are supported by facts. Bobo (1998) additionally explains that women in general had different reactions to the film, but "that on the whole Black females have found something progressive and useful in the film," a finding she highlighted given the film was directed by a white man whose work "will lead the viewer to see it in a certain way, because of the way the film is made. The film's producers are under both commercial and ideological constraints to structure an expensive media production in a manner that is familiar and therefore non-threatening to mainstream society."

The film's focus on Black women's stories was celebrated because it offered an alternative to the Black women stereotypes and underdeveloped characters often depicted in films. Although scholar Sharon Jones (1998) argues the film fails to fully explore the lesbian relationship detailed in the book and, as a result, Black women's sexuality, it does "attempt to portray the lives of African-American women strongly enduring and ultimately transcending racial, sexual, and class oppression" (37). As a result, Black women showed up to watch the film, many of whom watched it again and again when it became available for home viewing (Bobo 1998; Bond 2015). As the *New Republic*'s Victoria Bond (2015) writes, "When you see Whoopi Goldberg [who plays Celie] in close-up, a loving close-up, you look at this woman, you know that in American films in the past, in the 1930s, 1940s, she would have played a maid. She would have been a comic maid. Suddenly, the camera is focusing on her and we say I've seen this woman some place, I know her." The strong performances inspired some young Black women to believe they could pursue acting as a career (Darrisaw 2018).

In 2020, *The Color Purple* marked its thirty-fifth anniversary. Its longevity is complemented by a Broadway musical first launched in 2005, and plans for a movie adaptation of the musical are underway (Darrisaw 2018). As filmmaker and film critic Tambay Obenson (2020) explains, "The film remains a cultural touchstone for African American women, due in large part to its depiction of female relationships as a form of sanctuary, in a patriarchal world filled with violence. When it was released, it shattered the widespread cultural resistance to talking openly about domestic abuse." Both Whoopie Goldberg and Oprah Winfrey were at the beginnings of their careers when they made their film debuts in *The Color Purple*, and representations of Black women in Hollywood films in the 1980s were slim and often problematic (Toby 2020). Some of the film's stars believe that the story—both Walker's novel and the film adaptation—are ultimately inspirational in their message that women can claim their power, are not disposable, and are able to survive abuse (Toby 2020).

And yet, thirty-five years later, the film's legacy is complicated. In general, scholars acknowledge the strong focus on Black women's experiences, the celebration of Walker's narrative, the presentation of Black queer women, and the portrayal of resilience (Obenson 2020). At the same time, some are critical of the fact that the novel was adapted by a white screenwriter and white director because the story is told through their frame, which privileges a broad, mainstream audience (Obenson 2020). As director and screenwriter Tanya Steele notes, "We have to have Black women telling Black women's stories. I'm tired of Black men, white men, and white women telling Black women's stories" (Obenson 2020).

Sex and the City (1998–2004)

Created by Darren Star, *Sex and the City* (*SATC*) is a popular comedy-drama that aired on HBO from 1998 to 2004. It centers on the stories of four women: Carrie Bradshaw (Sarah Jessica Parker), Samantha Jones (Kim Cattrall), Charlotte York (Kristin Davis), and Miranda Hobbes (Cynthia Nixon). The women's story lines center around their romantic and sexual experiences, and elements of the narratives highlight their experiences as successful professionals. A central characteristic of the show is the explicit way the women talk about their sex lives, their experiences, and their desires. The show also prioritizes female friendships as central to the women's lives, and it privileges this friendship over familial bonds and romantic relationships (Dykes 2011).

SATC is honored with multiple Emmy, Golden Globe, and Screen Actors Guild Awards. It appears on best television series lists, prompted two *Sex and the City* feature films and a television series prequel called *The Carrie Diaries*, and is the subject of numerous articles and books by television critics and scholars. *SATC* remains popular in worldwide syndication, and commercial outfits in New York City offer *Sex and the City* tours. A sequel titled *And Just Like That . . .* debuted on HBO in December 2021 and features three of the four main characters, who are now in their fifties, as they navigate their current life challenges and friendships.

Critics and scholars identify *SATC* as a landmark show, a "cultural touchstone" that builds upon such previous women-centered situation comedies as *The Mary Tyler Moore Show* (Dykes 2011, 49). The program is women focused, and while men certainly tuned in, it is the featuring of women's candid experiences in new ways that informed much of its popularity. As scholar Ashli Dykes (2011) writes, the representation of female friendships and the "frank discussion of female sexuality" is central to the program; *SATC* offers a contemporary view of single women, friendship, and intimacy, and in doing so, it reveals a "space for discussion and introspection about the place of the contemporary single women in our society" (49). One of the show's stars, Cynthia Nixon, eludes to this idea in one of her takes on the show's popularity by saying, "When a show hits big, it's because it's showing something true that the culture hasn't caught up with yet. *Sex and the City* showed the world unmarried women in their 30s who weren't upset about it" (Galanes 2014). At the same time, as Naomi Wolf (2009) suggests, the show did not shy away from showing the characters' "search for love." Wolf also suggests the series was "radical" in a number of ways: it features women who are "compelling on their own terms," challenges the stereotype of the "slut" by portraying the character of Samantha as a woman who favors her sexual encounters and career over romantic commitments, and centers Carrie's writing voice as the one who shares the philosophical reflections that anchor each episode.

These themes resonated with audiences and with the culture at large. On August 28, 2000, *Time* magazine's cover featured the four *SATC* stars with the question, "Who Needs a Husband?" and the text "More women are saying no to marriage and embracing the single life. Are they happy?" Scholar Deborah Jermyn (2009) argues that *SATC* is a television milestone, noting, "Throughout its run, *SATC* captured the imagination and attention of modern-day women like no other television text of its time, attaining a currency that has continued beyond the show's finale in 2004. . . . For millions of female viewers *SATC* was (and remains) part of the cultural fabric of everyday life" (6). She suggests that *SATC* pushed against "the boundaries governing television's representation of sex and its exploration of female sexuality, language and the intricacies of friendship" more than any show that came before it (Jermyn 2009, 91–92).

The show is not absent criticism. Some of the episodes advanced depictions of the queer community that are deemed problematic, while other episodes are seen as racially insensitive, moments that current viewers have reflected on as awareness of issues connected to representations in popular culture have increased (Jones 2018). The show is also criticized for its "whiteness" in a city as diverse as New York City and for its celebration of materialism (Jones 2018). At the same time, however, *SATC* is about women in New York that "exist in a very white and affluent world," a world that does exist (Galanes 2014).

In the series finale, the characters end up in romantic unions rather than as the single women in the city the show celebrated, an ending criticized by some. However, Deborah Jermyn (2009) suggests that this critique of the series ending is not faithful to the narratives, often fanciful narratives themselves, that dominate the show and that the characters' friendships remained steady throughout. While elements of the show's representations will likely be continually discussed, especially after the sequel premieres, the initial ninety-four episodes remain anchored in television history as advancing contemporary representations of women for women. Finally, *Sex and the City*'s legacy includes opening the door for additional "edgy" television programming featuring multiple women characters to be produced and embraced by audiences, including *Desperate Housewives*, *The L Word*, and *Girls* (Jermyn 2009; Galanes 2014).

The Dove Campaign for Real Beauty

The Dove Campaign for Real Beauty, often referred to as Dove's Real Beauty Campaign, is a personal care product advertising campaign that emerged in 2004 to address societal body insecurities with which many women struggle. Its "Real Beauty" campaign links positive messages about women and their bodies with Dove products. The idea for the campaign was informed by the company's multicountry research inquiry into women's interests and perspectives, which found that just a small percentage of the 3,000 women they engaged with believe themselves to be beautiful (Etcoff et al. 2004). Dove's choice to push back against the status quo of traditional constructions of beauty resulted in a campaign that has been described by supporters as a game changer and success story. Critics, meanwhile, have called the campaign inauthentic and accused it of capitalizing on "women's poor body images" (Bahadur 2014).

The most recognizable visuals from the early years of the campaign are photographs of a group of diverse women in their underwear. In these images, "real" women—women who are not professional models, are from various backgrounds, and have various body types—are spotlighted in an attempt to challenge "the myopic view of feminine beauty as it was portrayed by then models with perfectly applied makeup" (Brooks, Chanland, and Cox 2020, 18). Some ads featured a single woman, sometimes in her underwear and other times in clothes. Other ads focused on challenging traditional beauty standards that view particular breast sizes, height, or freckles as flaws (Heiss 2011). While these images are a departure from what is typically seen in beauty advertising, some observers assert that the shapes and sizes of the women featured in these images are not all that transformative. As scholar Sarah Heiss argues, "Though the bodies depicted were not typical of fashion models, many of the differences were close enough to pre-existing ideals that they would be accepted by most beauty standards." Heiss suggests, for example, that the overweight model "hardly looked overweight"; the older woman may have had a few wrinkles on her face, but her body appeared smooth and free of blemishes; and none of the images contained bodies with "visible disabilities, deformities or marks" (Heiss 2011).

Dove is owned by the company Unilever; the campaign arose from a partnership with the advertising company Ogilvy & Mather and was led by a mostly female team (Brooks, Chanland and Cox 2020). The group aimed to "revolutionize the culturally driven female self-perception of beauty" (Brooks, Chanland, and Cox 2020, 18). In 2006, the campaign released an "Evolution" video that writer Nina Bahadur describes as "the tipping point, turning the Campaign for Real Beauty into a household name" (Bahadur 2014). The video—which went viral, a novel concept in 2006—showed how image retouching and image manipulation could be employed to transform a photograph of a woman into an image representing what is idealized as beautiful. To complement the messaging and awareness raising present in their ads, Dove also partnered with organizations to engage girls and boys in discussing self-esteem and other issues (Brooks, Chanland, and Cox 2020). It also provides resources on its website for parents, educators, and youth leaders through the Dove Self-Esteem Project program.

Since 2004, the campaign has evolved with new steps and missteps discussed by industry professionals and scholars along the way. For example, controversy ensued after some criticized the placement of Black women in particular advertising images. Critics argue the presentations had racist overtones or implicitly suggested white skin was superior to darker skin (Brooks, Chanland, and Cox 2020). Others debated whether the company is victimizing women and capitalizing on their anxieties for promotional purposes (Brooks, Chanland, and Cox 2020; Molloy 2015). The campaign has been criticized for advancing a message of female empowerment and self-acceptance that Dove's parent company, Unilever, does not uphold with some of its other brands, including SlimFast (a diet product), Axe (men's body spray products whose ads are often sexist), and Fair and Lovely skin-whitening cream (internationally marketed to women with darker skin; Bahadur 2014). Additionally, the Real Beauty Campaign's focus is beauty, which by default prioritizes appearance as a way to evaluate oneself.

Subsequent components of the Real Beauty campaign and other campaigns, however, effectively acknowledge that a focus on one's appearances is a common cultural practice. Others have urged women to let go of harsh self-judgments. The 2013 video "Real Beauty Sketches" and a series of video campaigns posted on the Dove US YouTube channel, including #MyBeautyMySay and #BeautyBias, address this issue. A campaign launched at the sixtieth anniversary of Dove's beauty bar (what the company's calls its bars of soap) "asks women to pledge to redefine beauty for themselves and young girls to challenge preconceived notions about attractiveness" (Cooney 2017). In 2021, Dove released "Reverse Selfie," a sequel to their "Evolution" video, where the creation of a social media post is shown in reverse, emphasizing the work that goes into crafting image and highlighting how young the girl in the image is after the staging is removed. In this campaign, Dove aims to challenge young people's practices of using retouching apps to create a perfect selfie, pointing out that one's self-esteem is compromised when unrealistic images permeate social media (Campaigns of the World 2021).

Despite the criticism that it has received at times, Dove campaigns have also been recognized for prompting a messaging shift in marketing and advertising industries. Some credit the Real Beauty campaign for pioneering images of women that are not airbrushed or digitally enhanced (Cooney 2017). Other industry insiders note that brands are now "more conscious of how they portray women and who they choose as 'models,'" and campaigns such as "World's Toughest Job" from American Greetings and "Run Like a Girl" from Always have followed Dove's lead (Laird 2014). Pantene's #ShineStrong film called "Sorry, Not Sorry" addressed women's tendency to apologize, and CoverGirl's #GirlsCan campaign addressed female empowerment.

For Dove's part, the campaign team believes consistently having conversations about self-esteem, beauty, and body image might ultimately "change a generation" (Bahadur 2014). Now often referred to as "femvertising," the more current use of feminist-oriented ideas to promote products and services "can be considered novel in that it focuses on questioning female stereotypes acknowledged to be (at least partially) created by advertising" (Åkestam, Rosengren, and Dahlen 2017, 796).

Orange Is the New Black (2013–2019)

Orange Is the New Black (*OITNB*) is a television drama found on the streaming service Netflix. It debuted at a time when streaming services were in the formative stages of producing their own original content. The show is set in a prison and was inspired by Piper Kerman's memoir of the same name, detailing her experiences serving time at a Danbury, Connecticut, prison for drug smuggling and money laundering. While the TV show features a character named Piper Chapman, includes details that reflect Kerman's own legal transgressions, and portrays a prison environment similar to Kerman's descriptions, the program's narratives diverge from Kerman's life (Damico and Quay 2016). Show creator Jenji Kohan and her team completed extensive research to supplement Kerman's account to create a realistic television prison setting, which in turn highlights the dysfunction in the prison system (Radish 2013). While *OITNB*'s popularity was aided by the binge-watching phenomenon that was a novel concept in 2013 (Netflix released the entire first season all at once), the show demonstrates that stories about women and women in marginalized communities can be successful, challenging those "who argue that television must pander to the 18–35 male demographic" (Householder and Trier-Bieniek 2016, 1). The show cleared the path for subsequent programming by other innovative creators, such as *GLOW* and *Pose* (Berman 2019).

OITNB is notable for its representation of a developed multiracial and LGBTQ cast of characters and its success in developing an entertaining show focusing on women's stories. Kohan, who successfully created *Weeds* for the premium cable channel Showtime, first pitched the show to Showtime and then to HBO. Both turned it down, believing that a show featuring a "multiracial cast of female criminals" would not interest audiences (Press 2018, 236). Netflix picked it up, and in casting the fictional version of Piper, Kohan famously noted that the white, blond character was "her Trojan Horse," that Piper's story "was a gateway to all the stories" (Press 2018, 236). As *Time* magazine's Judy Berman (2019) points out, the Trojan Horse concept smuggled in "dozens of women Hollywood historically ignored—poor women, Black women, brown women, trans women, immigrant women, elderly women, mentally ill women, women with double-digit dress sizes" (50). In casting, Kohan pointedly selected relatively unknown actors from all demographic backgrounds, of all shapes and sizes, and of all ages; television writer Joy Press (2018) explains that "Jenji wanted to steer *Orange* into cinema verité territory: having the 'Hollywood pretty' Piper character at the show's center would only accentuate *Orange*'s realistic depiction of the other women's bodies" (238). Piper also represents the middle-class white woman who is not aware of her privilege.

This inclusive casting coupled with deep character development and narratives informed a number of accomplishments. The show addresses complex issues connected to gender, race, social class, power, privilege, and sexual orientation, and though some of these portrayals are criticized by critics and scholars, there is broad agreement that the show's success in casting is significant. *OITNB* is the first show to feature a transgender character played by a transgender actor, Laverne Cox. Cox's character, Sophia Burset, is complex and stereotype defying but not perfect, perhaps educating viewers a bit on the humanity of an often misunderstood, misrepresented, and marginalized group. Kohan, while asserting that her goal is to entertain, describes the choices she made in crafting the program as a form of activism (Press 2018). Scholars April Kalogeropoulos Householder and Adrienne Trier-Bieniek (2016) explain that as a show made by and for women, it, among other things, "features a host of diverse female characters including women of color who challenge stereotypes and have depth and narrative development. Its female friendships pass the Bechdel test—characters form deep relationships and talk to one another about things other than men. Older women are given a voice and a sexuality. Class issues are at the surface, and are honestly portrayed, sometimes uncomfortably so. Queer and lesbian characters are not only visible but sex and gender are complicated rather than simplified" (6). At the same time, as the show progressed, some became critical of the way *OITNB* appropriates challenges marginalized people face into exploitive television that is written to target the white viewer over a diverse audience (VanDerWerff and Ray-Harris 2019). While debates about elements of the show's legacy persist, few deny that in the early days of streaming television, *OITNB* was a game changer.

Bibliography

Adams, Todd. 2020. "USA Today's Christine Brennan Recipient of 2020 APSE Red Smith Award." APSE, March 6, 2020. https://www.apsportseditors.com/x-2/

Adewunmi, Bim. 2017. "How Oprah Got Her Acting Groove Back." BuzzFeed News, April 10, 2017. https://www.buzzfeednews.com/article/bimadewunmi/how-oprah-got-her-acting-groove-back

Advertising Age. 2012. "The 100 Most Influential Women in Advertising." *Advertising Age* 83 (28): 18–44.

Åkestam, Nina, Sara Rosengren, and Micael Dahlen. 2017. "Advertising 'Like a Girl': Toward a Better Understanding of 'Femvertising' and its Effects." *Psychology of Marketing* 34: 795–806. https://doi.org/10.1002/mar.21023

American Film Institute. 2020. "AVI Movie Club: *The Color Purple*." May 27, 2020. https://www.afi.com/news/afi-movie-club-the-color-purple/

Bahadur, Nina. 2014. "Dove 'Real Beauty' Campaign Turns 10: How a Brand Tried to Change the Conversation about

Female Beauty." *HuffPost*, January 21, 2014. https://www.huffpost.com/entry/dove-real-beauty-campaign-turns-10_n_4575940

"Barbara Walters: The Exit Interview." 2004. *New York Times*, September 5, 2004. https://www.nytimes.com/2004/09/05/arts/television/barbara-walters-the-exit-interview.html

Berman, Judy. 2019. "*Orange Is the New Black* Is Ending. TV Will Never Be the Same." *Time*, August 5, 2019: 49–51.

Betancourt, Bianca. 2021. "Soledad O'Brien Is Flipping the Narrative on Racism in America." *Harper's Bazaar*, February 25, 2021. https://www.harpersbazaar.com/culture/film-tv/a35616750/soledad-obrien-disrupt-and-dismantle-interview/

BFFoundation. n.d. "The Mission." Accessed January 1, 2021. https://bentonvillefilm.org/about/

Blyth, Antonia. 2019. "Mindy Kaling on How 'Late Night' Was Inspired by Her Own 'Diversity Hire' Experience & the Importance of Holding the Door Open for Others—Deadline Disrupters." *Deadline*, May 18, 2019. https://deadline.com/2019/05/mindy-kaling-late-night-the-office-disruptors-interview-news-1202610283/

Bobo, Jacqueline. 1998. "Black Women's Responses to *The Color Purple*." *Jump Cut* 33: 43–51. https://www.ejumpcut.org/archive/onlinessays/JC33folder/ClPurpleBobo.html

Boehm, Mike. 2001. "Generations of Genocide." *Los Angeles Times*, April 2, 2001. https://www.latimes.com/archives/la-xpm-2001-apr-02-me-45772-story.html

Bond, Victoria. 2015. "'The Color Purple' Is a Cultural Touchstone for Black Female Self-Love." *New Republic*, March 17, 2015. https://newrepublic.com/article/121311/color-purple-has-remained-cultural-touchstone-black-women

Brandchannel. 2015. "What She Knows: 5 Questions with Chief Revenue Officer Samantha Skey." Brandchannel,

August 5, 2015. https://www.brandchannel.com/2015/08/06/5-questions-sheknows/

Brennan, Christine. 2020. "Opinion: Allegations against Washington NFL Team Are Nothing New for This Organization—It Happened to Me Too." *USA Today*, July 17, 2020. https://www.usatoday.com/story/sports/columnist/brennan/2020/07/17/redskins-revelations-nothing-new-cesspool-nfl-franchise/5455505002/

Brooks, Bradley, Dawn Chanland, and Steven Cox. 2020. "Dove's Advertising Campaign Highs and Lows: From Real Beauty to Real Success to Real Controversy." *Business Case Journal* 27 (1): 16–31.

Brown, Les. 1976. "What Makes Barbara Walters Worth a Million?" *New York Times*, May 2, 1976. https://www.nytimes.com/1976/05/02/archives/what-makes-barbara-walters-worth-a-million.html

Byrne, John. 2011. *World Changers*. New York: Penguin.

Campaigns of the World. 2021. "Dove: Reverse Selfie | Help Girls Positively Navigate Social Media." Campaigns of the World, April 23, 2021. https://campaignsoftheworld.com/digital/dove-reverse-selfie/

Carter, Bill. 2004. "Barbara Walters to Leave '20/20' after 25 Years, Show's Last Season of Emotion Laden Interviews." *New York Times*, January 26, 2004. https://www.nytimes.com/2004/01/26/business/barbara-walters-leave-20-20-after-25-years-show-s-last-season-emotion-laden.html

Conkling, Winifred. 2020. *Ms. Gloria Steinem: A Life*. New York: Feiwel and Friends.

Cooney, Samantha. 2017. "Dove Wants Women to Redefine Beauty." *Time*, January 10, 2017. https://time.com/4629671/dove-raise-the-beauty-bar/

Cordero, Rosy. 2021. "Everything to Know about the *Sex and the City* Revival *And Just Like That*." *Entertainment Weekly*,

January 19, 2021. https://ew.com/tv/everything-we-know-about-the-sex-and-the-city-revival-and-just-like-that/

Damico, Amy, and Sara Quay. 2016. *21st Century TV Dramas: Exploring the New Golden Age*. Santa Barbara, CA: Praeger.

Darrisaw, Michelle. 2018. "*The Color Purple* Is Getting the Movie Musical Treatment—Here's Our Dream Cast." Oprah Daily, November 5, 2018. https://www.oprahdaily.com/entertainment/tv-movies/a24663258/the-color-purple-musical-movie-adaptation/

Davis, Judy Foster. 2013. "Beyond 'Caste-Typing'? Caroline Robinson Jones, Advertising Pioneer and Trailblazer." *Journal of Historical Research in Marketing* 5 (3): 308–333. https://doi.org/10.1108/JHRM-03-2013-0011

Dykes, Ashli L. 2011. "'And I Started Wondering . . . .': Voiceover and Conversation in *Sex and the City*." *Studies in Popular Culture* 34 (1): 49–66.

Egge, Sara. 2015. "'I Love Lucy' Confronts the American Housewife Ideal." Norton Center for the Arts, February 2, 2015. http://nortoncenter.com/2015/02/02/i-love-lucy-confronts-the-1950s-american-housewife-ideal/

Elliot, Stuart. 2001. "Caroline Jones, 59, Founder of Black-Run Ad Companies." *New York Times*, July 8, 2001. https://www.nytimes.com/2001/07/08/nyregion/caroline-jones-59-founder-of-black-run-ad-companies.html

Etcoff, Nancy, Susie Orbach, Jennifer Scott, and Heidi D'Agostino. 2004. *The Real Truth about Beauty: A Global Report*. Commissioned by Dove. https://www.clubofamsterdam.com/contentarticles/52%20Beauty/dove_white_paper_final.pdf

"Film Star, USC Team Up to Weed Out Gender Bias: Viterbi Researchers Create AI Tool Collaborating with Actress Geena Davis." 2020. *ISE: Industrial & Systems Engineering at Work* 52 (7): 16.

Fontoura, Maria. 2021. "The Wanderlust of Chole Zhao." *Rolling Stone*, January 26, 2021. https://www.rollingstone.com/movies/movie-features/chloe-zhao-director-nomadland-marvel-eternals-interview-1115696/

Freeman, Hadley. 2020. "Geena Davis: 'As Soon as I Hit 40, I Fell Off the Cliff, I Really Did.'" *The Guardian*, August 9, 2020. https://www.theguardian.com/culture/2020/aug/09/geena-davis-as-soon-i-hit-40-i-fell-off-the-cliff-i-really-did

Galanes, Philip. 2014. "Sex? Yes. The City? Yes. But Things Have Changed." *New York Times*, January 17, 2014. https://www.nytimes.com/2014/01/19/fashion/Allison-Williams-Cynthia-Nixon-Girls-Sex-and-the-City.html

Giago, Tim. 2007. "Three Courageous Native Women Newspaper Publishers." *HuffPost*, December 5, 2007; updated May 5, 2011. https://www.huffpost.com/entry/three-courageous-native-w_b_75414

Giago, Tim. 2014. "Remembering the Great Native American Journalists." *HuffPost*, March 16, 2014. https://www.huffpost.com/entry/remembering-the-great-nat_b_4912651

Grant, Jordan. 2015. "Caroline R. Jones: Trailblazer Ad Woman." National Museum of American History, May 18, 2015. https://americanhistory.si.edu/blog/caroline-r-jones-adwoman

Heiss, Sarah. 2011. "Locating the Bodies of Women and Disability in Definitions of Beauty: An Analysis of Dove's Campaign for Real Beauty." *Disability Studies Quarterly* 31 (1). https://dsq-sds.org/article/view/1367/1497

The History Makers. 2014. "Soledad O'Brien." Interview, February 21, 2014. https://www.thehistorymakers.org/biography/soledad-obrien

Householder, April Kalogeropoulos, and Adrienne M. Trier-Bieniek. 2016. *Feminist Perspectives on* Orange Is the New Black*: Thirteen Critical Essays*. Jefferson, NC: McFarland.

James, Caryn. 2019. "Lois Weber: The Trailblazing Director Who Shocked the World." BBC, March 20, 2019. https://www.bbc.com/culture/article/20190318-lois-weber-the-trailblazing-director-who-shocked-the-world

Jermyn, Deborah. 2009. *Sex and the City.* Detroit: Wayne State University Press.

Jones, Ellen. 2018. "'That Show Was as White as It Gets!' Sex and the City's Problematic Legacy." *The Guardian*, April 21, 2018. https://www.theguardian.com/tv-and-radio/2018/apr/21/that-show-was-as-white-as-it-gets-sex-and-the-citys-problematic-legacy

Jones, Sharon L. 1998. "From Margin to Centre? Images of African-American Women in Film." *Social Alternatives* 17 (4): 35–39.

Kanfer, Stefan. 2003. *Ball of Fire. The Tumultuous Life and Comic Art of Lucille Ball.* New York: Alfred A. Knopf.

Kelly, Kitty. 2010. *Oprah: A Biography.* New York: Crown Publishers.

Koblin, Josh. 2018. "Shonda Rhimes Describes Her Grand Netflix Ambitions." *New York Times*, July 20, 2018. https://www.nytimes.com/2018/07/20/business/media/shonda-rhimes-netflix-series.html

Kohn, Eric. 2018. "Chloe Zhao's 'The Rider' Is a Welcome Antidote to the Age of Trump." *IndieWire*, November 14, 2018. https://www.indiewire.com/2018/11/chloe-zhao-the-rider-the-eternals-1202020696/

Laird, Kristin. 2014. "The Real Impact of Real Beauty." *Marketing Magazine* 119 (9): 20–23.

Le Rougetel, Amanda. 2018. "Documentary Gives Voice to Ms. Magazine Letters." *Herizons* 32 (3): 7–8.

Lipsitz, Raina. 2011. "'Thelma & Louise': The Last Great Film about Women." *The Atlantic*, August 31, 2011. https://www.theatlantic.com/entertainment/archive

/2011/08/thelma-louise-the-last-great-film-about-women/244336/

Lipton, Joshua. 2001. "Barbara Walters." *Columbia Journalism Review* 40 (4): 80.

Little Eagle, Avis. 1999. "OPINION: Journalism Needs More Minorities." *Indian Country Today* (Rapid City, SD), May 3, 1999.

Little Eagle, Avis, and Georgianne Nienaber. 2017. "Legitimizing Plunder at Standing Rock." *Teton Times*, February 1, 2017. https://www.facebook.com/thetetontimes/posts/legitimizing-plunder-at-standing-rockby-avis-little-eagle-and-georgianne-nienabe/1355972131126733/

Macaulay, Scott. 2013. "Chloé Zhao." 2013. *Filmmaker Magazine*. https://filmmakermagazine.com/people/chloe-zhao/

Mahar, Karen Ward. 2001. "True Womanhood in Hollywood: Gendered Business Strategies and the Rise and Fall of the Woman Filmmaker, 1896–1928." *Enterprise & Society* 2 (1): 72–110. https://doi.org/10.1093/es/2.1.72

Mahler, Jonathan. 2014. "As Barbara Walters Retires, the Big TV Interview Signs Off, Too." *New York Times*, May 15, 2014. https://nyti.ms/1nSQRVm

McEntegart, Pete. 2002. "The Top 100 Sports Books of All Time." *Sports Illustrated*, February 16, 2002. https://vault.si.com/vault/2002/12/16/the-top-100-sports-books-of-all-time

McLeland, Susan. 2004. "Walters, Barbara." In *The Encyclopedia of Television*. 2nd ed., edited by Horace Newcomb, 2473–2475. New York: Routledge.

McNary, Dave. 2019. "Mindy Kaling, Priyanka Chopra Teaming on Wedding Comedy for Universal." *Variety*, April 12, 2019. https://variety.com/2019/film/news/mindy-kaling-priyanka-chopra-wedding-comedy-1203188802/

Messina, Judith. 2018. "Asked & Answered." *Crain's New York Business* 34: 7.

Meyer, Michaela, and Rachel Griffin. 2018. "Riding Shondaland's Roller Coasters: Critical Cultural Television Studies in the 21st Century." In *Adventures in Shondaland*, edited by Rachel Griffin and Michaela Meyer, 1–19. New Brunswick, NJ: Rutgers University Press.

Molloy, Parker. 2015. "When Dove Tries: The Latest 'Real Beauty' Gimmick." *Bitch Magazine: Feminist Response to Pop Culture* 67 (Summer): 5.

Moore, Kasey. 2021. "Every Shonda Rhimes Show & Movie Coming Soon to Netflix." What's on Netflix, May 17, 2021. https://www.whats-on-netflix.com/coming-soon/every-shonda-rhimes-shondaland-project-coming-to-netflix-05-2021/

Movshovitz, Howie. 2019. "Lois Weber, Hollywood's Forgotten Pioneer, Has Two Films Restored." National Public Radio, January 5, 2019. https://www.npr.org/2019/01/05/682372051/lois-weber-hollywoods-forgotten-early-pioneer-has-2-films-restored

Ms. n.d. "About *Ms.*" https://msmagazine.com/about/

Murray, Susan. 2005. *Hitch Your Antenna to the Stars: Early Television and Broadcast Stardom*. New York: Routledge.

Nelson, Rebecca. 2019. "Mindy Kaling Didn't Sign Up to Be a Role Model." *ELLE*, October 9, 2019. https://www.elle.com/culture/a29340748/mindy-kaling-interview-2019

Nijhawan, Amita. 2015. "Mindy Calling: Size, Beauty, Race in *The Mindy Project*." *M/C Journal 18* (3): 1. https://doi.org/10.5204/mcj.938

Norlian, Allison. 2021. "From Anchoring the News to Becoming an Outspoken Critic, Journalist Soledad O'Brien Continues to Hold People Accountable." *Forbes*, January 18, 2021. https://www.forbes.com/sites/allisonnorlian/2021/01/18/from-anchoring-the-news-to-becoming-an-outspoken-critic-journalist-soledad-obrien-continues-to-hold-people-accountable/

NPR. 2006. "Dad Was Christine Brennan's Biggest Fan. 'Best Seat in the House' Is Writer's Tribute to a Good Sport." National Public Radio, June 14, 2006. https://www.npr.org/templates/story/story.php?storyId=5485175

Nsiah-Buadi, Christabel. 2018. "A Trailblazing Filmmaker Wants to Make Sure Native Stories Have Their Place in the American Narrative." *The World*, Public Radio International, March 8, 2018. https://www.pri.org/stories/2018-03-08/trailblazing-filmmaker-wants-make-sure-native-stories-have-their-place-american

Obenson, Tambay. 2020. "'The Color Purple' Revisited: Why Spielberg's Movie Is Still Problematic and Meaningful to Many Black Women." *IndieWire*, April 3, 2020. https://www.indiewire.com/2020/04/the-color-purple-debate-anniversary-1202217786/

O'Brien, Soledad. 2009. "Soledad O'Brien Explores Latino Experience, Mixed-Race Heritage." CNN, October 6, 2009. http://www.cnn.com/2009/LIVING/personal/10/06/lia.soledad.obrien.excerpt/index.html

O'Brien, Soledad. 2018. "Very terrible! But, uh, walk me through the senior black staff at @CNNPolitics or @cnn or, hey, I'll take cable news." Twitter, August 13, 2018. https://twitter.com/soledadobrien/status/1029176597780328448

O'Brien, Soledad. 2021. *Hearing on "Fanning the Flames: Disinformation and Extremism in the Media."* Testimony before the House Committee on Energy and Commerce, February 24, 2021. https://energycommerce.house.gov/committee-activity/hearings/hearing-on-fanning-the-flames-disinformation-and-extremism-in-the-media

Otterson, Joe. 2018. "Oprah Winfrey, Apple Sign Multi-Year Content Partnership." *Variety*, June 15, 2018. https://variety.com/2018/tv/news/oprah-winfrey-apple-content-partnership-1202848061/

Otterson, Joe. 2019. "Mindy Kaling Exits Universal for New Overall Deal at Warner Bros. TV." *Variety*, February 21,

2019. https://variety.com/2019/tv/news/mindy-kaling-overall-deal-warner-bros-tv-1203145124/

Penrice, Ronda Racha. 2018. "Oprah Winfrey Network's 'Queen Sugar' Has Quietly Become One of TV's Most Racially Progressive Shows." NBC News, June 20, 2018. https://www.nbcnews.com/think/opinion/oprah-winfrey-network-s-queen-sugar-has-quietly-become-one-ncna882926/

Pogrebin, Abigail. 2011. "How Do You Spell Ms.: Forty Years Ago, a Group of Feminists, Led by Gloria Steinem, Did the Unthinkable: They Started a Magazine for Women, Published by Women—and the First Issue Sold Out in Eight Days: An Oral History of a Publication that Changed History." *New York*, November 7, 2011. https://nymag.com/news/features/ms-magazine-2011-11/

Press, Joy. 2018. *Stealing the Show: How Women Are Revolutionizing Television*. New York: Simon & Shuster.

Quintanilla, Carl. 2013. "The Oprah Effect." CNBC, June 21, 2013. https://www.cnbc.com/the-oprah-effect/

Radish, Christina. 2013. "Creator Jenji Kohan Talks *Orange Is the New Black*, Her Research into Prison Life and Graphic Sex Scenes." Collider, July 7, 2013. https://collider.com/jenji-kohan-orange-is-the-new-black-interview/

Rave, Jodi. 2005. "Challenges Native and Non-Native Journalists Confront." *Nieman Reports* 59 (3): 7–9. https://niemanreports.org/articles/challenges-native-and-non-native-journalists-confront/

Rave, Jodi. 2018a. "American Indian Media Today." Democracy Fund, November 20, 2018. https://democracyfund.org/idea/american-indian-media-today/

Rave, Jodi. 2018b. *American Indian Media Today: Tribes Maintain Majority Ownership as Independent Journalists Seek Growth*. Indigenous Media Freedom Alliance. http://democracyfund.org/wp-content/uploads/2020/06/2018_DF_AmericanIndianMediaToday.pdf

Red Nation International Film Festival. n.d. "#WhyWeWearRed Native Women in Film Take on the Subject of Murdered & Missing and Lack of Inclusion of Native Women in Film & Television." Accessed May 1, 2021. https://www.rednationff.com/why-we-wear-red/

Rhimes, Shonda. 2015. *Year of Yes*. New York: Simon & Shuster.

The Root. 2018. "Soledad O'Brien Is Tired of Journalists Sugar-Coating Racism." YouTube video, 0:2:48. August 10, 2018. https://www.youtube.com/watch?v=upLQiD9tnZs

Rose, Lacey. 2020. "Shonda Rhimes Is Ready to 'Own Her Own S***': The Game-Changing Showrunner on Leaving ABC, 'Culture Shock' at Netflix, and Overcoming Her Fears." *Hollywood Reporter*, October 21, 2020. https://www.hollywoodreporter.com/features/shonda-rhimes-is-ready-to-own-her-s-the-game-changing-showrunner-on-leaving-abc-culture-shock-at-netflix-and-overcoming-her-fears

Schulman, Sandra Hale. 2019. "Joanelle Romero: From Hollywood to the Red Nation." Medium, October 29, 2019. https://sandraschulman.medium.com/joanelle-romero-from-hollywood-to-the-red-nation-f4f59a5caa65

Setoodeh, Ramin. 2017. "'The View' Turns 20: ABC to Re-Air First Episode with Barbara Walters." *Variety*, August 7, 2017. https://variety.com/2017/tv/news/the-view-20-anniversary-barbara-walters-meredith-vieira-joy-behar-rosie-o-donnell-whoopi-goldberg-1202517303/

SheKnows Living Editors. 2014. "SheKnows Unveils Results of Its Femvertising Survey (Infographic)." Sheknows.com, October 30, 2014. https://www.sheknows.com/living/articles/1056821/sheknows-unveils-results-of-its-fem-vertising-survey-infographic/

Sittenfeld, Curtis. 2011. "A Long Day at 'The Office' with Mindy Kaling." *New York Times*, September 23, 2011. https://www.nytimes.com/2011/09/25/magazine/a-long-day-at-the-office-with-mindy-kaling.html

Sochen, June. 2008. *From Mae to Madonna: Women Entertainers in Twentieth-Century America*. Lexington: University Press of Kentucky.

Stafford, Zach. 2016. "The Oprah Winfrey Show: 'Hour-Long Life Lessons' That Changed TV Forever." *The Guardian*, September 8, 2016. https://www.theguardian.com/tv-and-radio/2016/sep/08/oprah-winfrey-show-30-year-anniversary-daytime-tv

Stamp, Shelley. 2010. "Lois Weber and *The Hand That Rocks the Cradle*." Starts Thursday!, August 6, 2010. http://www.starts-thursday.com/2010/08/shelley-stamp-lois-weber-and-hand-that.html

Stamp, Shelley. 2013. "Lois Weber." In *Women Film Pioneers Project*, edited by Jane Gaines, Radha Vatsal, and Monica Dall'Asta. New York: Columbia University Libraries. https://doi.org/10.7916/d8-zsv8-nf69

Stampler, Laura. 2014. "Here's How Women Respond to All Those 'Female Empowerment' Ads." *Time*, October 14, 2014. https://time.com/3502904/heres-how-women-respond-to-all-those-female-empowerment-ads/

Stark, Steven. 1997. *Glued to the Set: The 60 Television Shows and Events That Made Us Who We Are Today*. New York: The Free Press.

Stein, Lindsay. 2014. "Cmo Q&A." *PRWeek* 17 (7): 12.

Steinem, Gloria. 1990. "Sex, Lies and Advertising." *Ms.* (July/August): 18–28. https://www.academia.edu/31540089/STEINEM._Sex_lies_e_advertising.pdf

Stroud, Court. 2019. "How Playing Sports Helped SHE Media's Samantha Sky Become a Powerful CEO." *Forbes*, December 30, 2019. https://www.forbes.com/sites/courtstroud/2020/12/30/how-playing-sports-helped-one-woman-become-a-powerful-ceo/?sh=5da88aec426d

Thorne, Will. 2020. "Mindy Kaling on Featuring Indian Characters 'Who Are Not All Like Princess Jasmine' in

Netflix's' 'Never Have I Ever.'" *Variety*, February 25, 2020. https://variety.com/2020/tv/news/mindy-kaling-indian-characters-never-have-i-ever-netflix-1203515520/

Toby, Mekeisha Madden. 2020. "Reflecting on 'The Color Purple' 35 Years after It Hit Theaters." Shondaland, December 18, 2020. https://www.shondaland.com/inspire/a35009902/the-color-purple-35-anniversary/

Toby, Mekeisha Madden. 2021. "*Delilah* EP Previews New OWN Drama ('Black Women Hold So Many Worlds Together'), Teases *Greenleaf* Spinoff." TVLine, March 9, 2021. https://tvline.com/2021/03/09/delilah-own-preview-season-1-interview-craig-wright-oprah-winfrey-greenleaf-spinoff/

Trent, Sydney. 2015. "Soledad O'Brien on Starbucks and Race: It's Okay to Ask and It's Okay to Answer." *Washington Post*, March 3, 2015. https://www.washingtonpost.com/news/inspired-life/wp/2015/03/25/dont-hate-starbucks-when-it-comes-to-race-its-ok-to-ask-and-its-ok-to-answer-says-journalist-soledad-obrien/

Tupica, Rich. 2020a. "Film Industry Veteran Joanelle Romero Launches 'Indigenous New Media' to Boost Native Entertainment Deals." *Native News Online*, March 2, 2020. https://nativenewsonline.net/currents/film-industry-veteran-joanelle-romero-launches-indigenous-new-media-to-boost-native-entertainment-deals

Tupica, Rich. 2020b. "Q&A: Joanelle Romero talks Native Women in FILM Festival." *Native Knot*, February 4, 2020. https://www.nativeknot.com/news/Native-American-News/QAndA-Joanelle-Romero-talks-Native-Women-in-FILM-Festival.html

VanDerWerff, Emily, and Ashley Ray-Harris. 2019. "*Orange Is the New Black* Celebrated Diverse Women. It Also Exploited Their Stories." Vox, August 7, 2019. https://www.vox.com/2019/8/7/20754146/orange-is-the-new-black-diversity-final-season-review

Wagmeister, Elizabeth. 2020. "'Grey's Anatomy' Showrunner Confirms Patrick Dempsey Will Be Back—Again—and Teases Show's Future." *Variety*, December 18, 2020. https://variety.com/2020/tv/news/greys-anatomy-final-season-patrick-dempsey-returns-1234865876/

Waldman, Dan. 2015. "USA Today Columnist Christine Brennan Speaks about the Role of Women in Sports Media." *Daily Northwestern*, September 27, 2015. https://dailynorthwestern.com/2015/09/27/campus/usa-today-columnist-christine-brennan-speaks-about-the-role-of-women-in-sports-media/

Walters, Barbara. 2008. *Audition: A Memoir*. New York: Alfred A. Knopf.

Warner Bros. 2019. "Mindy Kaling Inks New Overall Deal with Warner Bros. Television Group." February 21, 2019. https://www.warnerbros.com/news/press-releases/mindy-kaling-inks-new-overall-deal-warner-bros-television-group

Watson, Emma. 2016. "Geena Davis." *Interview* 46 (4): 26–111. https://www.interviewmagazine.com/culture/geena-davis

Weitzman, Elizabeth. 2019. *Renegade Women in Film & TV*. New York: Clarkson Potter Publishers.

Williams, Mary Elizabeth. 2013. "There Will Never Be Another Barbara Walters." *Salon*, May 5, 2013. https://www.salon.com/2013/05/13/there_will_never_be_another_barbara_walters/

Willmore, Alison. 2021. "Cholé Zhao's America: The Creator of Quiet Indie Dramas Is Now the Most-Sought-After Director in Hollywood." *New York*, February 15, 2021. https://www.vulture.com/article/chloe-zhao-nomadland.html

Wolf, Naomi. 2009. "Carrie Bradshaw: Icons of the Decade." *The Guardian*, December 21, 2009. https://www.theguardian.com/world/2009/dec/22/carrie-bradshaw-icons-of-decade

ESPN
Bristol-Myers Squibb
NFL
THE SPORTS
AWARDS

Introduction

This chapter presents information and visuals that provide insights into the subject of women in American media. The "Data" section presents summaries of research reports focused on different aspects of the representation of women in film, scripted television, news, and advertising industries. Information about underrepresented demographic groups is also shared. The "Documents" section culls together a series of texts that build on subjects explored in the book. First, some early twentieth-century texts are presented and discussed. Government documents then highlight some specific ongoing concerns identified by critics, scholars, and industry insiders. Here, readers will find testimonial excerpts addressing such topics as mediated representations of older American women, stereotypical images of women in the media, and challenges women journalists face. The chapter ends with an explanation of proposed legislation that aims to address disparities in media diversity.

Data

Film

In the early 1900s, film studios in Hollywood began to establish themselves as industry leaders. At this time, women worked as

---

Hannah Storm attends the 4th Annual Sports Humanitarian Awards. Storm is an experienced television sports journalist. She and colleague Andrea Kremer made history as the first female duo broadcasting team to cover NFL games. (Hutchinsphoto/Dreamstime.com)

producers, writers, directors, editors, and actors (Mahar 2001). However, while women continued to act in films as the industry grew, the establishment of the Hollywood studio system resulted in decreased female participation in the industry in other areas (Amaral et al. 2020). The Hollywood studio system was a business model that dominated the production, distribution, and exhibition of films in theaters. The Big Five major film production companies—MGM, Warner Brothers, Paramount, Twentieth Century Fox, and RKO—controlled all aspects of the industry and produced 90 percent of fiction films in the United States; additionally, American films were featured on 80 percent of international screens during the first part of the twentieth century (Giannetti 2008). This state of affairs lasted until 1948, when the U.S. Supreme Court required studios to divest themselves of their theaters.

Figure 5.1 shows percentages of women working as film producers, directors, and writers over 100 years of the film industry, beginning in 1910 and ending in 2010, sixty-two years after the 1948 ruling. The presented data is from an analysis of more than 26,000 movies produced in the United States. The researchers note the "dearth of female representation among movie producers during the heydays of the studio system is strongly associated with lower levels of female representation among directors, screenwriters and actors" (Amaral et al. 2020, 2). However, this data may not convey the full story. J. E. Smyth's (2018) research suggests that women's roles as producers, creatives, and writers were not always credited or documented in film histories. She argues that crediting the directors of films as sole creative leaders erases the complex collaborative process that informs the making of a film, a process in which many women were engaged.

Other examinations of women in the film industry document the representation of women in twenty-first-century movies. For example, the University of California's Annenberg Inclusion Initiative is focused on documenting the portrayals and contributions of typically underrepresented groups

Figure 5.1. Percentages of Women Working in Hollywood: 1910–2010

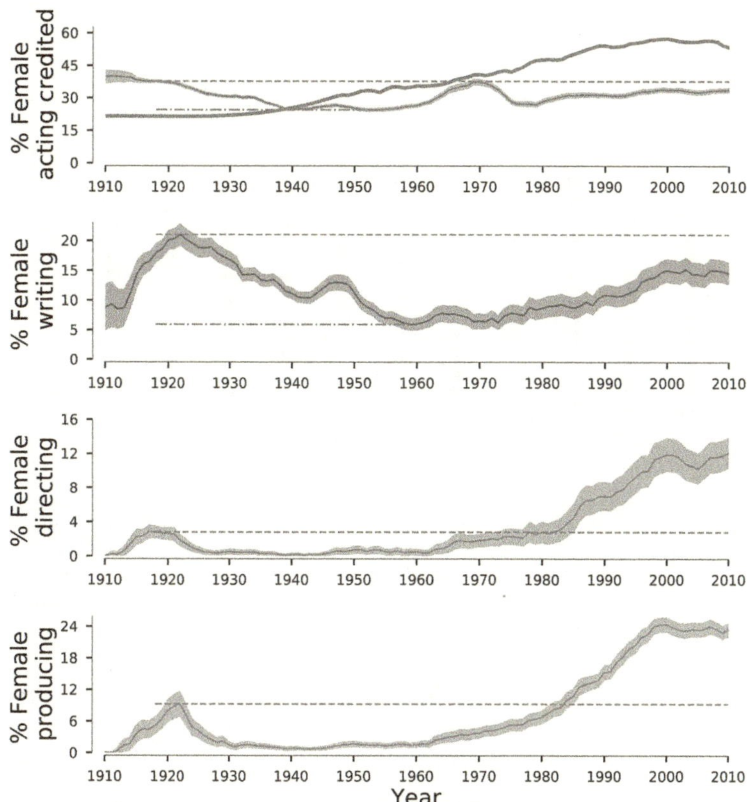

Source: Amaral, Luis Nunes, Joao Moreira, Murielle Dunand, Heliodoro Tejedor Navarro, and Ada Lee Hyojun. 2020. "Long-Term Patterns of Gender Imbalance in an Industry without Ability or Level of Interest Differences." *PLoS ONE* 15 (4): e0229662. https://doi.org/10.1371/journal.pone.0229662.

in Hollywood. Figure 5.2 displays the percentages of named or speaking male and female characters seen in the 100 top-grossing films of each year from 2007 to 2018, demonstrating that male characters continue to outnumber their female counterparts.

Complementing this analysis is the team's calculation of how many films feature gender-balanced casts, where 45–54.9 percent of the total cast is female. The scholars point out that

Figure 5.2. Percentages of Male and Female Characters in the Top Films of Each Year: 2007–2018

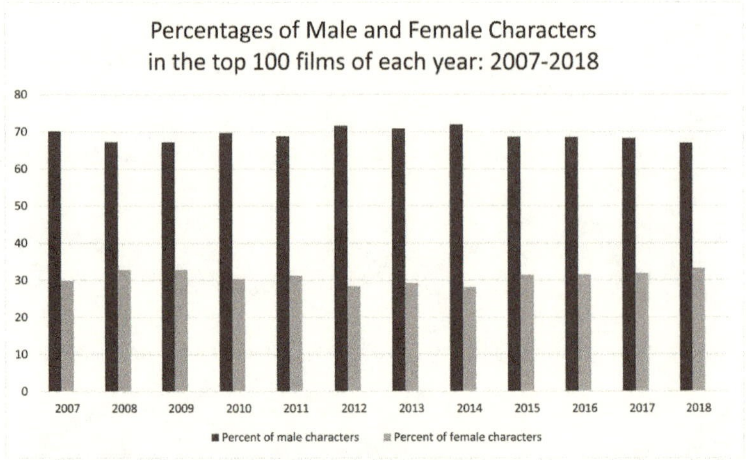

Source: Smith, Stacy, Marc Choueiti, Katherine Pieper, Kevin Yao, Ariana Case, and Angel Choi. 2019. *Inequality in 1,200 Popular Films: Examining Portrayals of Gender, Race/Ethnicity, LGBTQ & Disability from 2007 to 2018*. Annenberg Inclusion Initiative at USC Annenberg's School for Communication and Journalism. http://assets.uscannenberg.org/docs/aii-inequality-report-2019-09-03.pdf.

although girls and women comprise about half of the population and are half of the movie ticket–purchasing audience, the representation of them on-screen remains lacking. Between 2007 and 2018, the highest percentage of films with gender-balanced casts was 19 percent in 2017. In 2018, just 9 percent of the 100 top-grossing films feature gender-balanced casts. Figure 5.3 displays the percentages of films with gender-balanced casts in the top 100 films of each year from 2007 to 2018. Readers should note that the percentage tops out at 20 percent on the graph, as no year exceeded the 19 percent of films featuring gender-balanced casts that was achieved in 2017.

Despite the current cultural focus on diversity and inclusion in Hollywood over the past few years, the top 100 box office films of 2018 did not feature especially diverse casts. As table 5.1 demonstrates, there is notable exclusion of women from underrepresented groups in these films.

A subsequent report focused on Latinos in film, both in front of and behind the camera, suggests that Latinos are "erased" in

Figure 5.3. Percentages of Films with Gender-Balanced Casts in the Top 100 Films of Each Year: 2007–2018

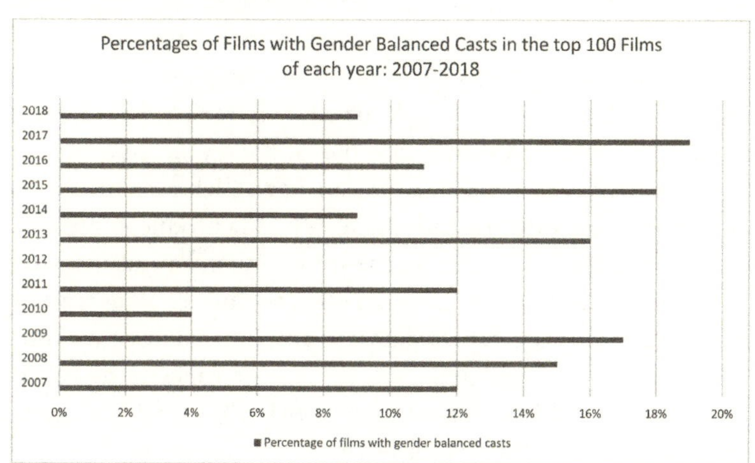

Source: Smith, Stacy, Marc Choueiti, Katherine Pieper, Kevin Yao, Ariana Case, and Angel Choi. 2019. *Inequality in 1,200 Popular Films: Examining Portrayals of Gender, Race/Ethnicity, LGBTQ & Disability from 2007 to 2018*. Annenberg Inclusion Initiative at USC Annenberg's School for Communication and Journalism. http://assets.uscannenberg.org/docs/aii-inequality-report-2019-09-03.pdf.

Table 5.1. Exclusion of Underrepresented Women in the Top 100 Films of 2018

Underrepresented Group	Number of Films *without* These Characters
LGBT females	89
Latinas	70
Asian or Asian American females	54
Black or African American females	33
Multiracial females/females from other groups	51
Female characters with disabilities	83
American Indian/Alaska Native females	99
Native Hawaiian/Pacific Islander females	97
Middle Eastern or North African	92

Source: Smith, Stacy, Marc Choueiti, Katherine Pieper, Kevin Yao, Ariana Case, and Angel Choi. 2019. *Inequality in 1,200 Popular Films: Examining Portrayals of Gender, Race/Ethnicity, LGBTQ & Disability from 2007 to 2018*. Annenberg Inclusion Initiative at USC Annenberg's School for Communication and Journalism. http://assets.uscannenberg.org/docs/aii-inequality-report-2019-09-03.pdf.

the film industry. It found that the population of Latinos in the United States "outpaces Hollywood" in that a higher percentage of Latinx populations are present in 77 percent of the fifty states and two territories than are present in Hollywood films (Smith et al. 2019, 5). This study further documents that among the 1,200 top-grossing films from 2007 to 2018, just 3 percent, or thirty-five, feature leads or coleads who are Latinx. Seventeen of these characters are women, and five of the seventeen characters are played by one actress, Cameron Diaz. Behind the camera, only one Latina director and nineteen Latina producers are identified across the 1,200 films in the study. When Latinx characters are present, their portrayals often align with three long-running stereotypes: they are depicted absent any cultural or community context, they are depicted as criminals, or they are associated with religion. Additionally, the majority (54%) of Latinx characters are portrayed holding jobs that do not require a college education, with only 4 percent of characters depicted in educated professional positions. Finally, Latina characters are more likely to be sexualized than their Latino counterparts in film and are more likely to be sexualized than Black or Asian women.

Scripted Television

The scholars and organizations examining the representation of women on scripted television from broadcast, cable, and streaming services routinely document categories of portrayals of gender, race, and ethnicity. Martha Lauzen's 2019 sample of television programs from broadcast networks, cable, and streaming platforms in 2018–2019 included a data set of over 5,100 characters. Of the major characters, defined as characters who are part of the story narrative and are present in more than one scene, 45 percent were female, a "historic high." In the sample of television programs collected from the 2017 to 2018 season, 40 percent of the major television characters are female. However, the majority of the major female characters in the 2018–2019 sample are white. Figure 5.4 displays the demographic breakdown of female television characters across broadcast networks, cable, and streaming platforms in a sample of programs from the 2018 to 2019 season.

Figure 5.4. Race/Ethnicity of over 5,100 Female Characters on Television: 2018–2019

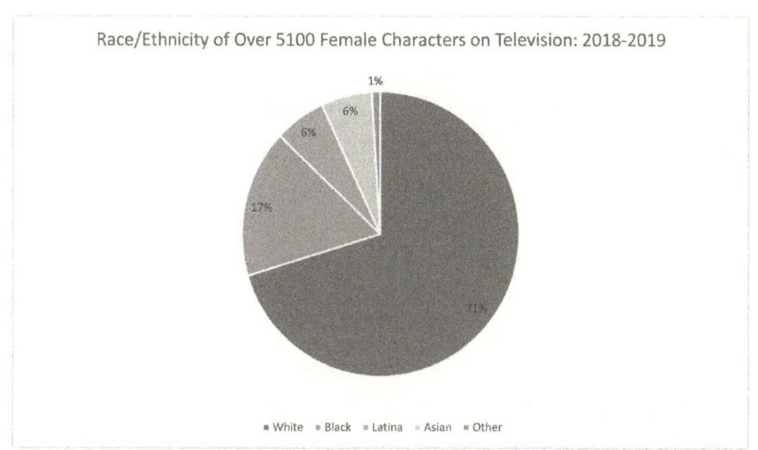

Lauzen, Martha. 2019. *Boxed In 2018–19: Women on Screen and behind the Scenes in Television*. Center for the Study of Women in Television & Film at San Diego State University. https://womenintvfilm.sdsu.edu/wp-content/uploads/2019/09/2018-19_Boxed_In_Report.pdf.

However, a 2019 GLAAD Media Institute report examining the 2019 television season notes that the number of racially and ethnically diverse characters on broadcast prime-time television continues to increase, a trend documented over several years (Townsend et al. 2019). The study identifies 264 white men and 203 white women as series characters, a bit of an unbalance. This unbalance is not as present among characters of color. The study authors write, "The gender balance between characters of colors overall comes closer to parity, 199 series regular women of color and 210 men of color. There are 85 Black women series regular characters, and 111 Black men characters. In all other demographics, women outnumber men. Latinx women outnumber the men, 43 women to 37 men; while there are 36 Asian Pacific-Islander (API) women and 31 API men, and there are 35 women characters of another race or multiracial compared to 31 men." On broadcast network television, 23 percent of all series regulars are women of color, and "women of color represent 49 percent of all characters of color, and 49.5 percent of all women characters" (Townsend et al. 2019, 14).

Where LGBTQ characters have historically not been routinely represented on television, many twenty-first-century scripted television programs feature reoccurring and regular LGBTQ characters. A recent GLAAD report documents this increasing amount of LGBTQ characters on television. It finds that in 2019, 33 percent of regular or reoccurring LGBTQ+ characters on broadcast television were lesbians, 30 percent of LGBTQ+ characters were lesbians on cable, and 30 percent of LGBTQ characters were lesbians on streaming; the numbers were 25 percent, 26 percent and 33 percent, respectively, in 2018 (Townsend et al. 2019). Across all television platforms, gay male characters outnumber lesbian women. The research report also notes the existence of few trans women on broadcast (two characters) and streaming television (five characters), but there were fourteen trans women characters on cable programming. Table 5.2 displays the numbers of LGBTQ characters on television platforms during the 2019 television season, and table 5.3 displays the sexual orientation of these LGBTQ characters.

Table 5.2. Number of LGBTQ Characters on Network, Cable, and Streaming Television Platforms in the 2019 Television Season

	Network (ABC, CBS, CW, Fox, NBC) Prime-Time Television Shows	Cable Television Prime-Time Television Shows	Streaming Television Shows on Netflix, Hulu, and Amazon Prime
Number of LGBTQ series regular characters	90	121	109
Number of LGBTQ reoccurring characters	30	94	44
Total regular and reoccurring LGBTQ characters	120	215	153

Source: Townsend, Megan, Raina Deerwater, Nick Adams, and Monica Trasandes. 2019. "Where We Are on TV: 2019–2020." GLAAD Media Institute Report, GLAAD. https://www.glaad.org/sites/default/files/GLAAD%20WHERE%20WE%20ARE%20ON%20TV%202019%202020.pdf.

Table 5.3. Sexual Orientation of Regular and Reoccurring LGBTQ Characters in the 2019 Television Season

	Network (ABC, CBS, CW, Fox, NBC) Prime-Time Television Shows (120 Total LGBTQ Characters)	Cable Television Prime-Time Television Shows (215 Total LGBTQ Characters)	Streaming Television Shows (153 Total LGBTQ Characters)
Number of lesbian characters	40 (33%)	65 (30%)	46 (30%)
Number of gay characters	46 (38%)	74 (34%)	64 (42%)
Number of bisexual characters	30 (25%)	61 (28%)	36 (24%)
Number of straight LGBTQ characters	4 (3%)	13 (6%)	5 (3%)
Number of asexual characters	0	0	1 (1%)
Number of characters whose orientation is unknown	0	1 (0.5%)	2 (1%)

Source: Townsend, Megan, Raina Deerwater, Nick Adams, and Monica Trasandes. 2019. "Where We Are on TV: 2019–2020." GLAAD Media Institute Report, GLAAD. https://www.glaad.org/sites/default/files/GLAAD%20WHERE%20WE%20ARE%20ON%20TV%202019%202020.pdf.

News

A recent Women's Media Center (WMC; 2019) report, *The Status of Women in the U.S. Media 2019*, documents gender disparity between men and women journalists working on evening television broadcasts, in print, on internet platforms, and for wire services. The report finds a majority of journalists who report the news are men, accounting for 63 percent of all bylines and credits across all media platforms. The research also documents that more news is written by men than women online (60% of stories) and in print (59% of stories). In its review of prime-time broadcast news programs on ABC, CBS, NBC, and PBS, the WMC notes that men report twice as much as women in their roles as anchors and correspondents overall, contributing to a large gender gap in the industry. Table 5.4 presents the WMC's gender breakdown of anchors, correspondents, and reporters at each of these networks. Readers should keep in mind that this data was collected before Nora O'Donnell became the *CBS Evening News* anchor in 2019. As of 2021, two of the national evening network news broadcasts are anchored by women (O'Donnell and PBS's Judy Woodruff), and two are anchored by men (ABC's David Muir and NBC's Lester Holt).

The *Status of Women in the U.S. Media 2019* notes that the gender gaps are additionally present when it comes to who reports what type of news. In general, men are more likely to report on such topics as international news, technology, and elections, while women are more likely to report on topics such as lifestyle and leisure. Table 5.5 displays WMC's analysis of the percentages of women reporting on specific categories of news in print news, internet news, and newswire services.

On the local television news front, the trend of hiring women and women of color has produced gains in equitable representation. The *2021 RTNDA/Newhouse School at Syracuse University Newsroom Survey* report, authored by Bob Papper, indicates that 43.9 percent of the local television news force are women. Although this is a decrease from the 44.7 percent reported the year before, the decrease is attributed to the trend of women leaving the workforce as a result of the impact of COVID-19 (Papper 2021). Additionally, Papper notes, "For the first time in more than 25 years of the annual survey, all local TV newsroom respondents have women on the news team" (6). The

Table 5.4. Who Is Delivering News on Prime-Time Evening Broadcasts?

National Prime-Time News Broadcast Program	Percentage of Anchors, Correspondents, and Reporters Who Are Women	Percentage of Anchors, Correspondents, and Reporters Who Are Men
ABC World News Tonight	35%	65%
CBS Evening News	38%	62%
NBC Nightly News	38%	62%
PBS NewsHour	36%	64%

Source: Women's Media Center. 2019. *The Status of Women in the U.S. Media 2019*. https://womensmediacenter.com/reports/the-status-of-women-in-u-s-media-2019.

Table 5.5. Percentages of Women Journalists Reporting in Different News Areas

News Category	Percentage of Women Reporting in Print News	Percentage of Women Reporting in Internet News	Percentage of Women Reporting in News Wire Services
Sports	10%	21%	14%
Technology and media	33%	43%	7%
International news and politics	34%	41%	30%
Business and economy	36%	43%	43%
Arts and culture	37%	48%	29%
U.S. elections	39%	26%	37%
U.S. policy	41%	40%	41%
Legal	41%	35%	20%
Weather	43%	39%	34%
Crime and police	44%	41%	27%
Science and environment	45%	40%	40%
Religion	46%	45%	40%
Social and justice	46%	47%	37%
Education	48%	48%	58%
Entertainment	49%	47%	65%
Lifestyle and leisure	52%	57%	50%
Health	58%	59%	39%

Source: Women's Media Center. 2019. *The Status of Women in the U.S. Media 2019.* https://womensmediacenter.com/reports/the-status-of-women-in-u-s-media-2019.

report additionally found that 39.1 percent of news directors are women, continuing increases documented over the past six years. However, just 22.8 percent of television general managers are women. When considering the breakdown of women of color working in television news, Papper found that "of people of color, women are better represented among Hispanic/Latino Americans, African Americans and Asian Americans. Native Americans in TV news are predominantly men" (4). Table 5.6 describes the overall presence of women and men of color working in local television news per the RTNDA/Newhouse School survey.

Table 5.6. Women and Men of Color Working in Local Television News

	Percentage of the Local TV Workforce (Over 1,300 Stations)	Percentage of Women	Percentage of Men
African American	12.3%	56.6%	43.3%
Hispanic/Latino	12.2%	50.8%	49.2%
Asian American	2.8%	62.5%	37.5%
Native American	0.4%	30.6%	69.4%

Source: Papper, Bob. 2021. "Local Broadcast Newsroom Diversity." *2021 RTDNA/Newhouse School at Syracuse University Newsroom Survey*. https://www.rtdna.org/uploads/files/2021%20RTDNA-Syracuse%20Research%20-%20Local%20News%20Diversity.pdf.

Sports Media

Overall, sports media coverage of women's sports pales in comparison to sports media coverage of men's sports. Some argue coverage of women's sports is lacking because sports media outlets do not think there are audiences for women's sports and because shrinking newspaper budgets and staff result in attention by sports journalists and columnists focusing on men's professional teams with known fan bases (Lamke 2013; Springer 2019). Social media platforms, however, provide opportunities for additional, and diverse, reporting on women athletes and sports. As scholars Miles Romney and Rich Johnson point out, "Social media platforms (SMPs) differ from traditional media in that space is not a finite resource restricted to time (broadcast) or print space (newspapers). These limitations are often used by SNs [sports networks] to justify the abundance of popular or profitable sports content" (Romney and Johnson 2020, 739). Romney and Johnson examined whether there is gender-equitable sports coverage on the main Instagram platforms from ESPN, Fox Sports, NBC Sports, and CBS Sports from a sample of 1,587 images gathered between July 2015 and July 2016. Their analysis shows that women and women athletes are underrepresented compared to men and men athletes and that women are more likely to be seen passively in images, reinforcing established trends in gendered sports reporting. Figure 5.5 summarizes some of their findings.

Figure 5.5. Gender and Athlete Breakdown of 1,587 Instagram Images from ESPN, Fox Sports, NBC Sports, and CBS Sports

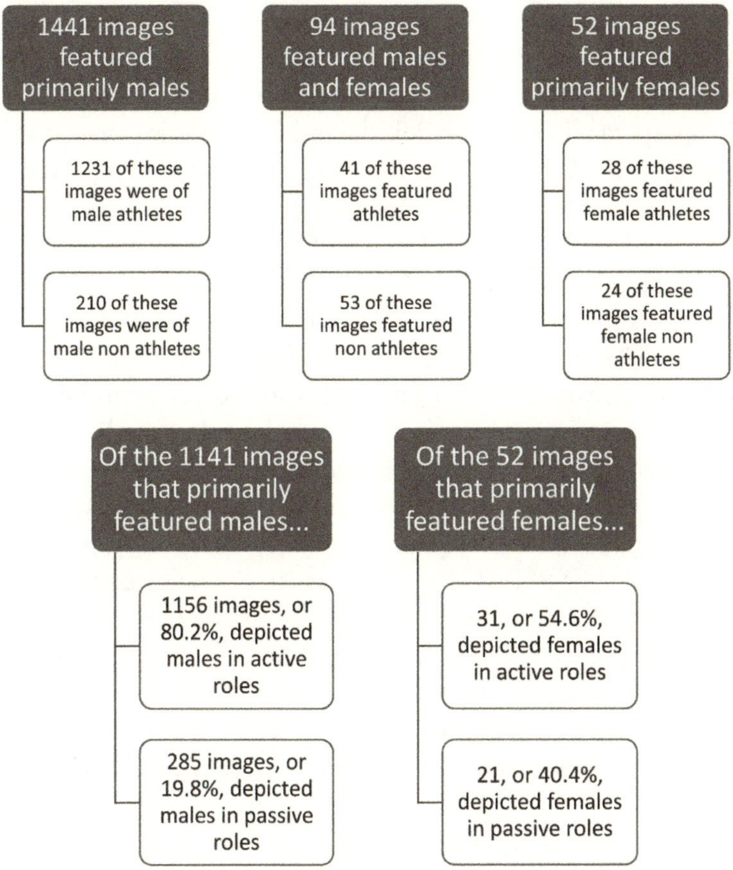

1441 images featured primarily males

- 1231 of these images were of male athletes
- 210 of these images were of male non athletes

94 images featured males and females

- 41 of these images featured athletes
- 53 of these images featured non athletes

52 images featured primarily females

- 28 of these images featured female athletes
- 24 of these images featured female non athletes

Of the 1141 images that primarily featured males...

- 1156 images, or 80.2%, depicted males in active roles
- 285 images, or 19.8%, depicted males in passive roles

Of the 52 images that primarily featured females...

- 31, or 54.6%, depicted females in active roles
- 21, or 40.4%, depicted females in passive roles

Source: Romney, Miles, and Rich G. Johnson. 2020. "The Ball Game Is for the Boys: The Visual Framing of Female Athletes on National Sports Networks' Instagram Accounts." *Communication & Sport* 8 (6): 738–756. https://doi.org/10.1177/2167479519836731.

The demographics of who is covering both men's and women's sports provides additional insight into the industry. The *Associated Press Sports Editors Racial and Gender Report Card* evaluates the demographic breakdown of sports media staff at over seventy-five newspapers and websites. This report is published by the Institute for Diversity and Ethics in Sport (TIDES) at the University of Central Florida and was requested by the

Associated Press Sports Editors (ASPE). The analysis, one that is completed every few years, looks at racial and gender hiring practices, noting shifting percentages of sports media staffs that are women or people of color. Data from 2014, 2017, and 2021 demonstrate that although more women have been hired in sports media roles, overall, the industry remains male dominated. Table 5.7 shows the percentage of women employed as sports reporters, columnists, editors, and assistant or deputy editors in 2014, 2017, and 2021 at APSE newspapers and websites.

Richard Lapchick, the study's author, identifies ESPN as a leader in hiring women in all key positions, notably as sports columnists and assistant sports editors. Removing ESPN employees from the data sets results in a decrease in percentages of women working in these roles at other media outlets. For example, although the largest area of growth for women from 2014 to 2017 is the assistant/deputy sports editor position, "of the 89 women who were assistant sports editors, 75 worked for ESPN. If the ESPN assistant sports editors were removed, the percentage of female assistant sports editors would drop from 30.1 percent to 6.3 percent" (Lapchick 2018, 8). A similar trend was noted in the 2021 report, where data shows "25.0 percent (five of 20) of all the women who were sports editors worked at ESPN; 51.8 percent (43 of 83) of all

Table 5.7. Percentages of Women Employed at Associated Press Sports Editor (ASPE) Newspapers and Websites: 2014, 2017, and 2021

	2014	2017	2021
Sports reporters	12.6%	11.5%	14.4%
Sports columnists	12.4%	16.6%	17.8%
Sports editors	8.6%	10%	16.7%
Assistant/deputy sports editors	9.8%	30.1%	24.2%

Sources: Lapchick, Richard. 2018. *The 2018 Associated Press Editors Racial and Gender Report Card*. Institute for Diversity and Ethics in Sport at the University of Central Florida, May 2, 2018. https://www.tidesport.org/associated-press-sports-editors; Lapchick, Richard. 2021. *The 2021 Associated Press Editors Racial and Gender Report Card*. Institute for Diversity and Ethics in Sport at the University of Central Florida, September 22, 2021. https://www.tidesport.org/associated-press-sports-editors.

the women who were assistant sports editors worked for ESPN; 38.1 percent (8 of 21) of all the women who were columnists worked at ESPN; 20.5 percent (30 of 146) of all the women who were reporters worked for ESPN; and 15.9 percent (7 of 44) of all the women who were copy editors/designers worked for ESPN" (Lapchick 2021, 3).

Advertising

The advertising industry is frequently criticized for objectifying women as sexual objects, in large part because it glorifies and glamorizes only a narrow range of female ages, body types, and other characteristics. A 2020 Geena Davis Institute study examines 251 Cannes Lions Film and Film Craft advertisements from 2019, finding that 38.4 percent of characters in ads are women, 7 percent are over sixty years old, 38 percent are characters of color, 1.7 percent are LGBTQ+ characters, 2.2 percent are characters with disabilities, and 7.2 percent are characters with large body types.

In examining the contexts of the portrayals, the research identified the following trends: women are more likely to be sexualized, larger women are more likely to be seen as funny or lazy, and older women, while often positively portrayed as smart leaders, are rarely seen. Pointing out that better representation of traditionally underrepresented groups should remain a focus in the industry, the report calls for companies to "write and cast more female characters, sexualize them less, and show them as funny and having authority" (Geena Davis Institute on Gender in Media 2020, 8). Table 5.8 summarizes the report's findings on instances where women are framed as sex objects in the sample of ads that were examined. While the percentages are not large overall, it is notable that women are much more likely to be sexually objectified than their male counterparts.

In 2015, SHE Media launched an advertising industry awards program to recognize campaigns defying stereotypical images of gender and implicitly encouraging the promotion of goods and services that do not rely on such tropes. According to the Femvertising Awards website, SHE Media wanted to

Table 5.8. Percentage of Advertising Characters Framed as Sex Objects in 251 Cannes Lions Film and Film Craft 2019 Advertisements

	Women	Men
Characters shown in revealing clothing	10.8%	2.2%
Characters shown as partially nude	8.1%	4.5%
Characters shown as visually objectified	1.8%	0.6%
Characters who are verbally objectified	1.2%	0.2%

Source: Geena Davis Institute on Gender in Media. 2020. *Bias & Inclusion in Advertising: An Analysis of 2019 Cannes Lions Work*. https://seejane.org/wp-content/uploads/bias-and-inclusion-in-advertising-cannes-lions.pdf.

"honor brands that are challenging gender norms by building stereotype-busting, pro-female messages and images into ads that target women and girls." Campaigns are recognized in such categories as humor, inspiration, and social impact. The establishment of the awards emerged from surveys distributed by SHE Media (then known as SheKnows Media) that found 94 percent of women respondents agreed that depicting women as sex objects in advertising is problematic; 52 percent indicated they bought a product because they like the pro-female ad approach in the product's promotion; and 62 percent believed any brand can enter the "pro-female space" (SheKnows Living Editors 2014). While some scholars are critical of appropriating feminist ideals in advertising, the approaches and imagery used in femvertising campaign nominees and winners challenge often seen gender tropes. Table 5.9 lists the names of the winning femvertising campaigns since the award's inception.

Table 5.9. #Femvertising Award Winners: 2015–2019

2015 Award Winners	First Moon Party (HelloFlo), Courage Inside (Ram Trucks), #LikeAGirl (Always), Speak Beautiful (Dove and Twitter), Daily Business (Sayfty), This Girl Can (Sport England), Women of Worth (L'Oreal Paris)
2016 Award Winners	Dad-do (Pantene), The Bud-Light Party: Equal Pay (Bud Light), Rule Yourself: Women's Gymnastics (Under Armour), Why Girls Can't Code (Girls Who Code, the Red Elephant Foundation), #WomenNotObjects (Badger & Winters)

Table 5.9. *(continued)*

2017 Award Winners	#ThisBody Is Made to Shine (Lane Bryant), Daughter (Audi), Raising an Olympian: Simone Biles, "Guide and Trust" (P&G), Just Dad (Angel Soft), Being a Woman Transcends the Body (L'Oreal Paris), Fearless Girl (State Street Global Advisors), #MoreThanMean (Just Not Sports), #UnitedByHalf (United Colors of Benetton, Calia), "What Sports Taught Me" (Dick's Sporting Goods)
2018 Award Winners	I'm No Angel (Lane Bryant), #MoreRoleModels (Mattel/Barbie), Your Hair Talks, Make a Statement (John Frieda), I Am What I Make Up (Cover Girl), #SheDrives (Nissan), The Wonder of Us (Coca-Cola), Dippers (Oreos)
2019 Award Winners	The Ball Is in Her Court (Bumble), Cheer for Each Other—All Strength, No Sweat (Secret), We All Win (Microsoft), Her First Baseball Game (Facebook Groups), RITAS Spritz—Subtle Notes (Bud Light), A PSA by Monica Lewinsky (#DEFYTHENAME)

Sources: Business Wire. 2015. "SheKnowsMedia Announces Winners of the Femvertising Awards and the Pitch at #BlogHer15: Experts among Us." July 21, 2015. https://www.businesswire.com/news/home/20150721005752/en/SheKnows-Media-Announces-Winners-of-the-Femvertising-Awards-and-The-Pitch-at-BlogHer15-Experts-Among-Us; Business Wire. 2016. "SheKnowsMedia Announces Winners of the 2016 #Femvertising Awards at Advertising Week New York." September 26, 2016. https://www.businesswire.com/news/home/20160926006445/en/SheKnows-Media-Announces-Winners-of-the-2016-Femvertising-Awards-at-Advertising-Week-New-York; Joskowitz, Lauren. 2017. "The Winners of the 2017 #Femvertising Awards Are In." SheKnows, September 26, 2017. https://www.sheknows.com/entertainment/articles/1136262/femvertising-award-winners-2017/; SHE Media. 2018. "SHE Media Announces 4th Annual #Femvertising Awards Winners." August 8, 2018. https://www.shemedia.com/she-media-announces-4th-annual-femvertising-awards-winners; SHE Media. n.d. "Celebrating 5 Years of Femvertising." Femvertisingawards.com. Accessed November 1, 2020. https://www.emvertisingawards.com/.

Documents

Document 5.1. *Picturesque America, Anywhere in the Mountains* by Charles Dana Gibson, c. 1900

Scholars point to the nineteenth-century magazine as the first form of mass media developed for a national audience (Kitch 2001). Such magazines prioritized the images and experiences of white women, and their depictions of women on their covers and in their pages led to the establishment of the first mass media stereotypes of

women. One of the first of these stereotypical images that defined the "ideal" woman was the "Gibson Girl," an image of a slim, well-dressed, beautiful, and confident woman imagined in a series of pen-and-ink drawings by Charles Dana Gibson (Kitch 2001). Gibson's drawings permeated the culture for about twenty years, advancing images of the ideal woman while also reflecting changing ideas about women in the culture.

The image in this document, featured in the Library of Congress's exhibit "Gibson Girl's America: The Gibson Girl as the New Woman," is described by the Library of Congress in the following way: "With casual grace, two elegantly dressed young women repose on the rocky ledges of a rugged mountainside. The hikers who hail or wave to one another frame the central pair and animate the expansive scene. Gibson's meticulous depiction of their hats accentuates the Gibson Girls' stylish attire and visually reinforces the impression of height, leading the eye to the mountains. In this classic, often reproduced image, Gibson shows off the classic Gibson Girl as a figure who embraced outdoor physical activities."

Source: Gibson, Charles Dana. c. 1900. *Picturesque America, Anywhere in the Mountains*. Pen and ink over graphite. Retrieved October 1, 2020, from the Library of Congress. https://www.loc.gov/pictures/item/2010716157/.

Document 5.2. O'Hara, Neal R. 1920. "Those Fluttering Flappers: The Demi-Dame Who Is Too Young to Marry and Too Old to Believe in Santa." *New York Evening World*, April 20, 1920

In the 1920s, the dominant image of the New Woman was the "flapper," a slim, youthful, fashionable woman who was comfortable with her independence, sexuality, and role as a consumer. The popularity of the flapper style marked a shift in ways women were conceptualized in popular culture and in the culture itself.

The 1920 commentary on flappers below references figures who likely were recognizable to readers at the time. They include the novelist Louisa May Alcott, author of Little Women (1868); *author Elinor Glyn, whose romantic fiction was considered scandalous at the time; Terpsichore, one of the nine muses in Greek mythology and the goddess of dancing and chorus; the Arctic explorer Robert Peary; and the author Robert W. Chambers, known for his gothic horror stories.*

Those Fluttering Flappers: The Demi-Dame Who Is Too Young to Marry and Too Old to Believe in Santa by Neal R. O'Hara

Something they didn't have in the hoopskirt era was the flapper you see to-day. Up to the time Taft slipped from President to professor and Wilson went vice versa, the flapper was practically unknown. But in the last seven or eight years she's been busting into more prominence than a red nose and more trouble than a Red agitator.

All the world's a stage to-day, and the flapper is the ingenue. She is the demi-dame that's too young to be married and to [*sic*] old to believe in Santa Claus, hair ribbons and Louisa May Alcott. She runs from sweet sixteen to twinkling twenty but that's all she does run from.

Flappers are born not made up, but it doesn't take them long to hit the red paint stride. Most of 'em graduate from low heels to high heels and high necks to low ones before they graduate from high school.

They get double meanings a long time before they get double chins, but they still get by with their baby faces. There is as much difference between a flapper and a vamp as there is between an Easter egg and a hard-boiled one.

But don't overlook the fact that to-day's Easter egg can be to-morrow's breakfast with only a little alteration.

Twenty years ago the flappers thought fairy tales were Big Stuff. Cinderella stood out as the last word in literature, and

Jack and the Beanstalk was packed with thrills. To-day the juvenile smart set has different ideas. Little Red Riding Hood is little read but Elinor Glyn hits on all eight cylinders. To-day the flappers pass up the circus to take in the latest bedroom farces. They can keep track of the plot and all that happens behind the six doors.

On a ballroom floor, the flap is neither handicapped nor shoulder bound. She has more steps than the State Capitol and more stamina than an army mule. From tiara to toes, she's Terpsichore. She understands men and horses and literature and bridge. And she knows New York from the Aquarium at Battery Park to the Zoo in the Bronx. She may be rusty on ham and eggs, but she does know life and the nine shades it's colored in.

Flapperism is still young, but no more so than the flappers. It has spread like the flu and it's awful catching. A gal in a gingham dress has only to grab off a lavaliere, a low-neck gown and a lipstick, and right away she's a fluttering flapper. Peary never discovered anything colder than a chiffon frock but the flappers like 'em just the same. Eve was created too old to be a flapper, but she had flap ideas about clothes and pneumonia.

The flapper at eighteen is practically harmless, but she's got a large future looming before her. With all her girlish curves, she grows up to be an angle in some eternal triangle. The dames that get too much attending on the blushing side of twenty very often get too little alimony on the wrinkled side of thirty. However, eternal triangles are spicier for a boarding school Beatrice to think about plane geometry.

But what happens after flapper-hood can't scare a dame that's studied Robert W. Chambers. A jane that isn't a flapper before she's a bride ain't ever a bride! Flap and the world flaps with you, flop and you flop alone.

Source: O'Hara, Neal R. "Those Fluttering Flappers: The Demi-Dame Who Is Too Young to Marry and Too Old to Believe in Santa." *New York Evening World*, April 20, 1920.

Document 5.3 Congressional Hearing: "The Image of Aging in Media and Marketing"

As *numerous studies of the ways older women and men are represented in American media have documented, American movies, television shows, and other popular culture outlets did not often feature diverse representations of older Americans in the early 2000s. Few such developed characters appeared on prime-time television programming or in popular films. Excerpts from this congressional hearing, which took place on September 4, 2002, describe the issues connected to the absence of quality representations of older men and women in the media, despite the fact that members of this demographic make up a notable percentage of the population. Data suggests members of this demographic hold significant consumer spending power—something for-profit media industries might better consider. The hearings included testimony from actor Doris Roberts, who played actor Ray Romano's mother in the long-running hit television series* Everybody Loves Raymond *(1996–2005).*

Excerpt of: OPENING STATEMENT OF SENATOR JOHN BREAUX, CHAIRMAN

We have all sat through films in which a 60-something leading man is paired together with a 20-something leading lady. We have also seen older people mocked and younger people celebrated for the purposes of selling a product.

It is clear that entertainment, marketing and news industries value youth. What this hearing will address today is the fact that often the media's obsession with youth comes at the expense of older Americans. In fact, 75 percent of older consumers are dissatisfied with the marketing efforts that are directed at them, and often even avoid buying products whose ads are negative and stereotypical.

In the quest to target youth, the media and the marketing industries ignore the purchasing power and the preferences of millions of American baby boomers and seniors across our country, the population that incidentally controls about three-fourths of the wealth of our nation.

Statistics are disturbing from what our committee has learned. As an example, adults 65 and older comprise 13 percent of the U.S. population, but only 2 percent of the characters on prime time television. An example further is that 77 of the 122 prime time television series did not employ a single writer over the age of 50. Also, less than 10 percent of today's advertising in our media focuses on people over 50, although this is a group [that] by the year 2040 will be 40 percent of the entire population of the United States of America.

Also, 50 and over adults buy 41 percent of all the new cars and 48 percent of all the luxury automobiles. Today 50-plus adults represent 80 percent of all luxury travel and spend 74 percent more on a typical vacation than Americans between the ages of 18 and 49. Older consumers, for example, are also spending three times the national average on health care products and services.

* * *

Excerpt of: STATEMENT OF DORIS ROBERTS, EMMY AWARD WINNING ACTRESS, "EVERYBODY LOVES RAYMOND," LOS ANGELES, CA

Thank you. Mr. Chairman, members of the committee, thank you very much for inviting me to talk with you about ageism. I am in my seventies, at the peak of my career, at the height of my earned income, and my tax contributions, I might add. When my grandchildren say that I rock, they are not talking about a chair.

Yet society considers me discardable. My peers and I are portrayed as dependent, helpless, unproductive and demanding rather than deserving. In reality, the majority of seniors are self-sufficient middle-class consumers with more assets than most young people and the time and talent to offer society.

This is not just a sad situation, Mr. Chairman. This is a crime. In the next 25 years, more than 115 million Americans will be 50 and over. They will become the largest older population in history. I am here to urge you to address the devastation, cost and loss that we as a nation suffer because of age discrimination.

Age discrimination negates the value of wisdom and experience, robs us of our dignity and denies us the chance to continue to grow, to flourish, and to become all that we are capable of being. We all know that medical advances have changed the length and the quality of our lives today, but we have not, however, changed our attitudes about aging or addressed the disabling myths that disempower us.

I would like the word "old" to be stricken from our vocabulary and replaced with the word "older." My contemporaries and I are denigrated as "old," old coots, old fogies, old codgers, old geezers, old hags, old timers and old farts.

In truth, the minute you are born, you are getting older, and the later years can be some of life's most productive and creative. For the last 100 years, the average age of the Nobel Prize winner is 65. Frank Gehry designed Seattle's hip new rock museum at the age of 70. Georgia O'Keefe was productive way into her eighties. Add to the list Hitchcock, Dickens, Bernstein, Fosse, Wright, Matisse, Picasso and Einstein, just to mention a few people who produced some of their best work when they would be considered over the hill by current standards.

The entertainment industry, these image makers, are the worst perpetrators of this bigotry. We must change the negative stereotypes of aging that exist in the media, and when I was a young woman, some of the most powerful and popular actresses were women way in their forties, women such as Joan Crawford, Bette Davis, Katherine Hepburn and Barbara Stanwyck, who continued to work, getting better and better in their craft as they got older, and many of my friends, talented actresses in the 40- to 60-year-old range, are forced to live on unemployment or welfare, because of the scarcity of roles for women in that age bracket.

A Screen Actor Guild's employment survey showed that there are three times as many roles for women under 40 as there are for women 40 years old and older, even though 42 percent of Americans are older than 40. This is why some of my spectacularly talented actress friends have been forced into humiliating positions of borrowing money to just meet their mortgage payments and health insurance or begging me to see if there is a tiny part on "Everybody Loves Raymond."

It also explains why younger and younger actresses are visiting plastic surgeons; actresses in their 20s are getting Botox injections to prevent wrinkles from forming. Women start getting tummy tucks and face lifts in their thirties to forestall the day when the phone stops ringing.

When a woman hits the age of 40 in Hollywood, executives think she is too old. Well, I have got news for them. I have been fortunate to be one of a handful of actresses who has continued to work throughout my career, but it has not been easy. When I was in my forties, I heard of a great part on a new series called "Remington Steele." But I was not considered for it because I was thought to be too old, and because I was very persistent and knew the casting director, I read for it, and I got it.

The roles for women my age frequently show seniors in insulting and degrading ways. They make cartoons of the elderly. I recently turned down a role in a movie for me to play a horny grandmother who spewed foul language, exposed herself and chased after young boys. Well, I turned that one down. But I know someone who took that part.

There is a coalition to protect the way every other group is depicted in the media, but no one protects the image of the elderly. Hollywood clearly is clueless when it comes to understanding today's seniors. They are blind to the advances in medicine and self-care, and the increases in personal income have made us a force to be reckoned with and a market to be exploited.

Source: "The Image of Aging in Media and Marketing." Congressional Hearing, S. Hrg. 107–797, September 4, 2002.

https://www.govinfo.gov/app/details/CHRG-107shrg83476/CHRG-107shrg83476.

Document 5.4. House Committee on the Judiciary Hearing: "Diversity in America: The Representation of People of Color in the Media"

Numerous studies have documented that only limited progress has been made toward representative media representation of the various demographic groups in the United States. Activists, actors, and researchers argue that while there is increased awareness around this issue, more needs to be done to encourage more diverse representation in the U.S. media industry. During this September 24, 2020, hearing, multiple stakeholders provided testimony documenting the current state of media representation and explained why diversity is important. The following testimony was provided by Erika Alexander, an actor, director, and producer and the cofounder and chief creative officer of Color Farm Media, at a September 24, 2020, congressional hearing on "Representation of People of Color in the Media."

Excerpt from Ms. Erika Alexander's testimony

Now, I'm a girl from Flagstaff, Arizona. My mother was a teacher. My father was an itinerant preacher. They were both orphans. They had six kids. We lived in the Starlite hotel's two-bedroom shack, off Route 66. So of course, I expected to testify before congress. ;)

But seriously folks, perhaps some of you know me from my television work on *The Cosby Show* as Cousin Pam or as Maxine Shaw on *Living Single*. Maybe you know me from Oscar-winning film *Get Out*, or *Wu-Tang: An American Saga*. I am a two-time, NAACP Best Actress winner. I've traveled with the Royal Shakespeare Company and done six plays at the Public Theater in New York City. You may even know me as the Producer of the recent John Lewis documentary, *Good Trouble*. I'm proud to be a working actor, proud to have made my living in entertainment, but I'm one of the lucky ones.

For too long, people of color, women, LGBTQ people, [and] people with disabilities were not represented in mainstream media, or if they were, it was through harmful stereotypes. Media images have power, power to shape opinion and lives, for good or for ill.

That's why Representation Matters. We know this qualitatively and also through quantitative research from the Geena Davis Institute on Gender in Media.

I know first-hand that representation matters because of what I call the "Maxine Shaw Effect." The character of Maxine Shaw, the lawyer that I portrayed on the hit television series *Living Single* has inspired thousands of people to pursue education and careers in law and politics. The character even inspired Stacey Abrams and your esteemed colleague, Congresswoman Ayanna Pressley. These phenomenal women, and countless everyday people, have told me that the character of Maxine Shaw inspired them to pursue the law. They tell me that the only Black female attorney they saw growing up, that resonated with them, was Maxine Shaw. A ground-breaking fictional Black character inspired trail-blazing, real-life Black achievers.

And when we say representation matters, we don't just mean on-screen, but behind the camera, in the trades, in the departments, and most importantly in "the room where it happens," where decisions are made.

Let's talk about the Big Picture for a second. I have seen and experienced the structural racism and discrimination that is part of the unwritten fabric of Hollywood. When a television show can only have so many Black characters before it becomes a "Black show," and is relegated to the cultural ghetto, that's structural racism. When a certain foreign country's (China's) presumed prejudices lead to the casting of only light-skinned Black actresses in shows or films that need to make part of their profit there, that's structural racism. Most crucially, since we know that representation matters, when the faces and body types we see represented in film and television are selected and cast by a largely white executive cadre, the baked-in biases of yesterday persist, though we live in an increasingly diverse world.

Here's my experience: As a dark-skinned, Black actress, certain doors would never be open to me, no matter my accomplishments. When I was young I would never be cast as an ingenue like my white age peers. When I starred, for five years, on a hit network comedy, *Living Single*, my pay and that of my costars was only a small fraction of what our white counterparts were making on *Friends*, from the same studio. I mentioned that I was "one of the lucky ones." Here I was, a "success" by some lights, and yet I was having a hard time making a living.

My friend Viola Davis put it well in a 2018 interview with *Porter* magazine: "If Caucasian women are getting 50 percent of what men are getting paid, we're not even getting a quarter of what white women are getting paid."

Frustrated with the opportunities available, I had to expand my skill set and I taught myself how to write, to create my own entertainment properties, but here too, I encountered structural racism. I created a science fiction film and pitched it around town. I was dismayed and disheartened when a white male studio head told me I was wasting my time, that "Black people don't like science fiction," because they "don't see themselves in the future." He's saying this to me, a daughter of the people who created jazz, rock and roll, hip hop. We are the original futurists in American culture, but this well-paid white gatekeeper was telling me he knew better, and I meet those same people in the talent agencies and management companies that set the tone for the town, and set the value and the price of my work.

That's the last thing I want to address: If you want to see what and who Hollywood values, follow the money. Yes, there has been some change, yes, *Black Panther*, *Hamilton* and *Crazy*

Rich Asians made a lot of money, talk about "one of the lucky ones," but for every extraordinary exception like that, there are hundreds of mediocre films with white casts that get greenlit, filmed, marketed and awarded each year. The lack of diversity in the executive suite leads to this ongoing pandemic of exclusion on the cultural stage.

What would I suggest to remedy this state of affairs?

Well, the one super villain Black Panther would not defeat is the racist infrastructure of this industry. So the hero we need is us. We the people. And to address this complex issue it will take more than a village, it will take a nation.

The government should incentivize companies to support and fund marginalized content creators. Though artists and entertainers have been vilified as everything from radicals to spoiled babies, what we really are is small business people who make America's number one export and key to our soft power in the world, entertainment. I say, support minority small businesses.

Here's what I've done: I created Color Farm Media, a company dedicated to finding new voices. We call ourselves the "Motown of film, television and tech." Our goal is to rebrand Blackness. It's why we made the John Lewis documentary *Good Trouble*, why I'm making a film about the legendary Boys Choir of Harlem, and why I'm directing a documentary about reparations.

The seeds of the future are planted in the stories of today. If only certain stories are told, only certain lives matter. Going forward, diversity and true representation in our stories, in our entertainment will ensure that Black Lives Matter, too. Thank you.

Source: "Diversity in America: The Representation of People of Color in the Media." U.S. House Committee on the Judiciary Hearing, September 24, 2020. https://judiciary.house.gov/calendar/eventsingle.aspx?EventID=3354.

Document 5.5. Reporter Sulome Anderson Speaks Out on Challenges for Women Journalists

Women journalists face sexism, access issues, and potentially violent situations that their male colleagues may not have to endure in many countries, including the United States. In these remarks, American journalist Sulome Anderson, who has reported from Beirut, Lebanon, and New York City during her career, elaborates on some of the specific challenges women journalists encounter in their work as well as the gender pay gap among women and men in her profession. She asserts that the American government should address these issues. Anderson delivered this testimony at a hearing of the Tom Lantos Human Rights Commission, a bipartisan commission of the House of Representatives that promotes, defends, and advocates for international human rights. A component of the commission's work focuses on the treatment of journalists throughout the world.

First, I'd like to thank the Committee to Protect Journalists for asking me to speak, and the members of the Tom Lantos Human Rights Commission for their interest in this important topic.

"What's it like being a female journalist in the Middle East?" is one of the most common questions I'm asked, and my least favorite. I dislike it because I'm lucky enough to have been raised by parents who taught me I could do anything a man can do, and because it so often reflects well-meaning ignorance about the region. Yes, many parts of the Middle East are restrictive and oppressive towards women. Yes, there are places I simply cannot go and people I am unable to speak with because I'm not a man.

But I've personally managed to interview ISIS members, Hezbollah fighters, military leaders and all manner of people in situations that may seem entirely inaccessible to females from the perspective of someone unfamiliar with the Middle East.

The truth is, women actually have a few advantages over men in this context. Not only are we less threatening to sources, we're able to draw aside the curtain of cultural taboo and access other women who would not feel comfortable sharing their personal stories and traumas with male journalists. I believe that's part of the reason why so much excellent reporting out of conflict zones right now is by female correspondents. Their work helps shape public perception of these conflicts, and they give us a crucial window into the pressing issues women face in every country.

But the fact is that women in journalism face unique risks, and that's something none of us can afford to forget. Conflict reporting itself obviously carries a fair amount of danger regardless of gender; something I am acutely aware of. In March 1985, my father Terry Anderson was Middle East bureau chief of the Associated Press, covering the civil war in Lebanon, where I am now partly based. Three months before I was born, he was kidnapped by an Islamist militia and held in captivity for almost seven years. That event shaped the course of my life and career. The stories of his brutal treatment at the hands of his captors have haunted me since childhood.

What particularly disturbs me about that scenario is the knowledge that, as horrific as my father's captivity was, it pales in comparison to what I, or any female journalist, would experience in the same situation. And yet, women all over the world risk that outcome every day to report important stories, and dozens are killed or imprisoned every year. I've been fortunate enough to escape sexual assault while doing my job—at least twice, quite narrowly—but many female correspondents are not so lucky. In an industry that frowns upon perceived weakness, it is particularly difficult for women who have had such experiences to process them, heal, and continue to work.

The death of Kim Wall [a Swedish journalist murdered in August 2017 by the man she was interviewing] underscores the risks faced even by women reporting stories that appear not to be life threatening at first glance. It should also sound the alarm for an industry struggling to find a business model that provides adequate support and compensation for all journalists, especially freelancers, but particularly women. In addition to experiencing the same gender pay gap of most industries, when a reporter is being paid $250 a story—the going freelance rate for many prominent American outlets—she can't afford someone qualified to keep her safe in dangerous situations. So there needs to be an effort on the part of the media to establish satisfactory industry standards, especially for independent journalists.

At a government level, funding for programs that provide grants to women in journalism would be extremely helpful. But more generally, there needs to be an effort not to undermine and disparage the job that so many female correspondents risk their lives and bodies for. "Fake News" has become a rallying cry for dictators across the globe seeking to escape unflattering news coverage—many of whom are currently jailing or otherwise silencing women working to expose their corruption. The American government should appreciate the perils faced by these brave reporters and empower them instead of making their jobs more dangerous.

Thank you for your time.

Source: Anderson, Sulome. "Remarks for Tom Lantos Human Rights Commission." Tom Lantos Human Rights Commission briefing: "Women in Journalism: Unique Perspectives, Unique Threats," March 8, 2018. https://humanrightscommission.house.gov/events/hearings/women-journalism-unique-perspective-unique-threats.

Document 5.6. Congressional Resolution on Media Diversity

Introduced in both the House of Representatives and the U.S. Senate in September 2019, the following resolution is a response to calls for more diversity in media organizations, particularly news organizations. Led by Senators Jacky Rosen (D-NV) and Marco Rubio (R-FL) and by Representatives Val Demings (D-FL) and Jennifer González-Colón (R-PR), the resolution aims to support media messages that reflect the diversity of the nation and that are chosen and delivered by a team of professionals who represent diverse demographic groups. Senator Rosen (2019) discussed the importance of the resolution by noting, "We must make an effort to ensure that our newsrooms, production offices, and media boardrooms are reflective of America's diversity, in terms of background, identity, and ideology. This is critical now, more than ever. This resolution encapsulates these sentiments, allowing us to empower individuals to break through barriers and to ensure our nation realizes that diversity is our strength. I'm proud to join my colleagues in taking steps toward building a more diverse media landscape."

House Resolution 549/Senate Resolution 306: A resolution reaffirming the commitment to media diversity and pledging to work with media entities and diverse stakeholders to develop common ground solutions to eliminate barriers to media diversity.

Whereas the principle that an informed and engaged electorate is critical to a vibrant democracy is deeply rooted in our laws of free speech and underpins the virtues on which we established our Constitution, "in Order to form a more perfect Union, establish Justice, insure domestic Tranquility, provide for the common defence, promote the general Welfare, and secure the Blessings of Liberty to ourselves and our Posterity . . .";

Whereas having independent, diverse, and local media that provide exposure to a broad range of viewpoints and the ability to contribute to the political debate is central to sustaining that informed engagement;

Whereas it is in the public interest to encourage source, content, and audience diversity on our Nation's shared telecommunications and media platforms;

Whereas the survival of small, independent, and diverse media outlets that serve diverse audiences and local media markets is essential to preserving local culture and building understanding on important community issues that impact the daily lives of residents;

Whereas research by the American Society of News Editors, the Radio Television Digital News Association, the Pew Research Center, and others has documented the continued challenges of increasing diversity among all types of media entities;

Whereas with increasing media experience and sophistication, it is even more important to have minority participation in local media to ensure a diverse range of information sources are available and different ideas and viewpoints are expressed to strengthen social cohesion among different communities; and

Whereas the constriction in small, independent, and diverse media outlets and limited participation of diverse populations in media ownership and decision making are combining to negatively impact our goal of increasing local civic engagement and civic knowledge through increased voter participation, membership in civic groups, and knowledge of local political and civil information: Now, therefore, be it *Resolved*, That the Senate—

(1) reaffirms its commitment to diversity as a core tenet of the public interest standard in media policy; and

(2) pledges to work with media entities and diverse stakeholders to develop common ground solutions to eliminate barriers to media diversity.

Source: "A resolution reaffirming the commitment to media diversity and pledging to work with media entities and diverse stakeholders to develop common ground solutions to eliminate barriers to media diversity." H. RES. 549 (September 10,

2019). https://www.congress.gov/bill/116th-congress/house-resolution/549/text; S. RES. 306 (September 10, 2019), https://www.congress.gov/bill/116th-congress/senate-resolution/306/text.

Bibliography

Amaral, Luis Nunes, Joao Moreira, Murielle Dunand, Heliodoro Tejedor Navarro, and Ada Lee Hyojun. 2020. "Long-Term Patterns of Gender Imbalance in an Industry without Ability or Level of Interest Differences." *PLoS ONE* 15 (4): e0229662. https://doi.org/10.1371/journal.pone.0229662

The Coalition for Women in Journalism. 2020. "Detailed Reports of Threats." https://womeninjournalism.org/threats

Geena Davis Institute on Gender in Media. 2020. *Bias and Inclusion in Advertising: An Analysis of 2019 Cannes Lions Work*. https://seejane.org/wp-content/uploads/bias-and-inclusion-in-advertising-cannes-lions.pdf

Giannetti, Louis 2008. *Understanding Movies*. 11th ed. Upper Saddle River, NJ: Prentice Hall.

Kitch, Carolyn. 2001. *The Girl on the Magazine Cover: The Origins of Visual Stereotypes in American Mass Media*. Chapel Hill: University of North Carolina Press.

Lamke, Sheree, prod. 2013. *Media Coverage & Female Athletes*. University of Minnesota Tucker Center and Twin Cities Public Television, December 1, 2013. https://video.tpt.org/video/tpt-co-productions-media-coverage-female-athletes/

Lapchick, Richard. 2018. *The 2018 Associated Press Editors Racial and Gender Report Card*. Institute for Diversity and Ethics in Sport at the University of Central Florida, May 2, 2018. https://www.tidesport.org/associated-press-sports-editors

Lapchick, Richard. 2021. *The 2021 Associated Press Editors Racial and Gender Report Card*. Institute for Diversity and Ethics in Sport at the University of Central Florida, September 22, 2021. https://www.tidesport.org/associated-press-sports-editors

Mahar, Karen Ward. 2001. "True Womanhood in Hollywood: Gendered Business Strategies and the Rise and Fall of the Woman Filmmaker, 1896–1928." *Enterprise & Society* 2 (1): 72–110. https://doi.org/10.1093/es/2.1.72

Papper, Bob. 2021. "Local Broadcast Newsroom Diversity." *2021 RTDNA/Newhouse School at Syracuse University Newsroom Survey*. https://www.rtdna.org/uploads/files/2021%20RTDNA-Syracuse%20Research%20-%20Local%20News%20Diversity.pdf

Romney, Miles, and Rich G. Johnson. 2020. "The Ball Game Is for the Boys: The Visual Framing of Female Athletes on National Sports Networks' Instagram Accounts." *Communication & Sport* 8 (6): 738–756. https://doi.org/10.1177/2167479519836731

Rosen, Jacky. 2019. "Rosen, Rubio Introduce Bipartisan, Bicameral, Media Diversity Resolution." September 10, 2019. https://www.rosen.senate.gov/rosen-rubio-introduce-bipartisan-bicameral-media-diversity-resolution

SheKnows Living Editors. 2014. "SheKnows Unveils Results of Its Femvertising Survey (Infographic)." SheKnows, October 30, 2014. https://www.sheknows.com/living/articles/1056821/sheknows-unveils-results-of-its-fem-vertising-survey-infographic/

Smith, Stacy, Marc Choueiti, Katherine Pieper, Kevin Yao, Ariana Case, and Angel Choi. 2019. *Inequality in 1,200 Popular Films: Examining Portrayals of Gender, Race/Ethnicity, LGBTQ & Disability from 2017 to 2018*. Annenberg Inclusion Initiative at USC Annenberg's School for Communication and Journalism. http://assets

.uscannenberg.org/docs/aii-inequality-report-2019-09-03.pdf

Smyth, J. E. 2018. *Nobody's Girl Friday: The Women Who Ran Hollywood*. New York: Oxford University Press.

Springer, Shira. 2019. "7 Ways to Improve Coverage of Women's Sports." *Nieman Reports*, January 7, 2019. https://nieman.harvard.edu/articles/covering-womens-sports/

Townsend, Megan, Raina Deerwater, Nick Adams, and Monica Trasandes. 2019. "Where We Are on TV: 2019–2020." GLAAD Media Institute Report, GLADD. https://www.glaad.org/sites/default/files/GLAAD%20WHERE%20WE%20ARE%20ON%20TV%202019%202020.pdf

Women's Media Center. 2019. *The Status of Women in the U.S. Media 2019*. February 21, 2019. https://womensmediacenter.com/reports/the-status-of-women-in-u-s-media-2019

Introduction

This chapter provides lists of additional resources for those wishing to explore and learn more about specific topics discussed in this book. First, the chapter provides brief annotations of a select list of books and articles that address specific aspects of representations of women in film, scripted television, advertising, sports, and news. On the list of twentieth-century works, readers will find contributions from foundational scholars as well as other sources that offer valuable historical content. Curated sources from the twenty-first century address contemporary topics or offer a contemporary analysis of historical texts. Second, the chapter offers annotations on contemporary research reports available to anyone with an internet connection. Third, a list of digital resources and audio/visual materials is provided. Some of these resources are easily located online, while others require a subscription to a streaming service or a rental fee paid to a distributor. Fourth, this chapter lists a group of relevant research and nonprofit organizations with websites that present information on current professional initiatives and contemporary research inquiries. Fifth, a section of relevant hashtags describes recent advocacy-oriented campaigns and

---

Laverne Cox presented at the 2015 Screen Actors Guild Awards and was honored for her performance in *Orange Is the New Black*. The cast of *Orange Is the New Black* took home the Actor in Outstanding Performance by an Ensemble in a Comedy Series. In addition to her talents as a performer and producer, Cox is also known for her advocacy for transgender rights. (Featureflash/Dreamstime.com)

initiatives that focus on elevating and empowering women in media industries. Finally, the chapter concludes with a list of relevant scholarly journals that publish peer-reviewed scholarly research on women in American media (both as participants and subjects) and related topics.

Selected Books and Articles: Twentieth Century

Butler, Judith. 1990. *Gender Trouble.* London: Routledge.

In *Gender Trouble*, philosopher and theorist Judith Butler challenges previously adhered to understandings of sex and gender, noting that one does not inform the other. She argues that one's biological sex does not inform one's gender and that gender is an act, or a performance, that can be considered in relation to societal and cultural constructs. Butler is often referenced when considering representations of gender in media texts.

Collins, Patricia Hill. 1991. *Black Feminist Thought: Knowledge, Consciousness, and the Politics of Empowerment.* New York: Routledge.

This book provides an overview of Black feminist theorists and explores how their ideas might be considered in light of feminist theory and Black women's lives. In her discussion of media stereotypes of Black women, such as the matriarch, the mammy, the welfare mother, and the Jezebel, Collins, a social theorist, argues that such representations allow for the normalizing of racism and subordination of Black women. Collins is also the author of other contemporary books and articles that explore issues of race from an intersectional perspective, including *Black Sexual Politics: African Americans, Gender, and the New Racism* (2004), and she coedited the ninth edition of *Race, Class, and Gender: An Anthology* (2016).

Creed, Barbara. 1993. *The Monstrous-Feminine: Film, Feminism, Psychoanalysis.* New York: Routledge.

In this influential book, Creed explores portrayals of women in horror films by focusing on how women's bodies are presented to viewers. Through her analysis of specific films, she argues that there are seven types of what she calls the "monstrous-feminine character": the archaic mother, the monstrous womb, the vampire, the witch, the possessed body, the monstrous mother, and the castrator.

Crenshaw, Kimberlé. 1989. "Demarginalizing the Intersection of Race and Sex: A Black Feminist Critique of Antidiscrimination Doctrine, Feminist Theory and Antiracist Politics." *University of Chicago Legal Forum* 1989 (1): Article 8. https://chicagounbound.uchicago.edu/uclf/vol1989/iss1/8

In this essay, Crenshaw uses the term "intersectionality" to emphasize that women's race and socioeconomic status inform their identities and experiences in interconnected ways. In so doing, Crenshaw challenges some of the assumptions inherent in simple categorization of Black women. Further, she emphasizes that individual women have unique, individual experiences, so an intersectional point of view is required when considering women's lives. Her work is often referenced when considering experiences of diverse women and, by extension, their media representations.

Dorenkamp, Angela, John McClymer, Mary Moynihan, and Arlene Vadum. 1985. *Images of Women in Popular Culture*. Fort Worth, TX: Harcourt Brace Jovanovich College Publishers.

This book presents a collection of diverse primary texts that explore how women have been portrayed in popular culture in the nineteenth and twentieth centuries. The organization of materials is thematic; the chapters present documents under the titles "Women's Nature," "Women's Place," "Women as Object," "Sweethearts and Wives," "Mothers," "Workers," "Sisters," and "Struggles and Visions." Each included primary text is introduced to provide the reader with appropriate context. Through this collection of materials, the book informs readers on how popular texts, from magazine articles to essays to speeches, convey evolving discourse about women in the United States.

Douglas, Susan. 1995. *Where the Girls Are: Growing Up Female with the Mass Media*. New York: Times Books.

In this book, media studies scholar, cultural critic, and writer Susan Douglas addresses the contradictory messages about feminism and equality in depictions of women in mainstream popular culture. She examines television shows, films, music, and advertising by humorously and critically discussing the representations of women in the broader historical context of the twentieth century. In so doing, she advances a cultural history of mainstream media's response to the second-wave feminist movement.

Goffman, Erving. 1976. *Gender Advertisements*. New York: Harper & Row.

Goffman analyzes how advertising images communicate and construct cultural expectations of gender in this now classic title. Using more than 500 advertisements as evidence, he points out that women in ads are presented as passive, submissive, childlike, or vulnerable, thus defining femininity along these lines. Goffman argues women are depicted in ways that suggest they are subordinate to men, whose masculinities are constructed in most advertising as confident, active, or intimidating. Much of Goffman's analysis is derived from his attention to the ways women and men are posed in advertising photographs.

hooks, bell. 1992. *Black Looks: Race and Representation*. Boston: South End Press; hooks, bell. 1996. *Reel to Real: Race, Sex and Class at the Movies*. New York: Routledge.

While the feminist intellectual bell hooks (the lack of capitalization is intentional) is the author of numerous books, these two titles specifically address media representations and are often referenced by scholars when considering representations of race and gender. In *Black Looks*, hooks offers a critique of the way "Blackness" is presented in popular culture. She argues, via a dozen essays drawing from some of her personal experiences and discussions of examples from popular culture, that the dominant white culture ultimately stereotypes and marginalizes Black culture. In *Reel to Real*, hooks's series of essays focus on various films and themes present in film culture. She argues that films are powerful teachers of the subjects of race, class, and gender and must be critically considered.

Marchetti, Gina. 1993. *Romance and the "Yellow Peril": Race, Sex, and Discursive Strategies in Hollywood Fiction*. Berkeley: University of California Press

In this book, Marchetti examines filmic representations of romance and sexual relationships between Caucasian and Asian characters in films from the twentieth century. She argues that such representations are problematic and are often linked to racial fears and misunderstandings of Asian culture.

Mulvey, Laura. 1975. "Visual Pleasure and Narrative Cinema." *Screen* 16 (3): 6–18. https://doi.org/10.1093/screen/16.3.6

In this famous essay, feminist film theorist Laura Mulvey argues that audiences are prompted by films to identify with the male protagonist in the story. Mulvey suggests that films advance a "male gaze," a viewing position held by audiences, or spectators, that sees women characters as subservient to the male characters in the film. Using psychoanalysis, Mulvey argues that typically male filmmakers capture women on-screen in ways that position them as objects of the male character's desire and in narrative power dynamics that privilege the man. As such, Mulvey theorizes that viewers adopt a male gaze as they watch the movie. Drawing from Hollywood films of the mid-twentieth century, Mulvey argues that the male gaze contributes to the objectification of women. This essay, which received numerous accolades as well as challenges to some of her ideas, is an important part of feminist film theory history. Although Mulvey both elaborated on and adjusted her ideas in subsequent work (see 1989's *Visual and Other Pleasures*), the concept of the male gaze is still referenced today.

Wolf, Naomi. 1991. *The Beauty Myth: How Images of Beauty Are Used against Women.* New York: William Morrow & Co.; reprint New York: Harper Perennial, 2002.

In this best-selling and often referenced book, Wolf explores "the beauty myth"—a term used to describe the idea that mainstream culture reinforces requirements that women and girls adhere to a standard of beauty that is unattainable by the majority of women. Wolf argues that despite the gains of twentieth-century feminism, women remain trapped in a quest to look a certain way because of images of women in advertising, media framing of women, and the diet industry.

Selected Books and Articles: Twenty-First Century

Adams, Katherine H., Michael L. Keene, and Melanie McKay. 2009. *Controlling Representations: Depictions of Women in a Mainstream Newspaper, 1900–1950.* Cresskill, NJ: Hampton Press, Inc.

This team of scholars examines images of women in daily newspapers in the first half of the twentieth century to explore how such depictions established and informed how women should behave. In focusing on the first half of the twentieth century, the book discusses how newspaper representations of women reflected such cultural moments as suffrage, flapperism, and World War II.

Specific attention is paid to newspapers' representations of women's socioeconomic class status.

Alley, Robert, and Irby Brown. 2001. *Women Television Producers: Transformation of the Male Medium*. Rochester, NY: University of Rochester Press.

After offering a brief history of the emerging television industry in the mid-twentieth century, Alley and Brown spotlight a number of female television producers, their career trajectories, their accomplishments, and their challenges in a historically male-dominated field. They accomplish this by interviewing the women themselves, giving them space to describe their experiences and viewpoints. The professionals they highlight include Marcy Carsey, Nancy Malone, Deborah Smith, and Lynn Roth.

Armstrong, Cory, ed. 2013. *Media Disparity*. Lanham, MD: Rowman & Littlefield.

This edited volume of essays synthesizes research and descriptions of contemporary media to offer an assessment of media and gender representations. Selections address topics such as women in the news, women in sports coverage, Wikipedia and gender, and women on reality-based television. The book ends with a discussion of the gendered media landscape via a contemporary feminist perspective.

Beirne, Rebecca, ed. 2008. *Televising Queer Women: A Reader*. New York: Palgrave Macmillan.

This series of accessible essays on such late twentieth-century and early twenty-first-century television programs as *Ellen*, *The L Word*, and *ER* offers perspectives on portrayals of queer women on television. Scholars here both celebrate and critique components of queer representations that are crafted to appeal to mainstream media audiences but are not always representative of the queer experience.

Bradley, Patricia. 2005. *Women and the Press: The Struggle for Equality*. Evanston, IL: Northwestern University Press.

This academic but accessible book tells the story of women working in all areas of the journalism field across centuries of the profession. Bradley focuses on the contextual inequalities in the newsroom and the larger culture itself, showing how women professionals persevered to work in often limiting environments.

Carter, Cynthia, Linda Steiner, and Stuart Allan, eds. 2019. *Journalism, Gender and Power*. Abingdon, UK: Routledge.

This international examination of journalism and gender examines such issues as sexism in the news industry, ways women are framed in news coverage, the impact of media oligopolies, and the sexualization of women in the news. Contributors address topics such as representations of women journalists, press coverage of women candidates for office, womanist news narratives, and sexism in the industry.

Chappell, Julie A., and Mallory Young, eds. 2017. *Bad Girls and Transgressive Women in Popular Television, Fiction, and Film*. Cham, Switzerland: Palgrave Macmillan.

Contributors to this book explore representations of women in popular television, fiction, and films that defy traditional cultural expectations of women and model resistance to the sexist status quo. Essays are thematically organized in the following subsections: "Crime and Punishment," "Domestic Arts," "Academic Performance," "Revisionist Perspectives," and "Alternative Realities." Within these sections, essay writers discuss such diverse works as *The Girl with the Dragon Tattoo*, *Bad Teacher*, *Bridget Jones: The Edge of Reason*, and *The Walking Dead*.

Cortese, Anthony. 2015. *Provocateur: Images of Women and Minorities in Advertising*. 4th ed. Lanham, MD: Rowman & Littlefield.

In this book about women, underrepresented groups, and advertising, Cortese includes numerous examples to support his arguments about the representations of gender, race, ethnicity, and the ideologies that inform them. The book provides an overview of such topics as advertising and sport, gay and lesbian advertising, symbolic racism in advertising, and visualizations of gender in advertising.

D'Amore, Laura Mattoon, ed. 2014. *Smart Chicks on Screen: Representing Women's Intellect in Film and Television*. Lanham: Rowman & Littlefield.

In this edited book, scholars discuss how educated, successful women are represented in film and television. Through discussions of movies and TV series such as *Born Yesterday*, *The Big Bang Theory*, *Elementary*, *Scandal*, *Madmen*, and *Grey's Anatomy*, the authors explore how smart women are marginalized, how beauty is prioritized over brains, and how intellect informs character actions. Contributors analyze how aspects of attractiveness, romantic relationships, and work inform how smart women are represented.

Douglas, Susan. 2010. *Enlightened Sexism: The Seductive Message That Feminism's Work Is Done*. New York: Times Books.

Douglas evaluates how media texts offer dueling narratives by pointing out that some depictions of women are "superhero" in nature—accomplished and in charge—while other portrayals conform to stereotypical tropes of characters focused on beauty and romance. Douglas explores how both types of portrayals are problematic and argues that marginalization of women, despite the gains made by the feminist movement, remains a significant problem in American popular culture.

Finneman, Teri Ann. 2015. *Press Portrayals of Women Politicians, 1870s–2000s: From "Lunatic" Woodhull to "Polarizing" Palin*. Lanham, MD: Lexington Books.

In this overview of women politicians and the media coverage they receive, Finneman specifically examines the newspaper coverage of four candidates for office, noting the various news frames and tactics used to challenge their candidacies and promote negative attitudes toward women candidates among voters. Finneman's book focuses on Victoria Woodhull (the first woman to run for president), Jeannette Rankin (the first woman elected to Congress), Margaret Chase Smith (the first woman to secure a national convention's nomination for president), and Sarah Palin (the first vice presidential candidate on a Republican ticket).

Goins, Marnel Niles, Joan Faber McAlister, and Bryant Keith Alexander, eds. 2020. *The Routledge Handbook of Gender and Communication*. Abingdon, UK: Routledge.

This reference book synthesizes and analyzes elements of the areas of gender studies, media studies, and the field of communication from an international perspective. The book is written by a diverse group of scholars who examine a comprehensive list of topics organized in the following sections: "Gendered Lives and Identities," "Visualizing Gender," "The Politics of Gender," "Gendered Contexts and Strategies," "Gendered Violence and Communication," and "Gender Advocacy in Action."

Grady, Constance. 2018. "The Waves of Feminism, and Why People Keep Fighting over Them, Explained." Vox, July 20, 2018. https://www.vox.com/2018/3/20/16955588/feminism-waves-explained-first-second-third-fourth

This article provides a useful overview of the history of feminist movements in the United States, discussing the wave metaphor as both helpful and problematic as an organizational mechanism. Included in the article are references to additional readings on so-called first-, second-, third-, and fourth-wave feminism.

Griffin, Rachel, and Michaela Meyer, eds. 2018. *Adventures in Shondaland.* New Brunswick, NJ: Rutgers University Press.

This edited academic compilation of essays explores aspects of television narratives created by television producer Shonda Rhimes and her production company, Shondaland. Different components of representation and identity politics are discussed, including selections that address bisexuality, Asian identity, and fan responses. Though the book is not completely focused on women, the inclusive casting on Shondaland-produced programs results in extensive scholarly discussion of many women characters.

Gross, Larry. 2001. *Up from Invisibility: Lesbians, Gay Men, and the Media in America.* New York: Columbia University Press.

Gross details the portrayals of gays and lesbians in news, television, film, and advertising during the second half of the twentieth century in this influential book. His analysis is anchored in the context of historic events, the profit-driven media industries, and cultural understandings of sexual minorities.

Halper, Donna. 2015. *Invisible Stars: A Social History of Women in American Broadcasting.* 2nd ed. New York: Routledge.

In this readable update to the first edition, Halper traces women's participation in the broadcasting industry from the twentieth century to the early twenty-first century, making connections to the changing cultural contexts of the decades. The book highlights women not frequently written about in broadcast history and discusses the connections between women's participation in the broadcasting field, both on and off the air, and public perceptions of women. While Halper documents and celebrates women's progress and growing industry power, she points out their participation still lags behind that of men in the field.

Harrod, Mary, and Katarzyna Paszkiewicz. 2017. *Women Do Genre in Film and Television*. New York: Routledge.

This scholarly anthology compiles essays that explore how women performers, directors, and writers use and engage with genre in the process of creating and contributing to television and film. The feminist analyses include examinations of international films and television programs and their authors.

Haskell, Molly. 2016. *From Reverence to Rape: The Treatment of Women in the Movies*. 3rd ed. Chicago: University of Chicago Press.

Now in its third edition, this book offers a critique of how women are depicted in Hollywood films in the twentieth century by examining film portrayals and the industry forces that were in place when specific films were made. Organized primarily by decade, Haskell offers an analysis of the treatment of women on-screen, explores the complexities of Hollywood, and identifies ways women worked within the patriarchal system.

Kitch, Carolyn. 2001. *The Girl on the Magazine Cover: The Origins of Visual Stereotypes in American Mass Media*. Chapel Hill: University of North Carolina Press.

Kitch's analysis of the evolution of images of women in popular magazines is accompanied by a discussion of women's history, demonstrating how representations of women were produced and advanced during periods of cultural transformation. Chapters explore how visual images in magazines present aspects of womanhood in magazines from the late 1800s through the close of the twentieth century. Through discussions of specific examples—from Gibson girls to flappers and visual conceptions of mothers to ideas about purity—Kitch looks at how magazine advertising and editorial content created, reflected, and maintained particular ideals about women over time.

Kosut, Mary, ed. 2012. *Encyclopedia of Gender in Media*. Thousand Oaks, CA: SAGE Publications.

This comprehensive encyclopedia is useful for those who wish to look up concise but well-researched entries on scholars and topics central to the exploration of the broad topic of gender in media.

Larson, Stephanie Greco. 2006. *Media & Minorities: The Politics of Race in News and Entertainment*. Lanham, MD: Rowan & Littlefield.

Larson examines how African Americans, Hispanic Americans, Native Americans, and Asian Americans are represented in news, radio, television, and film. Larson examines how stereotypical depictions are used in various media forms through her discussions of specific examples.

Levine, Elana. 2015. *Cupcakes, Pinterest, and Ladyporn: Feminized Popular Culture in the Early Twenty-First Century*. Feminist Media Studies. Urbana: University of Illinois Press.

In this edited compilation of essays, scholars discuss contemporary mediated representations of women and contemporary femininity. Levine argues that an examination of texts often dismissed as insignificant or "fluff" provides insight into how femininity is constructed and engaged with in the twenty-first century. The volume is organized into three sections: "Passions," "Bodies," and "Labors." Each section features a group of focused essays that speak to the topic at hand.

Magrath, Rory. 2019. *LGBT Athletes in the Sports Media*. Cham, Switzerland: Palgrave Macmillan.

This edited volume of essays written by scholars primarily from the United States and United Kingdom examines aspects of recent portrayals of LGBT athletes by the sports media, noting that shifts in cultural acceptance resulted in increased sports media coverage of this demographic group.

Mahar, Karen Ward. 2001. "True Womanhood in Hollywood: Gendered Business Strategies and the Rise and Fall of the Woman Filmmaker, 1896–1928." *Enterprise & Society* 2 (1): 72–110. https://doi.org/10.1093/es/2.1.72

Although women were active writers, producers, directors, editors, and actors during the rise of filmmaking in late nineteenth-century Hollywood through the 1920s, by 1925, their participation in areas other than acting and screenwriting had largely been erased. This article traces the evolution of this shift—what the author calls the "implicit gendering process of the industry"—by describing different evolutionary stages of the growing film industry.

Marubbio, M. Elise. 2006. *Killing the Indian Maiden: Images of Native American Women in Film*. Lexington: University Press of Kentucky.

Marubbio's discussion of twentieth-century depictions of Native American women in American movies reveals that from the silent film era onward, Native American women have largely been confined to what Marubbio calls the "celluloid maiden," a character who engages in some way with a white male protagonist and eventually dies. Her analysis of thirty-four films discusses how different versions of the celluloid maiden persist from the early 1900s into films from the 1990s.

Meyers, Marian. 2013. *African American Women in the News: Gender, Race, and Class in Journalism*. New York: Routledge.

Meyers describes her book as one that examines the representation of African American women in the news from an intersectional perspective—one that considers the ways gender, race, and class are connected to women's portrayals. Chapters focus on local news, cable news, and YouTube and are informed by qualitative research.

Pinedo, Isabel. 2021. *Difficult Women on Television Drama: The Gender Politics of Complex Women in Serial Narratives.* London: Routledge.

In this examination of women characters from dramas such as *The Killing, Orange Is the New Black, Big Little Lies,* and *Westworld,* Pinedo offers a feminist analysis of contemporary protagonists. In doing so, she considers issues of economics, sexual freedom, violence, and intersectionality.

Press, Joy. 2018. *Stealing the Show: How Women Are Revolutionizing Television.* New York: Simon & Schuster.

By focusing on women who are influential in creating scripted television programming, Press informs the reader about some of the backstories behind their successful television shows. The book's chapters include discussions of Amy Sherman-Palladino and *Gilmore Girls,* Jill Soloway and *Transparent,* Tina Fey and *30 Rock,* Lena Denham and *Girls,* and Jenji Kohan and *Weeds* and *Orange Is the New Black.*

Rodriguez, Clara E. 2008. *Latin Looks: Images of Latinas and Latinos in the U.S. Media.* New York: Routledge.

Essays in this edited book explore different aspects of twentieth-century media portrayals of Latinas and Latinos in the United States. The book is divided into three parts. In part one, contributors identify how members of this demographic are either misrepresented or erased in television narratives and news coverage. Part two explores representations of Latina and Latino film stars and their characters. Part three discusses how Latinas and Latinos choose to represent themselves. The book ends with a list of questions to promote discussion of the book's contents.

Rosewarne, Lauren. 2016. *Cyberbullies, Cyberactivists, Cyberpredators: Film, TV, and Internet Stereotypes.* Santa Barbara, CA: Praeger.

While Rosewarne's focus is on representations of internet users in general, her investigations into how gender is specifically constructed when television shows portray technology use provide the reader with insight into how particular stereotypes are constructed, reinforced, and sometimes defied. Rosewarne's analysis is informed by hundreds of depictions of internet users on television and in film; she ultimately argues that a preponderance of negative imagery of internet users is problematic.

Ross, Betsy. 2010. *Playing Ball with the Boys: The Rise of Women in the World of Men's Sports*. Cincinnati, OH: Clerisy Press.

Betsy Ross, a former ESPN news anchor, explores how women have become more prominent in the world of sports and sports broadcasting. Ross offers a behind-the-scenes examination of the sports industry and adds to this perspective with interviews with prominent women such as tennis great Billie Jean King, ESPN's Rebecca Lobo, *USA Today*'s Christine Brennan, and *Sports Illustrated*'s Selena Roberts.

Ruggerio, Alena Amato, ed. 2012. *Media Depictions of Brides, Wives, and Mothers*. Lanham, MD: Lexington Books.

This scholarly collection of essays examines how various media represent women in ways that advance and reinforce gender stereotypes. Scholars contributing to this title critically examine examples of popular culture, such as *Sex and the City*, *The Devil Wears Prada*, and *Mad Men* fan sites.

Savage, Ann M., ed. 2017. *Women's Rights: Reflections in Popular Culture*. Santa Barbara, CA: Greenwood.

This edited book explores the relationships between women's rights and representations of women, women's rights, and feminism in popular culture. Specific examples of popular culture are discussed in chapters that focus on television, popular music, film, literature, the news, and online resources. Essay writers establish clear connections between specific components of the women's movement and popular culture portrayals.

Smith, Kate McNicholas. 2020. *Lesbians on Television*. Bristol, UK: Intellect. https://library.oapen.org/handle/20.500.12657/47353

This title, which may be ordered in print or accessed for free online, explores representations of queer women on television via the discussion and analysis of five television programs: *The L Word*, *Skins*, *Coronation Street*, *Glee*, and *The Fosters*. The book is a result of the author's dissertation work, and her analysis is informed by cultural changes in the United Kingdom and United States that resulted in more inclusionary LGBTQ practices and policies.

Smyth, J. E. 2018. *Nobody's Girl Friday: The Women Who Ran Hollywood*. New York: Oxford University Press.

Challenging the narrative that film operations during the 1920s through about 1960 were largely dominated by men, Smyth profiles numerous powerful women in Hollywood, demonstrating their presence and power in multiple areas of the film industry, from costume creating to writing and producing to powerful administrative roles. A series of biographical profiles provide coverage of notable women such as the famous actress Bette Davis and Screen Writers Guild president Mary McCall Jr.

Sochen, June. 2008. *From Mae to Madonna: Women Entertainers in Twentieth-Century America*. Lexington: University Press of Kentucky.

In her examination of iconic women in American film, television, and music, Sochen examines the historical context in which their careers took place. Her book includes discussions of such well-known stars as Mae West, Lucille Ball, and Mary Tyler Moore. She also discusses nonwhite film and television stars such as Lupe Velez and Pam Grier. Sochen's critical discussion of this select group of women performers also includes commentary on the familiar typologies of roles in which these women were cast.

Tally, Margaret. 2016. *The Rise of the Anti-Heroine in TV's Third Golden Age*. Newcastle upon Tyne, UK: Cambridge Scholars Publishing.

After providing a brief history of the portrayals of women on television, Tally focuses on what she calls the "anti-heroine" in twenty-first-century television. Tally describes a number of women characters who are complex, accomplished, and flawed on shows airing on premium channels (Showtime and HBO), network channels (ABC primarily, but with nods to other network programming), and the streaming service Netflix. She argues that new types of television narratives and ensemble casting choices have provided for a range of different representations of women characters on television.

Valdivia, Angharad. 2010. *Latino/as in the Media*. Malden, MA: Polity Press.

Valdivia is a leading Latina media studies scholar whose previous work includes *A Latina in the Land of Hollywood, and Other Essays on Media Culture* (2000). In this book, Valdivia approaches the study of Latinos and Latinas in the media from a media and cultural studies perspective. She examines media representations while addressing such contemporary issues in the culture as immigration and societal status. While the book draws on a significant amount of research reports and scholarly analysis, Valdivia's synthesis is accessible to advanced undergraduate readers.

Weller, Sheila. 2014. *The News Sorority: Diane Sawyer, Katie Couric, Christiane Amanpour and the (Ongoing, Imperfect, Complicated) Triumph of Women in TV News*. New York: Penguin Books.

This book illuminates the career trajectories of some of the most famous and successful American female journalists, all of whom had to navigate sexism in the journalism industry in different ways.

Yousman, Bill, Lori Bindig Yousman, Gail Dines, and Jean McMahon Humez. 2020. *Gender, Race, and Class in Media*. 6th ed. Thousand Oaks, CA: SAGE Publications.

The sixth edition of this comprehensive reader features sixty-six essays that speak to ways gender, race, and socioeconomic class are represented in television, film, advertising, and social media platforms. While not all of this content connects to mediated representations of women, the book presents ideas from often referenced feminist scholars and essays that focus on specific media texts.

Contemporary Research Reports

Di Meco, Lucina. 2019. *#ShePersisted: Women, Politics & Power in the New Media World*. She-persisted.org. https://static1.squarespace.com/static/5dba105f102367021c44b63f/t/5dc431aac6bd4e7913c45f7d/1573138953986/191106+SHEPERSISTED_Final.pdf

In this report, Di Meco examines the 2020 Democratic presidential primaries via a gender lens, summarizes interviews with eighty-eight international women leaders, and provides an analysis of a sample of publications that report on women in politics. The report also considers the way social media contributes to women's participation in politics and details how social media both helps and hinders women, noting that while women are more likely to be attacked and targeted on social media platforms than men, they also successfully use these tools to connect with the public.

Geena Davis Institute on Gender in Media. 2020. *Bias and Inclusion in Advertising: An Analysis of 2019 Cannes Lions Work.* https://seejane.org/wp-content/uploads/bias-and-inclusion-in-advertising-cannes-lions.pdf

Every year, the Cannes Lions International Festival of Creativity, or Cannes Lions, celebrates creativity in advertising. This research report documents the representations of gender, race/ethnicity, LGBTQ+, disability, age, and body size in advertising submitted to Cannes Lions from 2006 to 2019. While the report documents some positive trends in representations, inequities are also noted and discussed.

Geena Davis Institute on Gender in Media, USC Viterbi School of Engineering, and TENA. 2020. *Frail, Frumpy and Forgotten: A Report on the Movie Roles of Women of Age.* https://seejane.org/wp-content/uploads/frail-frumpy-and-forgotten-report.pdf

This research report examines the representation of older women in 2019's top-grossing films from four countries: France, Germany, the United Kingdom, and the United States. The report shows that older women are rarely significant characters in the films studied, and when they are prominently featured, they are often depicted in stereotypical and ageist ways.

Hunt, Darnell, and Ana-Christina Ramon. 2020. *Hollywood Diversity Report 2020. A Tale of Two Hollywoods.* UCLA College of Social Sciences. https://socialsciences.ucla.edu/wp-content/uploads/2020/02/UCLA-Hollywood-Diversity-Report-2020-Film-2-6-2020.pdf

This comprehensive report examines representation and inclusion on- and off-screen in the top-grossing films of

2018 and 2019. While the report documents an increasing number of roles held by women and other underrepresented groups on-screen, the same trends are not evident in behind-the-scenes roles. The analysis discusses such findings as the demographic breakdowns of film leads, supporting characters, writers, and directors. It also examines overall cast and crew diversity.

Lauzen, Martha. 2019. *Boxed In 2018–19: Women on Screen and behind the Scenes in Television*. Center for the Study of Women in Television & Film at San Diego State University. https://womenintvfilm.sdsu.edu/wp-content/uploads/2019/09/2018-19_Boxed_In_Report.pdf

The *Boxed In* research initiative at the Center for the Study of Women in Television & Film at San Diego State University has been documenting women's participation in the prime-time television industry for over two decades. This recent report examines on- and off-screen representation in the 2018–2019 season, noting disparities between men and women.

Lauzen, Martha. 2020. "*The Celluloid Ceiling: Behind-the-Scenes Employment of Women on the Top 100, 250, and 500 films of 2019.*" Center for the Study of Women in Television & Film at San Diego State University. https://womenintvfilm.sdsu.edu/wp-content/uploads/2020/01/2019_Celluloid_Ceiling_Report.pdf

The Center for the Study of Women in Television & Film at San Diego State University has been documenting women's participation behind the scenes in the film industry for over two decades. This recent report examines how many women worked in jobs such as film directors, writers, producers, and cinematographers in a sample of films released in 2019. The disparities between employed men and women are noted.

Lauzen, Martha. 2021. *Boxed In: Women on Screen and behind the Scenes on Broadcast and Streaming Television in 2020-21.* Center for the Study of Women in Television & Film at San Diego State University. https://womenintvfilm.sdsu.edu/wp-content/uploads/2021/09/2020-21_Boxed_In_Report.pdf

This *Boxed In* report documents the most recent information around women's participation in the television industry. The time period covered overlaps with part of the COVID-19 pandemic, which may have disrupted elements of participation documented in the report.

Lauzen, Martha. 2022. *It's a Man's (Celluloid) World, Even in a Pandemic Year: Portrayals of Female Characters in the Top Grossing Films of 2021.* Center for the Study of Women in Television & Film at San Diego State University. https://womenintvfilm.sdsu.edu/wp-content/uploads/2022/03/2021-Its-a-Mans-Celluloid-World-Report.pdf

This report documents the participation of women in film during the top grossing films of 2021. Disparities between women's and men's participation are noted.

Papper, Bob. 2021. *Local Broadcast Newsroom Diversity.* RTDNA/Newhouse School at Syracuse University Newsroom Survey. https://www.rtdna.org/uploads/files/2021%20RTDNA-Syracuse%20Research%20-%20Local%20News%20Diversity.pdf

This report sponsored by the Radio Television Digital News Association (RTDNA) and Syracuse University's S. I. Newhouse School of Public Communication documents the demographic breakdown of people working in local news. Such reports are typically completed annually and provide comparative findings to studies from years prior.

Smith, Stacy, Marc Choueiti, Ariana Case, Katherine Pieper, Hannah Clark, Karla Hernandez, Jacqueline Martinez,

Benjamin Lopez, and Mauricio Mota. 2019. *Latinos in Film: Erasure on Screen & behind the Camera across 1,200 Popular Movies.* Annenberg Inclusion Initiative at USC Annenberg's School for Communication and Journalism. http://assets.uscannenberg.org/docs/aii-study-latinos-in-film-2019.pdf

This report focuses on the limited presence of Latinx people in top-grossing American films, despite the large and growing Latinx population in the United States. The report finds that in the 1,200 movies studied between 2007 and 2018, Latinx representation does not proportionally correspond with its share of the U.S. population. The report includes easy-to-understand infographics and a readable key summary.

Smith, Stacy, Marc Choueiti, Katherine Pieper, Kevin Yao, Ariana Case, and Angel Choi. 2019. *Inequality in 1,200 Popular Films: Examining Portrayals of Gender, Race/Ethnicity, LGBTQ & Disability from 2007 to 2018.* Annenberg Inclusion Initiative at USC Annenberg's School for Communication and Journalism. http://assets.uscannenberg.org/docs/aii-inequality-report-2019-09-03.pdf

Complete with easy-to-understand infographics and a key findings section, this report details representation metrics of women in men, racial and ethnic groups, LGBTQ characters, and characters with disabilities over top-grossing films from 2007 to 2018. The research team examines representation both in front of and behind the camera, identifying the types of characters and jobs held by various demographic groups in the industry.

Staurowsky, Ellen J., Nicholas Watanabe, Joseph Cooper, Cheryl Cooky, Nancy Lough, Amanda Paule-Koba, Jennifer Pharr, Sarah Williams, Sarah Cummings, Karen Issokson-Silver, and Marjorie Snyder. 2020. *Chasing Equity: The Triumphs, Challenges, and Opportunities in Sports for Girls and Women.* New York: Women's Sports Foundation. https://www

.womenssportsfoundation.org/articles_and_report/chasing-equity-the-triumphs-challenges-and-opportunities-in-sports-for-girls-and-women/

This comprehensive report examines the current state of women and girls in sport, highlighting trends in participation, access, safety, issues of equality, and media coverage. Content here relies on a literature review of over 500 research studies focused on the topic and results from the research team's survey of 2,356 women leaders in women's sport. The publication ends with informed calls to action that identify how equality might be better achieved in girls' and women's sport.

UNESCO. 2012. *Gender-Sensitive Indicators for Media: Framework of Indicators to Gauge Gender Sensitivity in Media Operations and Content.* https://unesdoc.unesco.org/ark:/48223/pf0000217831

This framework, developed over two years by an international team, was distributed to contribute to the goal of establishing gender equality across all media. In part one, the report outlines "actions to foster gender equality within media organizations." In part two, the report summarizes "gender portrayal in media content."

Women's Media Center. 2018. *The Status of Women of Color in the U.S. News Media 2018.* http://www.womensmediacenter.com/assets/site/reports/the-status-of-women-of-color-in-the-u-s-media-2018-full-report/Women-of-Color-Report-FINAL-WEB.pdf

This report compiles the most recent available data from news industry organizations to present a demographic picture of news professionals. Findings show that women and women of color hold few industry positions in comparison to their white male counterparts. The report also summarizes thoughtful interviews with several journalists who comment on relevant issues related to news coverage and diversity.

Digital Resources and Audio/Visual Material

Archer, John, prod. 2020. *Women Make Film: A New Road Movie through Cinema*. Hopscotch Films.

This comprehensive fourteen-episode documentary directed by Mark Cousins explores women's contributions to filmmaking. Each episode is narrated by a woman in the entertainment industry and focuses on women film directors across the globe, exploring how they tell stories. The accompanying website on Turner Classic Movies (TCM; https://womenmakefilm.tcm.com/) profiles women filmmakers and provides excerpts from the documentary and clips from films and director interviews. TCM also notes the broadcast schedule of documentary episodes and film screenings.

Cooky, Cheryl. 2016. "The Female Athlete: Missing in Action." TEDx Talks, May 24, 2016. https://www.youtube.com/watch?v=MPS2YoXWMSs

Cheryl Cooky's academic research on the portrayal of women athletes in media consistently shows that such sports coverage is lacking, when it does exist, it is often problematic. In this TED talk, she discusses elements of her research findings and highlights the #CoverTheAthlete campaign, which asks sports reporters to cover women athletes in the same way they cover athletes who are men.

Gee, Deborah, dir. 1988. *Slaying the Dragon* [film], and Kim, Elaine. 2011. *Slaying the Dragon: Reloaded* [documentary]. Produced by Asian Women United. Available via Kanopy for screening. *Slaying the Dragon: Reloaded* is available for institutional purchase at https://www.asianwomenunited.org/slaying-the-dragon-asian-women-in-u-s-television-and-film-1988/

Slaying the Dragon is an hour-long documentary that identifies the stereotypes of Asian women and men in early Hollywood cinema. The film demonstrates the prevalence of such common Asian stereotypes as the geisha and dragon lady and critiques the historical representation of this demographic. The follow-up thirty-minute documentary, *Slaying the Dragon: Reloaded*, builds on this discussion by examining more contemporary representations of Asians. Here the filmmaker looks at films, television shows, and content on YouTube, identifying changing trends and problematic material.

Feder, Sam, dir. 2020. *Disclosure: Trans Lives on Screen* [documentary]. Netflix.

After debuting at the Sundance Film Festival in 2020, Netflix made this film available on its streaming platform. The documentary explores the representation of transgender characters on film and television, pointing out problematic stereotypes and tropes. The filmmaker talks with prominent transgender people, primarily from the film industry, who share their perspectives.

Jhally, Sut, dir. 2010. *Killing Us Softly, 4: Advertising's Image of Women* [documentary]. Media Education Foundation. Amherst, MA.

This is the fourth in the *Killing Us Softly* series of films, which features Jeanne Kilbourne and her decades-long work examining the imagery of women in advertising. By presenting hundreds of examples from mainstream advertising, Kilbourne demonstrates how pervasive images of women in advertising convey problematic ideas about beauty, body size, sex, and self-worth. In 2019, Smith College marked the fortieth anniversary of the first *Killing Us Softly* film, and a panel of scholars discussed the impact of Kilbourne's work. At the time of this writing, the panel discussion, *Killing Us Softly: Then & Now*, is free to view on the Media Education Foundation's website (https://go.mediaed.org/killing-us-softly-then-and-now).

The Journalist's Resource at the Harvard Kennedy School's Shorenstein Center for Media and Public Policy. https://journalistsresource.org/

The "Race & Gender" section (https://journalistsresource.org/race-and-gender/) of this resource site provides useful information for journalists and interested readers on how members of different demographic groups are reported on and portrayed in the news media. Articles summarize research studies, offer guidance to journalists around reporting on particular groups and issues, and break down issues related to race and gender in digestible "explainers."

Judd, Ashley. 2016. "How Online Abuse of Women Has Spiraled out of Control." TED, October 2016. https://www.ted.com/talks/ashley_judd_how_online_abuse_of_women_has_spiraled_out_of_control

Providing an overview of her personal experience with being harassed online, Judd highlights the issue of sexual harassment and violent threats made against women in online environments and calls on elected officials and leaders at technology companies to address this problem.

Kamerik, Megan. 2011. "Women Should Represent Women in Media." TEDxABQ, September 2011. https://www.ted.com/talks/megan_kamerick_women_should_represent_women_in_media?language=en

In this TED talk, journalist Megan Kamerik advocates for a shift in the demographics of news departments so news stories are more equitably and completely covered. Kamerik suggests women journalists report on news stories in ways that challenge gender stereotypes that are sometimes perpetuated in stories written and edited by men.

Konner, Joan, producer. 2001. *She Says: Women in News* (TV). PBS, December 18, 2001. Available via the Independent

Production Fund. New York: Infobase [streaming video]. https://academiccommons.columbia.edu/doi/10.7916/D82F7NHC

This hour-long film features ten women journalists who share their stories of working in a male-dominated news environment. Through interviews and examples, the film displays the sexism, professional roadblocks, and institutional challenges these respected journalists had to navigate during their careers. Carole Simpson, Nina Totenberg, Helen Thomas, and Judy Woodruff are some of the journalists who offer their perspectives. The piece provides viewers with relevant aspects of the twentieth-century history of women in journalism through the eyes of professionals.

Lamke, Sheree, prod. 2013. *Media Coverage & Female Athletes* [documentary]. University of Minnesota Tucker Center and Twin Cities Public Television, December 1, 2013. https://video.tpt.org/video/tpt-co-productions-media-coverage-female-athletes/

Appropriate and equitable media representation of female athletes is a long-standing issue in the sports media industry. Running just under an hour, this documentary explores how female athletes and their sports are covered—or not covered—in the media. Coaches and athletes representing collegiate, Olympic, and professional teams share their experiences and offer perspectives on how media might better serve female athletes and teams and their fans. Scholars summarize key findings from recent research, and journalists provide some insight into how sports departments work.

Padnani, Amy. 2019. "How We Are Honoring People Overlooked by History." TED Salon: The Macallan, June 2019. https://www.ted.com/talks/amy_padnani_how_we_re_honoring_people_overlooked_by_history

In this short talk, *New York Times* editor Amy Padnani discusses the impetus behind the paper's project titled

Overlooked. As a dominant national newspaper, the *Times* has acknowledged that its published obituaries have historically neglected women and people of color who significantly contributed to the culture. Overlooked aims to better recognize these people and their accomplishments.

Picker, Miguel, dir. 2012. *Latinos beyond Reel: Challenging a Media Stereotype* [documentary]. Northampton, MA: Media Education Foundation.

This documentary explores how news and entertainment media in the United States neglect, misrepresent, and advance stereotypes of Latinas and Latinos. The film begins with a historical overview before exploring late twentieth-century and early twenty-first-century images present in news, television programs, and films. Adding to experts' discussion of such portrayals are interviews with Latina and Latino actors who reflect on elements of their work experience.

Rossini, Elena, dir. and prod. 2015. *The Illusionists* [documentary]. https://theillusionists.org/film/

This ninety-minute documentary explores how unrealistic beauty ideals are constructed and perpetuated by promotional imagery throughout the world. Featuring commentary from such notable feminist scholars and critics as Laura Mulvey, Gail Dines, and Susie Orbach, the film offers a contemporary cultural critique of how the beauty industry promotes insecurity and poor body image in girls and women. The film also documents the contradictions within the beauty industry itself.

Smith, Stacy. 2018. "The Data behind Hollywood's Sexism." TEDWomen, October 2018. https://www.ted.com/talks/stacy_smith_the_data_behind_hollywood_s_sexism

Stacy Smith of the Annenberg Inclusion Initiative discusses data from the organization's research reports that demonstrate problematic representations of women in film. This fifteen-minute talk, in which Smith explains key findings and asserts that more equitable representation should be a priority, is a useful supplement to published Annenberg research reports.

Studio Binder. 2020. "The Best 67 Female Film Directors Working Today." StudioBinder, May 31, 2020. https://www.studiobinder.com/blog/best-female-directors/

Though by no means a complete list, this blog post provides an informative summary of contemporary women film directors. Each entry features an image, a brief filmography, and some biographical details.

Women Come to the Front. https://www.loc.gov/exhibits/wcf/

This Library of Congress exhibition spotlights several women journalists and their contributions to World War II reporting and photography. Accompanying essays review cultural expectations of women in American society before, during, and after the war.

Women Film Pioneers Project. https://wfpp.columbia.edu/

This digital resource hosted by Columbia University is dedicated to advancing understanding of women's contributions to film. The site's content is primarily authored by scholars and features over 300 profiles of women who worked in film during the silent era. The resource also publishes peer-reviewed essays, research updates, articles, and multimedia projects.

Organizations

The Action Coalition for Media Education
https://acmesmartmediaeducation.net/

This independently funded media literacy network sponsors workshops, training sessions, keynotes, and summits (or conferences) to assist citizens, scholars, and educators in developing or furthering media education initiatives.

The Annenberg Inclusion Initiative
https://annenberg.usc.edu/research/aii

The Annenberg Inclusion Initiative is a research center at the University of Southern California Annenberg's School for Journalism and Communication. The center is focused on research that documents representations of gender, race/ethnicity, LGBTQ, disability, and age in entertainment and seeks to support inclusion and diversity both in front of and behind the camera. The organization also engages in work that promotes solutions for increasing equality in the industry. Full-text research reports and helpful infographics are available on the Annenberg Inclusion Initiative website.

Asian Pacific American Media Coalition (APAMC)
https://apamediacoalition.wordpress.com/

Founded in 1999, this organization advocates for the inclusion of Asian Pacific Americans in media industries. Composed of such organizations as the Asian American Justice Center and the Media Action Network for Asian Americans, the group releases an annual TV report card that grades television networks on their inclusion of Asian Pacific Americans on- and off-screen.

Center for the Study of Women in Television & Film
https://womenintvfilm.sdsu.edu/

Founded and directed by Dr. Martha Lauzen, this center at San Diego State University focuses on the representation of women in television and film industries through a variety of reports. The annual *Celluloid Ceiling* study, for example, identifies the number of women working as directors, writers, producers, cinematographers, and editors. Another annual study, *Boxed In*, looks at the portrayals of female characters on broadcast, cable, and streaming television, and it also documents women's employment behind the scenes. Additional analysis examines portrayals of women in film and the representation of women as film reviewers.

Geena Davis Institute on Gender in Media
https://seejane.org/

The Geena Davis Institute on Gender in Media was founded in 2004 by actor Geena Davis. This research-driven organization works to promote gender balance in family entertainment and produces comprehensive research reports that document the representation of demographic groups in various forms of media, with a focus on films, television shows and advertising seen by young people. The organization partners with allies in the entertainment industry to work toward creating gender balance and eliminating stereotypical depictions. Full-text versions of the institute's research reports, many of which include helpful and easy-to-read key summaries and infographics, can be accessed via the organization's website.

GLAAD
https://www.glaad.org/

GLAAD is an organization that advocates for positive media representations of the LGBTQ+ community. The GLAAD website makes available many resources, including a media reference guide, information about their events and initiatives to promote understanding and inclusion, and full texts of their research reports. Examples of GLAAD-sponsored research that examines media representations include the *Where We Are on TV* series, which documents the representation of LGBTQ+ characters on television each year, and the *LGBTQ Inclusion in Advertising and Media* report.

The Institute for Diversity and Ethics in Sport (TIDES)
https://www.tidesport.org/

This institute is part of the DeVos Sport Business Management Graduate Program in the University of Central

Florida's College of Business Administration. Its mission is to explore issues related to gender, race, and sport. The most notable of the research studies it publishes in these areas is the *Racial and Gender Report Card*, which documents hiring practices in sports and sports media.

The Journalism & Women Symposium
https://jaws.org/

This nonprofit, established in 1995, advocates for and supports women in journalism through providing networking and professional development opportunities. The group has engaged in diversity, equity, and inclusion (DEI) advocacy and has partnered with organizations such as the Poynter Institute and the International Women's Media Foundation.

Media Education Foundation (MEF)
https://www.mediaed.org/

This organization produces documentary films addressing issues related to media, culture, and society. Films are accompanied by educational resources that might be used in the classroom, but the documentaries stand alone as pieces that present perspectives on a variety of topics. Several documentaries address issues around gender representation in the media. MEF was founded by now retired University of Massachusetts professor and scholar Sut Jhally, and its board of advisors is composed of a team of well-known cultural writers and scholars, including Susan Douglas, Jean Kilbourne, and Naomi Klein.

Media Education Lab
https://mediaeducationlab.com/

Located at the University of Rhode Island, this center promotes media literacy and provides resources for educators, researchers, and learners.

National Association for Media Literacy Education (NAMLE)
https://namle.net/

NAMLE is a national organization focused on media literacy that runs conferences for educators and provides resources for parents and communities. While NAMLE's focus is on media literacy education as a whole, some of the work the organization promotes is focused on gender in the media.

The National Hispanic Media Coalition
https://www.nhmc.org/

The goal of this organization is to advocate for increased and more positive representations of Latinx people in U.S. media. Founded in 1986, the group initially focused on news and has since expanded to include a focus on the entertainment industries. The organization supports and advocates for policies that increase Latinx representation in front of and behind the camera and sponsors a variety of programs and events to that end.

Native Women in Film & Television in All Media
https://www.nativewomeninfilm.com/

This organization aims to increase opportunities for, and visibility of, American Indian and Indigenous women filmmakers. Pointing out that mainstream film and television narratives rarely feature American Indian and Indigenous characters, the group advocates for better inclusion using multimedia campaigns and calls to action. The group also sponsors film festivals and a screenwriting lab. The organization was founded by American Indian filmmaker Joanelle Romero.

The Representation Project
http://therepresentationproject.org/

Founded by documentary filmmaker Jennifer Siebel Newsom in 2011, this organization works to support gender equity, dispel gender stereotypes, and shift the culture's attitudes about gender itself. The project has supported several social media campaigns advocating for better media representation of women, produces educational films, and offers trainings. The website features a blog where current issues surrounding representation are discussed.

Women and Hollywood
https://womenandhollywood.com/

Established in 2007 by Melissa Silverstein, the organization describes itself as one that "educates, advocates, and agitates for gender diversity and inclusion in Hollywood and the global film industry." The website maintains lists of contemporary films featuring women's stories and identifies films directed by and written by women. Other resources include sourced data and statistics, a list of helpful databases for those in the industry, and a series of blog posts spotlighting women and their work.

Women in Media
https://www.womennmedia.com/

This organization aims to support and advocate for women working in film and other entertainment industries. It sponsors networking events and professional development opportunities for members. Membership options include a student membership for rising professionals.

Women's eNews
https://womensenews.org/

This nonprofit digital news service reports on topics that are particularly relevant to women. Initially created in 1999 with support from the NOW Legal Defense and Education Fund, Women's eNews became independent and self-sustainable in 2002. The site houses the former print publication *Teen Voices*, which featured articles written by young women.

Women's Media Center (WMC)
https://www.womensmediacenter.com/

Founded in 2005 by Jane Fonda, Robin Morgan, and Gloria Steinem, the Women's Media Center advocates for better representation of women in media. To do so, the WMC produces research that documents the presence of women (and other underrepresented groups) in media and makes these reports available on their website. The organization also works with media organizations to promote equity, monitors how news coverage represents women, and campaigns for news reports that represent women fairly and without relying on gender tropes. The WMC website makes numerous resources available for users.

Relevant Hashtags

#BodyPositive, #BoPo, #bodypositivity

The social media form of this body positive movement hopes to promote acceptance of all body sizes and challenge mainstream ideas about what an ideal body looks like. Posts marked with these hashtags feature women sharing pictures and conveying messages of empowerment. Though criticized by some for its focus on the body and appearance, the movement is popular on such social media platforms as Instagram, Twitter, and TikTok.

#CoverTheAthlete

The campaign, which began in 2015, urges news media to engage in more equitable coverage of women's sports and asks consumers to demand such coverage from their news outlets. Though the campaign is less active today, the short video that launched the campaign (found at https://www.youtube.com/watch?v=Ol9VhBDKZs0) makes a useful, and still relevant, point. The video poses questions to male athletes and comments about male athletes' performances using language that focuses on appearance versus performance that is typically heard when reporting on athletes who are women.

#FemaleFilmmakerFriday

Created by screenwriter, producer, and director Aline Brosh McKenna in 2018, this movement aims to post images of women working behind the scenes in film and television to diversify the images of directors that are circulated in the culture. McKenna notes that presenting women in such roles helps other women believe they can engage in the same work and be successful in a variety of entertainment industry professions.

#MeToo

The use of this Twitter hashtag in the late 2010s revealed patterns of widespread sexual harassment and abuse in the American entertainment industry. It became a cornerstone of a movement that supports those speaking out about sexual abuse and sexual harassment. Some current interpretations of this hashtag position it as advocacy for any marginalized group.

#SayHerName

This campaign, launched in 2014 by the African American Policy Forum's Center for Intersectionality and Social Policy Studies, aims to raise awareness about Black women and girls who are victims of police violence and whose experiences are not always reported in the mainstream media. The report that informs the campaign, titled *Say Her Name: Resisting Police Brutality against Black Women*, by Kimberlé Crenshaw and Andrea Richie, can be found on the African American Policy Forum website (https://aapf.org/sayhername).

#ThisIsWhatAFilmDirectorLooksLike

Created by Elena Rossini, the director and producer of the beauty industry documentary *The Illusionists*, this Twitter and Instagram campaign populates feeds with images and

GIFs of women filmmakers to elevate their visibility. One of the goals of the project is to diversify GIPHY's, a GIF search engine, results.

#TimesUp

This movement, founded by 300 women in the entertainment industry, focuses on highlighting issues women face in the workplace, noting that gender power imbalances in many industries can set the stage for sexual harassment. The campaign also advocates for policy changes and legislation promoting more equitable inclusion of women and other underrepresented groups.

#WhyWeWearRED

This campaign is described as an "initiative that aims to bring awareness to murdered and missing Native women & girls and the direct link of the lack of inclusion of Native women in film & television." The campaign emerged from the organization Native Women in Film & Television in All Media founded by Joanelle Romero.

Scholarly Journals

Empirical research, scholarly essays, and media critiques addressing topics related to representations of women in film, television, news, advertising, and social media platforms are routinely published in scholarly journals. The following is a partial list of journals that is useful to consult when trying to locate such sources:

- *Camera Obscura*
- *Communication and Sport*
- *Feminist Media Studies*
- *Film Quarterly*
- *GLQ: Journal of Lesbian & Gay Studies*

- *Journal of Advertising*
- *Journal of Cinema and Media Studies*
- *Journal of Communication*
- *Journal of Communication and Media Studies*
- *Journal of Health Communication*
- *Journal of Media Psychology*
- *Journal of Popular Film & Television*
- *Journalism & Mass Communication Quarterly*
- *Media, Culture & Society*
- *Media Report to Women*
- *New Media & Society*
- *Sex Roles*
- *Sexuality & Culture*
- *Sexualization, Media & Society*
- *Social Media + Society*
- *Television & New Media*
- *Women's Studies in Communication*

IWMF
Bank of Amer
Bank of Amer
IWMF

1830 *Godey's Lady's Book* begins publication. This magazine is the first of many magazines to construct ideas of womanhood in American culture. In the next several years, the magazine industry expands, and nationally distributed magazines become the first mass medium. By the end of the century, the magazine industry is thriving.

1848 The Seneca Falls Convention takes place at a church in upstate New York. Women gather and discuss the need for equal rights, including the right to vote. This gathering is often pointed to as the beginning of the first wave of feminism. So-called first wavers fought for the right to vote until the Nineteenth Amendment was passed in 1920. They also fought for reproductive freedom and educational and workplace equality.

Mid-1800s Magazines suggest that ideal women are holy, pure, domestically oriented, and submissive.

1868 Frustrated with newspaper reporting they view as unfair to women, dismissive of women's issues, and inconsiderate of women's progressive ideas, Elizabeth Cady Stanton and Susan B. Anthony start publishing their own newspaper titled *Revolution*.

1890–1920 A woman coming-of-age during this time period is known as the "New Woman" because she likely acted

---

Honorees Deborah Amos, Sanyia Toiken, and Michele Norris arrive at the 28th International Women's Media Foundation (IWMF) Courage in Journalism Awards in New York City on October 18, 2017. (Laurence Agron/Dreamstime.com)

and dressed in ways that challenge Victorian ideals. New ideas about women are incorporated in magazines.

1890 The Gibson Girl, a pen-and-ink drawing of a white woman, is featured in a series of magazine covers and images. Drawn by Charles Dana Gibson, the Gibson Girl and subsequent images of the "New Woman" that followed became early mass media stereotypes. They also reflected women's changing place in the culture.

1891 Julia Ringwood Coston begins publishing *Ringwood's Afro-American Journal of Fashion.*

1892 The first issue of the fashion magazine *Vogue* is published. In 1909, Condé Nast purchases the magazine and establishes it as a fashion magazine leader.

Early 1900s Hollywood establishes itself as a center of the fledgling film industry. Notable stars Mary Pickford and Gloria Swanson form their own production companies.

1920 Congress passes the Nineteenth Amendment, guaranteeing women the right to vote.

1920s The flapper emerges as a new mainstream image of women. Flappers, slim, youthful, and often sexually confident, are featured in magazines, advertisements, and films.

1920s Fashionable clothing choices, promoted in advertisements and glamorized on film, offer new ways for women to think about their bodies. To achieve the ideal look that is popular, women practice beauty regimens and dieting.

Late 1920s The age of classical Hollywood begins. Glamorous and powerful movie stars like Greta Garbo, Joan Crawford, and Katharine Hepburn begin successful careers.

Late 1920s The Hollywood studio system begins to become established. Eventually, five major studios control virtually all aspects of the industry.

1930 Hollywood enters a period of censorship when the Motion Pictures Producers and Distributors of America Production Code imposes restrictions on how women can be seen in films. The code commands that women adhere to conservative displays of gender roles and sexuality.

1942 The Office of War Information begins a propaganda campaign encouraging middle-class women to step up and work in jobs vacated by men who were fighting in World War II. After the war is over, women are encouraged to resume their prewar roles as homemakers.

1948 The Supreme Court's *Paramount* decision requires powerful film studios to divest their theater properties, prompting significant changes in the film industry.

1950s Though the technology was developed earlier, television becomes part of the American culture. Mainstream family situation comedies define the ideal family as white, nuclear, and adhering to traditional gender roles, where the father works and the mother manages the home and children.

1963 Betty Friedan's *The Feminine Mystique* is published. The book, which has since sold millions of copies, becomes a key text of the feminist movement, although critics take issue with its sole focus on white middle-class women. Some scholars mark the publication of this book as the beginning of the so-called second wave of feminism or the women's movement because of its impact on American culture.

Mid-1960s The women's movement, or feminist movement, gains momentum. Women advocate for equal rights, representations, and opportunities and challenge the sexist representations of women in the media.

1965 Helen Gurley Brown becomes the first female editor of *Cosmopolitan* magazine and transforms the magazine to appeal to young women.

1966 The women's liberation organization the National Organization for Women (NOW) is founded and the Media Workshop, an organization committed to challenging problematic images of race in the media, is established.

1968 The television show *That Girl* debuts, starring Marlo Thomas. The program is the first situation comedy to center on a single woman who lives alone.

1968 Women gather to protest the Miss America pageant in Atlantic City, New Jersey, for its allegedly demeaning treatment of women.

1970 The television program *The Mary Tyler Moore Show* debuts and breaks new cultural ground with a female title character who is career oriented rather than marriage minded.

1972 Gloria Steinem cofounds *Ms.* magazine, which is produced by women for women and offers alternatives to mainstream news and magazine content.

1972 John Berger cocreates *Ways of Seeing*, a British television series, and with four others publishes an accompanying book. The texts argue that there are gender power dynamics at play in advertising and art.

1972 Title IX of the 1972 Education Amendments requires equal opportunity for women and girls in education, including high school and college sports.

1974 *From Reverence to Rape* is published. Written by Molly Haskell, this book is one of the first feminist titles that focuses on images of women in film.

1975 Laura Mulvey's essay "Visual Pleasure in Narrative Cinema" is published in the film journal *Screen*. Mulvey develops the theory of the "male gaze" to explain how films are created to address the male viewer and represent a male point of view.

1976 Erving Goffman's book *Gender Advertisements* is published. Goffman asserts in the book that American advertising typically characterizes women as passive, submissive, childlike, and vulnerable.

1976 Barbara Walters becomes the first woman to coanchor a network evening newscast.

1980s The "supermom" and "superwoman" monikers are popularized as shorthand terms for women who can easily manage both home and career responsibilities. This construct is informed by media representations of working mothers.

1980s Cable television becomes part of the media landscape, providing audiences access to more diverse and innovative programming.

1981 *Ain't I a Woman: Black Women and Feminism*, by bell hooks, is published. The book examines issues of racism and sexism while providing an analysis of Black women in the media.

1986 After her success hosting the talk show *AM Chicago*, Oprah Winfrey begins broadcasting her national program *The Oprah Winfrey Show*. It becomes the most popular daytime talk show in the United States.

1988 The situation comedy *Murphy Brown* debuts, with Candice Bergen playing the part of the title character, a hard-driving, ambitious journalist. A story arc in the 1991–1992 season becomes part of the news headlines when Vice President Dan Quayle criticizes the story line of Brown's pregnancy and decision to raise her baby as a single mother as symbolic of the country's decaying family values.

1990s The riot grrrl movement challenges sexist practices in the punk music scene and prompts the creation and distribution of handmade *zines* (self-published fan magazines). Some scholars mark these events as the beginning of the so-called third wave of feminism.

1991 Anita Hill testifies before the Senate Judiciary Committee that Supreme Court nominee Clarence Thomas sexually harassed her. Thomas is eventually confirmed, but Hill's testimony prompts numerous women to come forward with their own workplace sexual harassment complaints. This controversy is seen by some scholars as a foundational event in the beginning of third-wave feminism.

1991 *Daughters of the Dust*, directed by Julie Dash, is released. Dash is the first African American woman to direct a mainstream feature film.

1995 Lucy Lawless stars in *Xena: Warrior Princess*, a television program that offers a new action-oriented image of a female heroine.

1996 *Bitch: Feminist Response to Pop Culture* begins publication. The magazine focuses on responding to antifeminist messages in mainstream culture.

1997 Actor Ellen DeGeneres comes out as gay on *The Oprah Winfrey Show*. Her character on the situation comedy *Ellen*, in which she stars, also comes out.

1998 The television show *Sex and the City* debuts on HBO. The series, which focuses on four women in New York, candidly explores their perspectives on sex, dating, fantasies, and relationships.

2004 The *L Word*, a groundbreaking drama featuring developed lesbian characters, debuts on Showtime.

2004 Facebook is established as a social networking site by Mark Zuckerberg and several others. While initially conceived as a closed network at Harvard University, the platform eventually opens up to anyone who wants an account.

2004 The Dove Campaign for Real Beauty is launched. The success of the promotion leads to other advertising that emphasizes women's self-confidence and empowerment.

2005 The cable channel Logo begins cablecasting programming. Logo's focus is on providing gay-, lesbian-, transgender-, and bisexual-oriented shows.

2005 YouTube begins as a video-sharing social media site. Users can watch, upload, and comment on videos.

2005 The *Huffington Post*, created by Arianna Huffington, Kenneth Lerer, and Jonah Peretti, is launched. This news aggregation website and publisher of opinion pieces and blogs becomes popular and influential, and Arianna Huffington becomes a powerful woman in American media.

2005 The Women's Media Center (WMC) is founded by Jane Fonda, Robin Morgan, and Gloria Steinem. The organization aims to use research to advocate for women's participation in media industries and for women's stories to be heard.

2006 Twitter begins as a microblogging social networking site.

2008 Some scholars and activists note the beginnings of fourth-wave feminism emerging around this time. Digital tools and platforms are used to communicate and advance ideas about contemporary women's issues.

2010 Kathryn Bigelow becomes the first woman to win the Academy Award for Best Director for the film *The Hurt Locker*.

2010 Instagram, a social networking site where users can share videos and photos, is launched. Uploaded images can be altered using filters. Facebook acquires Instagram in 2012.

2014 A hack of proprietary information at Sony Pictures reveals significant pay disparities between men and women who work at Sony, even when men and women are doing the same jobs.

2014 The African American Policy Forum and the Center for Intersectionality and Social Policy Studies launches the #SayHerName campaign to raise awareness of the number of Black women who are victims of police violence. The impetus for the campaign comes from media coverage that neglects reporting on women's stories.

2015 "OscarsSoWhite" becomes a popular phrase on Twitter to protest the lack of diversity in Hollywood. The phrase originates from the tweet "#OscarsSoWhite they asked to touch my hair" by April Reigh. Reigh tweeted the comment after seeing Academy Award nominations for twenty white actors, pointing out the lack of diversity among the nominees.

2017 The blockbuster film *Wonder Woman* opens in theaters. Directed by Patty Jenkins, this is the first time the iconic female comic book character is seen in a feature film.

2017 TikTok, the Chinese social networking video-sharing service, becomes available to iOS and Android mobile phone users. The app allows users to make, edit, alter, and share videos.

2017 The #MeToo movement takes hold after pervasive patterns of sexual misconduct are revealed in media industries.

2018 The organization Time's Up is founded by 300 women in the entertainment industry to address power imbalances, advocate for equitable inclusion of women and other underrepresented groups, and provide assistance to those dealing with sexual misconduct issues.

2018 At the Academy Awards, Best Actress–winner Frances McDormand famously calls for the use of "inclusion riders" in the film industry. Inclusion riders ensure that diverse hiring takes place for both on- and off-screen positions in movie productions.

2019 *The Status of Women in U.S. Media 2019*, a report by the Women's Media Center, documents that women are significantly less represented than men in every part of news, entertainment, and digital media.

2020 The COVID-19 pandemic sweeps across the United States and around the world, wreaking havoc with U.S. entertainment and media industries.

2020 George Floyd is killed by a white police officer in Minneapolis, prompting Black Lives Matter protests throughout the nation. The #SayHerName campaign points out that when an African American woman named Breonna Taylor was killed two months earlier by a white police officer in her own home in Louisville, Kentucky, her death did not garner nearly as much media attention. The campaign is successful in drawing awareness to Taylor's story.

2020 Democratic women leaders release an open letter to news outlets criticizing their sexist coverage of vice presidential candidate contenders and urging them to actively work to address sexist and racist elements of their coverage. Democratic presidential nominee Joseph Biden eventually names California senator Kamala Harris as his running mate.

2021 Kamala Harris is sworn in as vice president of the United States, the first woman and first Black and South Asian woman to hold the office.

2021 A number of "firsts" happen in awards celebrations. Chloé Zhao wins the Best Director prize at the Golden Globes for *Nomadland*, the second woman ever to win the award, and she becomes the second woman and first woman of color to be awarded Best Director at the Academy Awards. Youn Yuh-jung becomes the first Korean women to win a Best Supporting Actress Oscar for her role in *Minari*.

2021 Rashida Jones is hired as president of MSNBC, making her the first Black executive to run a news network.

2021 ABC News names Kimberly Godwin as the president of ABC News, making her the first Black executive to run a major U.S. broadcast news division.

2022 Jane Campion becomes the third woman to win Best Director at the Academy Awards for *Power of the Dog*.

2022 Ariana DeBose becomes the first queer woman of color to win Best Supporting Actress at the Academy Awards for her portrayal of Anita in *West Side Story*.

This glossary provides a list of key terms commonly used when discussing aspects of women, media, and gender representation in the United States.

agent of socialization (or socializing agent) An institution or group that communicates what social norms and expectations are. Media are considered socializing agents.

algorithm A set of rules, or a formula, developed to complete a task. Social media companies use computer algorithms to prioritize and filter information that is shown to individuals.

audience reception, active audience In a theoretical context, these terms are used to refer to the idea that audiences actively interpret media messages; individuals sometimes interpret messages differently from one another.

beauty myth A term coined by Naomi Wolf in her book by the same name that is used to describe or refer to the idea that a pervasive and ongoing slew of media messages routinely pressure women and girls to look beautiful, thin, and (for some) young. Wolf argues the unattainability of such beauty traps women in a destructive spiral of self-image critique.

Bechdel test Adapted from a comic strip by Alice Bechdel that comments on poor representation of women in films, this "test" determines its fundamental disposition toward women by asking whether movies have at least two women in it; whether the women talk to one another; and whether the women's conversation is about something other than a man.

color blind casting The practice of hiring actors regardless of their demographic profile. Sometimes this practice is in place when characters are conceived; they are written without demographic or physical characteristics ascribed to them.

cultural studies A field of study that looks at how news and entertainment media are produced and consumed in society. The field acknowledges that elements of society are inequitable and favor dominant ideas through economic, political, and social systems.

editorial content In the context of journalism, this term refers to content (like articles and photographs) that is independently produced by news reporters and editors rather than advertising or content commissioned by advertisers.

erasure In a media representation context, to ignore, remove, or marginally represent a group of people in media texts. Representations of demographic groups are often largely absent in mainstream media.

femme fatale In film noir, a woman character whose actions often lead to a man's death. This archetypal character is often defined by her sexuality, power, and dismissal of motherhood. In French, the term means "fatal woman."

femvertising A word that combines the ideas of female empowerment and advertising; this term refers to ads that celebrate female empowerment or other feminist ideas.

flapper The dominant image of a woman in the post–World War I United States; this slim, youthful, somewhat androgynous image celebrated women's sexual agency and freedom from domestic life.

gatekeeper In traditional media, the person or persons who filter and select information to be distributed and featured through various media formats.

gender ideology A set of ideas or beliefs about gender, often informed by societal standards at a particular historic moment.

gender inequality Social inequality that stems from gender.

hard news A category of news that includes breaking news, business, politics, and watchdog journalism. The information being reported is considered timely and essential.

hashtag Social media messages on a specific topic delineated by the pound (#) sign before the words being used to reference the topic. Social media campaigns use hashtags to organize and highlight their messages.

ideology A set of ideas or beliefs.

interactive marketing A promotional practice wherein companies or company representatives interact with consumers via digital platforms.

intersectionality A concept used in feminist theory that emphasizes the complexities of any individual woman's experience and deemphasizes such commonalities as race or socioeconomic class. The theory argues that identity is holistically informed and not informed solely by a demographic characteristic.

male gaze A term appropriated by feminist film scholar Laura Mulvey that theorizes film audiences are situated to watch films from the position of a male spectator.

media literacy The ability to access, analyze, evaluate, and create media messages. Media literacy education engages media consumers in thinking critically about the media they encounter, prompting them to ask critical questions about the message, its author, its purpose, and its reception.

misogyny Prejudice toward, dislike, or hatred of women.

MPPDA Production Code The Motion Pictures Producers and Distributors of America Production Code limited how women could be seen in films. The code commanded that women adhere to conservative displays of gender roles and sexuality.

objectification Treating a person like an object or a thing. Media representations often prioritize women's physical attributes over whom they are as a person. Advertisements have often been criticized for focusing on women's bodies or body parts rather than the whole person.

oligopoly An industry where only a few companies control the majority of the market. In the United States, only a few media companies control the majority of the industry, resulting in a structural media oligopoly.

participatory culture The ability of the public to create and distribute content in the culture rather than just being consumers of cultural content.

patriarchy A system controlled by men.

sexism Discrimination against women or men based on their biological sex.

soft news A category of news that includes reporting on aspects of the culture, including the arts, entertainment, lifestyle and human interest topics, sports, and celebrities.

stereotype A broad, underdeveloped generalization about people or groups. Stereotypical depictions of people and groups in the media often perpetuate ideas about race, ethnicity, and gender that are inaccurate and hurtful.

symbolic annihilation A term used in media studies to describe the absence or underrepresentation of demographic groups in media outlets and products.

vamp In the silent film era, a character who is an immoral or evil woman, often played by a "foreign" actress, whose actions lead to the male protagonist's downfall.

waves of feminism An imperfect metaphor that attempts to organize elements of feminist history. Scholars suggest categorizing feminism into waves is problematic and reductive. Nonetheless, different elements of feminist history are often marked as first wave (the movement that led to women's voting rights), second wave (the women's movement in the 1960s and 1970s), third wave (the 1990s focus on women's individual experiences), and fourth wave (a twenty-first-century focus on women's empowerment and intersectionality, often via the use of digital tools).

whitewashing In a media representation context, the prioritization of white culture over others. It also refers to a white actor portraying a character who, in the original narrative source material, is not white.

About the Author

Amy M. Damico, PhD, is a professor of communication and the faculty adviser to the Endicott Scholars Honors Program at Endicott College in Beverly, Massachusetts. She teaches a variety of classes in the areas of mass communication and media and cultural studies. Her previous authored and coauthored books are *Media, Journalism and "Fake News": A Reference Handbook*; *21st-Century TV Dramas: Exploring the New Golden Age*; and *September 11 in Popular Culture: A Guide.*